INSTRUCTOR'S MANUAL TO ACCOMPANY

ORGANIZATIONAL STRATEGY & POLICY

Text Cases and Incidents

FRANK T. PAINE
University of Maryland

WILLIAM NAUMES
Temple University

W. B. SAUNDERS COMPANY / Philadelphia / London / Toronto

Table of Contents

PREFACE

Organizational Strategy and Policy is designed to present students of Business Policy with both a framework for
forming and implementing strategic problems as well as real
world cases to practice application of those concepts. The
cases, whether disguised or actual representations, discuss
events that took place in an organization existing in our
society.

The concept of using cases to teach Business Policy
has been presented ably in the past. The purpose of this
instructor's manual is to assist the user of the cases presented in the companion text in developing and leading
viable class discussions based on the case materials.

The approach taken in developing the case notes is to
provide a broad overview of the general issues involved in
the case as well as a brief analysis of the case. In this
manner, the instructor can use the notes as a handy reference for questions and discussions.

The portion of the case notes referring to the suggested position in which the case should be presented in a
course, necessarily presupposes a particular format.
While we try to present alternative uses, a discussion of
our biases might be helpful.

The method that has been found useful for presenting
cases has been to start with a broad based case to show the
students the potential for interaction of strategic problems. The case should be "rich" in information as well as
problems. Both should draw on all the functional as well
as conceptual areas, once again to show how the different
areas interact and relate. A thorough analysis is not expected of the students at this point. The first case should
be used to assist the students in feeling their way through
an analysis of an integrative, top management decision
making process.

After this first exposure with a relatively complex
case, the students are presented with a series of more
well-defined, problem oriented cases. Typically, these
cases involve organizations faced with relatively narrow
problems or issues, traceable to a very few functional
or conceptual areas. In this manner, the students are able
to build up a base of experience and practice in spotting
problems and developing solutions for strategic decisions.
Typically the problems will combine a functional problem
with a conceptual issue, such as sales forecasting and the
effects of the economy on the products or services of the
organization.

The problem areas would get more complex and integrative as the course progresses. The last portion of the
course would be devoted to analyzing and discussing cases

with problems encompassing the full range of strategic issues. The cases or case series used at this point would be similar to the case used at the outset of the course. The difference would be in the expectation from the students. It would now be hoped that the students could analyze the total situation and develop comprehensive, well balanced strategies encompassing the full range of strategic problems. Moreover, the strategies developed would be highly cognizant of problems typically encountered in implementing as well as developing strategies in an organizational setting. The focus at this stage of the course would also be towards the future effects of environmental trends on the organization. This is as opposed to emphasis on the present situations in the earlier segment of the course.

To assist in presenting the cases for this purpose, the case notes have been structured in the following manner:

1. Purpose of the Case
2. Position in the Course
3. Key Issues
4. Analysis
5. Questions
6. Responses
7. Sample Case Reports

Where appropriate, this general format will be followed. Some variance may be necessary for some cases. This information is designed to assist the instructor to develop a well balanced discussion of the key issues that have developed from class testing of the cases. This is not to imply that any given instructor or class might not be able to discover alternative issues or uses for the cases, however. Experience has shown us that only through extensive use of any given case will a thorough understanding of all factors of a case ever be developed. In most instances, changing environmental conditions such as an energy shortage, may lead to new, evolving uses of standard cases.

The authors give thanks to the people who made the various cases available to us. Their names appear with the cases they supplied. We also wish to thank Kwame Ofinam who developed background information on which parts of many of these case notes are based. We take all responsibility for the accuracy of these notes, however.

THE ROLE OF THE PLANNER

Univis, Inc. is the only case in this category. It has been placed separately to demonstrate the interaction between the theoretical, social and political aspects of strategy and policy formation in organizations.

The different aspects of the Univis case mentioned in the following note are also used as the basis for discussion in the text portion of the book. Issues and problems apparent in the case are used as examples throughout the text. Particularly, the role of the planner and top management in the strategy formation process is emphasized. References made to the Univis case in the text compliment the comments in the following class note for instructors.

Univis, Inc.

Purpose

The Univis case can be used in several different ways. We have found it to be particularly effective in showing the potential problems facing the planner in designing and implementing a formal planning process.

Mr. Barber, President of Univis, states that formal planning is necessary for continued success. He hires a business trained planner, Mr. Cotton, to set up such a planning process. Only the top manager and the planner are involved. While involvement of the top manager in this process is a necessary condition, it is not a sufficient condition for successful planning.

The case can be used to explore the role of the planner in a formal planning process. The distinction and problems between the planner as a teacher and a doer can be profitably established through analysis of Cotton's actions and reactions to his moves by management.

Finally, the case can also be used on a broader basis to demonstrate the problems facing a relatively small firm in an oligopolistic industry. Opportunities and threats facing the firm in such a position frequently provide an interesting exercise in forming a feasible, acceptable strategy.

Position in Course

The case should be used at different positions in the course depending on the primary objective followed. If the purpose is to demonstrate an effective planning process, the case should be used early in the course. The case has been particularly effective at the third or fourth session, after the students have been exposed to much of the text portion of the book.

If the case is to be used in its broader context, it should be placed towards the end of the course. Here it can be used to provide the students with the necessity of forming and implementing a strategy given a relatively complete set of background information. The case is "rich" in information from this point of view.

Key Issues

The following points comprise some of the key issues to be found in the Univis case:
1. Need for formal planning procedures.
2. Proper organizational structure for implementing an effective planning process.

3. Behavioral objectives in forming an acceptable
   planning process.
4. Necessity to adequately communicate, in an
   understandable manner, the format by which an
   effective planning process is to be implemented.
5. Options open to a relatively small, non-diver-
   sified firm in an oligopolistic industry.

Analysis

The company's background: Univis started in 1911 as a
privately owned company in Dayton, Ohio. It was then called
the Standard Optical Company. It later became the Univis
Lens Company.

In 1955, four of its employees purchased a controlling
interest. In the first year of operation under the new
management, Univis, Inc. lost $290,000.

In 1960, the corporate headquarters was moved to
Ft. Lauderdale, Florida, and the name Univis, Inc. was
adopted. By 1966 only three of the original purchasers
formed the executive committee and 35% of the company's
common stock was owned by the directors and officers; the
remaining 65% belonging to about 2000 stockholders.

Sales in 1966 had reached $16.3 million with net earn-
ings at $1,005,118. Except for 1960 and 1963, net earnings
had been on a consistent rise at 33.5% a year compounded
with sales growth at 16.6% compounded.

Mission: to provide products and services that protect
and improve human sight.

Objectives: maximization of owners' common share price
through growth. Performance is to be geared towards the
image as a growth company with a growth stock hopefully resulting from this image.

Policy: the maintainence of "excellence in generalized professional management and growth should be through
being in tune with environmental changes and seizing the
right opportunities."

Flexibility: the corporate resources are 'put' in a
homogeneous pool and utilized whereever any business opportunity is found.

Dividend policy: to provide income for stockholders
and therefore "maintain cash dividend payout at the dollar
quantity already established" and to increase it when earnings justify it!

This policy was in line with the newly adopted (1963) "business planning" in the words of the President, R. O. Barber, for the "best way to grow."

Product line: it consisted of both glass and plastic lenses for all types of single lens glasses, through bifocal to cataract, and an innovator (1963) of the straight top bifocal plastic lens.

Diversification: In 1961, Univis's acquisition of the Bishop Company brought it into the frame business. With a 1962 takeover of the Zylite Corporation, productive capacity increased and Univis offered a full line -- both sexes and children -- of frames; roughly 2000 items.

Production facilities: Univis had four plants:
1. Fort Lauderdale produced special-purpose and single-vision glass lenses;
2. Guayama (Puerto Rico) produced standard bifocal glass lenses;
3. West Babylon (N,Y.) produced plastic lenses;
4. North Attleboro (Mass.) produced spectacle frames.

The total output of the four plants were centrally warehoused and distributed from Fort Lauderdale. Number of employees now was 1398.

Management: Univis had no management development program. Personnel motivated in this direction had to improve themselves the best way they could.

Exhibits 4 and 5 in the case give corporate officers' background and the organizational chart, respectively.

The ophthalmic industry and market: The U.S. retail market, as estimated by the Better Vision Institute, is over $1 billion per year. Factory sales of regular eyeglass products, including imports, exceed $150 million yearly -- at the retail end it is worth $1,050 million/year.

Industry potential was very high -- approximately 54% of U.S. population six years and older uses corrective lenses; in the past 4 years 40 million of these had not had their eyes reexamined. It was estimated that 28 million of these needed new corrections.

A 1970 forecast, by the Optical Manufacturers Association put ophthalmic lens sales at 39% above 1965; in absolute figures 40.8 million pairs. This provided an average growth rate of 6.8% per year compounded over that term.

Industry leaders: four firms dominate the industry: American Optical (also the price leader), Bausch & Lomb, the Shuron-Continental Div. of Textron, and Univis. Univis' major competitors are more highly diversified than it is.

Univis's channel of distribution is mainly through wholesalers and, infrequently, to the U.S. or state governments.

Planning at Univis: the company's view has always been that effective management is through planning. Formal controls were instituted in 1955 by the new management team mainly for more profitable operations.

The organizational manual then showed 8 divisions and a total of 124 job descriptions.

Performance standards for management and administrative personnel were set for the ensuing year after consultation between superiors and subordinates. For factory employees, a job rating system was instituted.

Incentive: a dollar bonus based on a point system was used (0-15) at Univis. The number of points scored was taken as a percentage of base pay (e.g. 10 means +10% of the salary). Two systems operated: 1. Difficult to rate positions were in the "Key Club" and informally rated with a maximum bonus of one month's pay or $8\frac{1}{2}$% base pay increment. 2. The "Funcrum Club" was for those managers who could directly affect Univis profits. The maximum bonus here was 15% plus excess percentage points over ROI set for the year -- e.g. if 10% was set and actual was 26%, they get 16% additional bonus.

Factory Positions: People were matched with their jobs, received no bonus, but a turkey each Christmas.

In 1963, the old system of centralized goal setting was changed, as was mentionned previously.

Corporate Planning: Structurally, this department directly reported to the president, for more effective support.

The purpose of Univis planning was primarily to achieve set corporate objectives and coordinate the development of company resources to be in line with the objectives.

Figure 1 in the case shows how planning determines "gaps" between objectives and expected performance. Theoretically action plans could be evolved to close these gaps.

Conceptual background of the plan: An organization is delineated from the societal system by members' interrelationships and goal orientation.

The human aspects involve substantive and procedural planning as well as routine duties within the determined structure.

The organizational goal structure became pyramidal with

a tri-layered horizontal hierarchy -- substantive, procedural, and routine goals.

Risk categories and levels -- conservative, normal and
speculative -- were set by experimentation, game and chance
analogies.

With acceptable risks established, required yields
were set on assets utilized.

Corporate goals: Quantitative goals, in line with the
basic objectives, all related to assets utilized -- amount,
risk, yield, and time involved.

At standard risk mix ROI should be a minimum of 20%.
" conservative "   "   "   "   " "   "   " 17%.
" normal   "   "   "   "   " "   "   " 21%.
" speculative   "   "   "   "   " "   "   " 25%.

Required per share earnings must increase at an average of 7% annually compounded.

By 1966 the % requirements were taken as pre-tax and
the per share was to be well above market averages over
time.

Progress to Date: Measurements of actual performance
was carried out on March 18, 1966 through the "Univis
Passive Projections 1966-1970." These were projections of
business activities over the next five years based on assumed normal market growth with no diversifications. A five
year plan replaced these projections for the period 1967-
1971.

The five year plan was a working paper allowing divisional managers to capitalize on opportunities subject to
constraints and management approval.

The planning department was responsible for providing
economic and basic guidelines. Each division then drew its
operational and functional plans.

Existing gaps and analysis were discussed by the executive committee in February and final plan presentations
were made on March 13, 1967.

Executive comments and reaction were highly mixed
depending on how each viewed planning.

Questions

1.   How successful has the implementation of a formal
     planning process been at Univis, Inc.?

2.   What problems could Mr. Cotton have avoided in imple-
     menting the planning process at Univis, Inc.?

3.	What inconsistencies are evident in the strategy used by Univis?

4.	What key environmental factors present the greatest opportunities and threats to Univis's ability to become a "growth" company? How can they be overcome?

5.	What should Mr. Cotton do to improve the effectiveness of the planning process and the strategy itself?

Responses

1.	The firm has been relatively successful to date. Their earnings have been erratic, however. Depending on the time period discussed, Univis has either performed spectacularly or just average. This points up the importance of the time factor in analysis as well as implementation.

The formal process has not really been implemented yet. This is true despite the fact that three years have passed at a cost of approximately $100,000 per year. This amounts to between 5% and 10% of earnings without any immediate payout. This helps to point out the long term nature of the investment in planning.

There is still resistance and lack of understanding of formal planning at Univis. Managers at the company are demonstrating confusion at the method which planning is being implemented.

Overall, Cotton has taken an inordinate amount of time to implement a costly,confusing, mainly theoretically oriented formal planning process.

2.	Mr. Cotton has looked primarily at Mr. Barber for guidance in setting up the planning process. Lower level managers haven't been consulted to any degree. The workings of the process haven't been communicated to them, thus the lack of understanding.

The central problem, however, is that Cotton hasn't decided what his own role should be. He has tried to combine the role of teacher and doer. Individually, the roles create problems. Combining them, the problems are almost insurmountable. He typically incurs the jealousy and fear of most managers without really giving himself an opening for him to step into in line management. Until this social and political problem of role definition is overcome, the other problems will persist.

3.	Among the inconsistencies apparent in the case is the desire to be thought of as a "growth" company while maintaining a high dividend rate (relative to other growth-oriented companies). Similarly, the risk table and expected returns noted in the case would lead the managers to choose conservative investments whenever possible.

All three categories, conservative, normal and speculative, when combined with expected yields under corporate-wide goals, lead to equivalent expected rate of return for each area, as should be. Combining this with the risk aversion of the top managers, as evidenced elsewhere in the case, it becomes clear that they would choose conservative investments. This is due to the fact that managers typically do not make decisions on purely quantitative grounds.

Other inconsistencies include the broad statement of mission as opposed to implementation of objectives. The mission states the firm's market is anything to improve and/or protect vision. Implementation later shows they are really looking at the ophthalmics industry, and, even narrower still, to eyeglasses. This continual narrowing of mission tends to give the managers "marketing myopia". Once again, this is inconsistent with the objective of being a growth oriented company.

Also, the Univis Creed states the company desires to develop professional management. There is no formal management development program in existence, however. It is clear from the case that it is up to the individual to motivate himself and find proper outlets for his own development.

4. The firm is relatively small and maintains the flexibility to adapt to a changing environment. It has not diversified away from its basic product area, and therefore is relatively free of constraints caused by ongoing operations.

Its competitors are large, diversified, research oriented firms. So far, Univis has been able to keep pace with new product developments. This could be a future threat, however. This is especially true since the market for their basic products is expected to grow at about 7% per year for the foreseeable future. This approximates Univis's initial growth objectives, but is hardly consistent with a growth company.

The economy is in an unsettled condition. Inflation is rising (about 5-6% at the time of the case). While the economy is presently flat, fiscal stimulation brought on by the war effort in Vietnam is expected to place the U.S. back on a growth track.

Growth oriented firms are looked upon with favor by the stock market, currently. The firm must show some results along these lines for their statements to be believed, however.

5. Cotton has to understand he is not talking about an intellectual process. Politically, he has to sell the

process, not only to Barber, but to the other managers as well. The description of the process must be worded in a way that managers with little academic training in business can understand. The managers at Univis mostly have scientific backgrounds.

He has to communicate to everyone that he is not trying to take their job. Also, he has to make it clear that <u>he</u> is not going to do the planning for them. He has to get a commitment from Barber to include all levels of management in the planning process. The different levels of management should be brought in at the stages most appropriate to them (as discussed in Chapter 5 of the text).

Finally, he has to help Barber and other managers to better define their objectives. Objectives and actions must be consistent if the strategy is going to be feasible, and acceptable.

SMALL BUSINESS

The cases in this section of the book all relate to problems faced by organizations which can legitimately be classified as small businesses. Problems tend to be highly focused in this kind of environment. Also, since their output is restricted, they tend to have little effect on the external environment. This combination of factors makes it somewhat easier to focus on key issues and concepts.

Since the number of people concerned is rather limited, it is easier to determine the value structure of all key individuals. This in turn helps in setting objectives consistent with the goals of the managers. Also, the strengths and weaknesses of the organization are more visible than in a large organization. Resources tend to be limited in small organizations.

This last point also limits the firm's ability to take advantage of external opportunities. Alternatives open to much larger firms with greater resources may be easily ruled out as infeasible for many smaller firms. On the other hand, smaller firms may find it easier to change direction than larger firms due to not having large amounts of resources fixed in current areas of operations which can't be used elsewhere.

Finally, the social and political relationships in small organizations tend to be more distinct. There are no large hierarchies to contend with. For these reasons, it is far simpler to trace the reactions to various moves and changes in strategic direction in a small organization than in a larger one.

We can see that all these factors demonstrate the potential effectiveness of using small business cases at early stages in the typical Business Policy course. As we stated in the Preface, the student can now be presented with manageable sized problems and issues, where the relationships are relatively clear.

Mitchell Nursery, Inc.

Purpose

Mitchell Nursery demonstrates the need for planning and integrated decision-making, even in a small unit. Mr. Oakes seems to be continually putting out fires while feeling that he should be doing more to ensure the continued long run success of his company.

The case points up the question of setting priorities for varying objectives. Oakes and Mitchell, the owners, don't want to relinquish control of their company. They also want to maintain profitability and financial reserves, however. They are finding that industry trends are requiring stronger financial backing for success.

Strict customer loyalty based on long standing, local friendships is no longer a guarantee of sales. Competition is now evolving into a standard, arms length, business relationship. The firm can no longer remain insulated from external effects.

The case can be used effectively to point up the relationship between objectives and the external environment. The industry is changing from a typical Mom and Pop operation to a professionally managed business enterprise. It appears to be heading for a standard shake-out phase where marginal producers will be forced out of the industry.

While Mitchell Nursery is not now a marginal operation it would only take one or two bad years to place it into that position due to undercapitalization. These weaknesses and threats are relatively easy to spot.

Matching strengths and opportunities are much more difficult, however. This leads to use of the case in two different formats. In the first, this case can be used simply to analyze the present situation facing the firm and the firm's reactions to that environment. It can also be used to try to develop strategies to enable the firm to meet its opportunities.

Position in Course

This case can be used at two stages in the course. The first would be at the early stages of the course where analysis is a critical segment of the objective of case discussion.

It is relatively easy to see what the objectives of the firm are. The internal and external environments are also relatively easy to explore due to the size of the firm and the regional nature of the industry. Also, the small number of people in the organization can be readily analyzed to show, in a microcosm, the relationships frequently found in much larger organizations.

The material in the case is mostly qualitative in nature. There is little in the way of number tumbling to be performed, although this leads to the need for outside references and information gathering to fill in the gaps in the case. This provides further reason for use at the early stage of the course. A useful technique is to ask the students to explore what types of information Oakes would need to decide on future alternative actions and then to find that information. In this way, the students can be shown the value and cost of added information.

Analysis

The company, located in Marysville, California, about 50 miles north of Sacramento, raised and sold grapevines, fruit and nut trees to commercial farmers and other nurseries.

The case presents highlights of an interview in April 1961 with the general manager, Carl Oakes. He states that he feels that the company's problem centers around the need for policies and goals; even though profits have been realized annually without them.

Oakes and John Mitchell (20 years nursery experience) founded the company in 1950, under Mitchell's name to capitalize on his excellent reputation. Incorporation followed seven years later, primarily for tax reasons. Growth has been from one employee, 50,000 trees, 25,000 grapevines, to 700,000 trees, 500,000 grapevines, eleven all-year employees, and $200,000/year in sales.

The corporation is organized strictly as a "Ma and Pa" operation. At 67 years of age, Mitchell is involved more in an advisory capacity with the active direction of operations delegated to Oakes.

Steve Taylor, field superintendent, directly reports to Oakes. He works on salary plus commission (%) on sales. Being used to Mitchell's management practices, he lacks initiative, even though he appears to know what to do.

Reporting to Steve Taylor are two key workers ($100 a week each) who supervise the workers when they are split into two gangs to tend the company's two separate fields -- 50 miles apart. Laborers earn $1.25 to $1.50 an hour.

The work force fluctuates throughout the year. At the height of the season it may reach a maximum of 25. The most tiring job -- planting grapevines -- is used as a self-selecting method for permanent employees because most

quit before the planging is over. Advancement is then to:
thinning out seedlings, weeding, pruning, and finally
grafting which requires some skill (See Exhibit 8 for company personnel).

Mexicans have proved to be the most dependable workers.
Workers have no fringe benefits but can earn 5¢ or 10¢ an
hour incentive raises.

In the office are a secretary -- Mary, Mitchell's sister, and a manager trainee. Mary has a rough approach
towards customers but Oakes feels he can't fire her, due to
family ties.

The manager-trainee, Bill Winters, was a commercial
high school accounting major. He is currently doing a cost
analysis of each plant variety cultivated and will be finished by June 1962.

It is noteworthy that vine cuttings are obtained for
free. The majority of Mitchell's trees, however, are
raised by grafting buds to "rootstock".

The most important product supplied by Mitchell Nursery
is the June bud (70% of sales), followed by the yearlings
(20% of sales). The yearlings are a little larger than the
June buds and more expensive. Exhibit 2 notes the differences between the two.

All sales to other nurseries are at wholesale, while
sales to farmers are at retail. The wholesale buyer gets a
40% discount. Presently, the retail sector is growing faster than the wholesale.

Annual and biannual forecasts are made for June buds
and yearlings respectively. The market demand for trees is
a function of market prices of the fruit that the trees bear.
Underestimating of tree needs may result from diseases
striking the plants. 1959 poor profits were primarily due
to this fact. Excess plants due to overestimation (from
10% to 50%) are burned. This is the primary reason for
granting discounts for placing orders ahead of time.

Pricing policy is strictly "follow the leader". Ad-
justments are made through discounting (to meet competition).
Replacement sales are discounts granted farmers equal to
50% of trees lost in the first year after sales.

Mitchell's chief competitor is the Bischoff Nursery in
nearby Yuba City. Bischoff buys most of its stock, has
four salesmen and a sales volume around $600,000 per year.

In terms of market share, Mitchell has 50-60% of the
June bud sales; other areas' and competitors' profitability
are not known. Most of Mitchell's sales are to customers
in neighboring counties.

Mitchell is considering employing a salesman because Oakes can't do as much direct selling as before. He now relies on repeat customers (80% of sales). He is losing some good customers to competitors, apparently due to lack of contact.

For the past two years, adversiting budgets have been between $2000 and $3000, mainly in direct mails and in the Marysville weekly. Competitors depend on newspaper and magazine advertising.

The quality of Mitchell's products is judged by customers to have a little edge over competitors. Orders are checked before dispatching and, in addition, 5 to 6 trees extra are included for every 1000 trees in each order. The State Department of Agriculture also exercises quality control through inspections. Also, buds are selected from healthy trees certified by the "Pathology Department" of the California Department of Agriculture.

Patented trees (23) are obtained through licensing agreements. Mitchell's nursery is experimenting haphazardly with raising new varieties but so far with no real success. Oakes maintains close contact with California School of Agriculture, the State Agricultural Department, and Shell Oil Research laboratory. Oakes would like to employ a full time researcher. The financial burden holds him back, however, and he is looking for an outsider with money to get the program off the ground.

Mitchell's growing is done on rented land. This allows for rotation and easy expansion and contraction when necessary.

While field laborers worked by hand (on knees 9 hours a day), mechanized operations included ploying, fertilizing, dusting, digging, and irrigation.

The company keeps little financial records apart from income tax statements. The only available balance sheet (Exhibit 7 in the case) was drawn in 1957 at the time of incorporation. Mitchell's management believes in incurring no debts, and paying off all bills on time. Needed funds are supplied from personal accounts (Oakes or John Mitchell) at 6% interest. Bank loans are not available since the company owns no land and exhibits a poor risk as inventory has no value. Issuing stock has not been considered a viable option for fear of losing control.

In analysis of the nursery's depreciation schedule -- buildings, trucks, tractors and equipment originally valued at $56,000 -- depreciation charges of $31,000 leave a net book value of $25,000 as of 1961.

Notes on the California Nursery Industry

The nursery industry is facing a difficult position due to rising costs and land usage. Labor costs, disease control, land values, real estate taxes and zoning restrictions are all adding to expenses. One method of lowering costs is through mechanization. This requires economies of scale and large capital expenditures. These kinds of outlays are already leading to consolidation of the many firms in the industry.

Another factor that is related to these involves the development of patented, disease free varieties. The larger firms are performing most of this work to improve profit margins. This also reduces competition due to differentiation of what had tended to be an undifferentiated product.

The industry does have outside help, however. County extension agents, university researchers and industry suppliers are all working on these problems for their own respective reasons.

Questions

1. What are the current objectives being pursued by Mitchell Nursery?

2. How do these objectives relate to environmental factors?

3. What internal strengths and weaknesses affect the firm's ability to take advantage of external opportunities?

4. What policies followed by Mitchell Nursery have inhibited its growth in the current market?

5. What specific policies should Oakes install to insure continued, long run viability and growth?

Responses

1. This is a clear situation where objectives really have not been formulated by the managers at Mitchell Nursery. Carl Oakes, in this extended interview, makes several comments from which a rudimentary set of goals can be pieced together.

Oakes is interested, primarily, in controlling his firm and keeping it operating into the future. His concept of how long into the future is rather vague. His planning horizon is fairly short term. It typically stretches only as far as the planting requirements for the

next one or two selling seasons. He is doing some experimentation with new varieties of trees, but this is being
carried on in a rather haphazard and unplanned manner.

A distinctively visible objective determined by Oakes'
discussion is his emphasis on quality. The firm has the
family name (John Mitchell is his father-in-law). The top
managers don't want their name muddied through sale of in-
ferior products. They also feel that this is the primary
reason that they can maintain sales, since they are selling
an otherwise undifferentiated, price competitive product.

Survival, control, quality, and meeting sales commitments, therefore, appear to be the unstated objectives of
the firm.

2.   The method of operations followed by Mitchell is
inconsistent with trends occurring in the external environment. Consolidation is starting among both customers (farmers) and competitors. The larger competitors are setting
policies designed for long term profitability. Pricing,
patented varieties, use of salesmen, etc. are designed to
increase sales and improve profitability.

The customer is also interested in profits. Long
standing relationships are becoming less important than
quality, service and pricing. Mitchell's insistence on
quality is consistent with this part of the environment.
Its policy of following the market with pricing could lead
to probelms if it gets caught off balance again as it did
when it tried to hold the line earlier. Also, if a price
war does develop, Mitchell could be in serious trouble due
to lack of financial reserves. The desire for absolute
control by the two owners leaves them little in the way of
options for generating cash outside of operations and
borrowing against their personal property.

3.   The two owners are experiences in their basic business.
They have an innate knowledge of how to develop products to
suit the needs of their customers. Mr. Oakes, particularly,
at least has the feeling that there are certain types of
information needed for long term success, such as cost for
each variety.

The owners also have a value system that says what is
good for the customer is good for the firm. This emphasis
on quality, service and price competitiveness keeps them
in good stead with their customers.

The firm does not maintain fixed assets. This allows
it to shift efforts between different areas of its immediate geographic regions. It also allows the firm to shift
emphasis to more promising varieties of trees due to either
demand or disease characteristics.

1 6

As discussed earlier, the firm lacks financial resources. It also lacks management depth or breadth. Mr.
Oakes has to do everything himself. Steve Teylor has been
unwilling, or unable, to take responsibility on himself yet.
Bill Winters, the trainee, has yet to prove himself capable
of any management tasks. Mary Mitchell could be classed as
a major liability considering her conversational style with
customers. Finally, the firm does not have anyone who can
lead a research effort into developing patented varieties
of trees.

4.   There are several symptoms that could be discussed
here. The lack of capital, management depth, planning deficiencies, pricing policies, all can be explored. They
all lead to the desire for absolute control of the firm by
the two owners, however. They mistake total ownership for
control.

    This question is one where the technicians are separ-
ated from the true policy analysts. The underlying problem
deserves the major emphasis. The symptoms deserve secondary comment to prove the major point.

5.   Once again, much time could be spent considering new
product development, pricing strategy, and present management weaknesses. The discussion has to eventually center
on the setting of priorities on the objectives of the firm.

    Currently, control is the primary objective. If the
owners want to insure the long term viability of the firm,
they have to accept the necessity of outside capital. The
question is how to get that capital at the least cost to
the present owners with the greatest gain. One way to do
this is to find an investor who also has one or more of the
management or research skills needed by the firm. A good
salesman, botanist, or management supervisor with capital
to invest would be ideal. This is not as difficult as it
may seem. There are always disillusioned managers of
larger firms with savings to invest who want to try their
hand at helping to run a firm.

    The present owners would still maintain control.
They are related and apparently getting along well. The
firm is still profitable, so they don't have to give up a
controlling interest to entice an investor in. Also, the
case mentions several firms, both direct and indirect competitors, that are much larger than Mitchell Nursery.
These could prove to be fertile ground for finding the
type of managers described above.

    After this initial problem is overcome, then the
managers can consider the other problem areas' policies.
The question of pricing will depend on a thorough cost
analysis. Better market forecasting should be developed.
The current management structure has to be rationalized.
All these policy recommendations will require further information and analysis. All these areas lead to

potentially profitable discussions depending on the time allotted to the case and the specific objectives of the case discussion.

Sea Life Park

Purpose

The Sea Life Park case series (A, B &C) can be used to trace the development of a strategy from the idea stage, through strategy formation to implementation of action plans. Since all the cases in this series are rich in information, the cases can be used either singly or in various combinations to provide insight into the various stages of strategy formation and implementation.

The Sea Life Park (A) case illustrates the efforts of an entrepreneur in trying to set up a company to fill various objectives. He seems to have struck upon a project which combines his personal areas of interest with a potentially profitable return to investors. The case should be used to demonstrate the problems of gathering information on market potential, production costs, profitability and general investor and consumer interest. Tap Pryor, the entrepreneur, attempts an information gathering process, assisted by a Stanford Business School professor. This method of accepting and rejecting various pieces of information is of more than passing interest. The whole concept of conflict resolution and cognitive dissonance is demonstrated quite well by this process.

Also, the case demonstrates what an entrepreneur, armed with a modicum of information, and an extremely persuasive personality, can do for a project. Tap's enthusiasm ends up carrying the day for initial acceptance of the Sea Life Park project. This can be used to show that a theoretically consistent and apparently feasible project still has to be sold to the social and political forces needed for implementation. Frequently a strong, persuasive backer is the key to acceptance of new projects or strategies.

The Sea Life Park (A) case can also be used as a lead in to the (B) and (C) cases, or as background information for these cases.

The Sea Life Park (B) case primarily traces Tap's efforts to secure financing for his new venture. The (B) case should be used to demonstrate problems and methods of finding risk capital for a new venture. It also shows the timing problems inherent in introducing a new strategy.

Tap Pryor makes a strategic decision in the case not to wait until financing is complete before implementing his strategic actions. This decision should be used to analyze the risks attendant with such a strategy. We frequently discuss the benefits of planning devices such as PERT and CPM, as mentioned in the text, to speed up strategic changes. What frequently is not discussed in such an analysis are the potential risks involved in carrying several actions simultaneously.

The trade-off should be explored between a desire by
Tap to get his project off the ground and the potential
risk of failure through starting too early. There is a
question as to just who would be assuming the risks involved in Tap's decision to go fast on the construction
project. This provides the opportunity to discuss the concept of values (in this instance, risk aversion) by various
members involved in the project. These members should include the investors as well as Tap Pryor.

Finally, the (B) case should be used to draw up contingency plans for the future. The students should be
asked to determine potential threats for the future of Sea
Life Park. After determining potential threats, the students could then be asked to develop contingency plans for
the future to overcome any weaknesses or threats, an action
which Pryor does not take in his enthusiasm to get going.

The contingency plans developed for the Sea Life Park
(B) case can now be compared with actual problems encountered during implementation discussed in the (C) case.
The question of timing is a key purpose for discussing this
particular case. The Sea Life Park has run into a series
of stumbling blocks. Anyone of them would have little or
no affect on the overall operations. Together, they can
lead to potentially damaging results for the combined Sea
Life Park/Oceanics Institute operations.

The practical problems encountered in implementing the
strategy should be discussed at this point in the course.
There are various "laws" stating how, if things can go
wrong, they will. This is usually tossed off to a capric-
ious fate. Deeper analysis of the various problems occurring in the (C) case should note why various problems
developed and, more importantly, how proper planning by
the managers involved could have overcome many of the problems.

Moreover, the Sea Life Park (C) case should be used
to note how objectives and missions can change over time.
The original objective noted by Tap Pryor is to set up an
Oceanic Institute supported by a marine amusement area.
By the time of the (C) case, the Sea Life Park area is
clearly the most important, and time consuming, area of the
project. Tap seems to be less interested in the project.
Discussion can now revolve around the question of whether
this change in emphasis is the reason for his lessened
interest. An alternative explanation is that his entrepreneurial enthusiasm is dampened by the drudgery of having to
oversee daily operations of an ongoing project.

This last point should provide a valuable area for
discussion at this point. The types of people likely to
start a strategic change may not be the same types needed
for implementing and overseeing those changes. The need

20

for professional management at various stages of strategic change can provide valuable insight into the problems encountered at this final stage of the Sea Life Park series.

Position in Course

The use of the Sea Life Park series can be either at the middle or end portions of a Business Policy course. Also, if a specific segment of the course is devoted to strategic planning in the small business, this case series would provide an ideal addition for this purpose.

The Sea Life Park series can be used singly to emphasize specific areas of the course if used in the middle. The Sea Life Park (A) case could be used in connection with the text materials relating to formation of new strategies and methods of gathering information to assess these strategies. Particularly, the (A) case should be used when developing the students' ability to scan the entire environment in relation to a new strategic move. Tap Pryor appears to look at only one side of the picture in developing his strategy (a common fault of students, as well). This may be necessary for an entrepreneur trying to sell an idea to which he appears totally committed. The case should be used at a point in the course where students have developed, but not fully tested, their analytical skills in exploring the total environment.

The Sea Life Park (B) case, if used separately, should come at the latter part of the first half of the course. It focuses on methods and problems of financing a new venture and the financial/accounting functions are key here. The (B) case can be used, profitably, with the sections of the text referring to financial analysis as well as risk analysis and timing. Tap has made the decision to proceed with construction before he has total financial resources to fund the entire project. In light of recent trends in the construction industry, this is indeed a risky approach. In 1963, this approach was not quite as risky as it may now seem, however.

The students should be able to discuss the actions taken by Tap Pryor in the (B) case in light of the crucial timing requirements of these actions. At this stage of the course, students should be able to integrate not only the stated present actions, but also potential future consequences of these actions. This case could be used as a "swing" case into the segment of the course devoted to developint alternative future courses of action based on current strategies followed by the various organizations discussed.

The Sea Life Park (C) case should be placed in that segment of the course dealing with implementation of strategies, if used separately. Typically, the question

of problems dealing with strategy implementation appears in
the last half of the course. Whereas problems concerning
timing, as discussed in an analysis of the (B) case would
involve contingency planning, they would concern applications in the (C) case. The plans developed by Tap Pryor
and his staff did not include much slack for implementation.

The (C) case demonstrates fairly well that unforseen
problems can come close to wrecking what otherwise would
seem to be feasible strategies. Problems of forecasting
future events (in this case, tourism and attendance) can
be brought into the discussion of the (C) case.

A thorough analysis of the problems facing the organization in the (C) case requires an understanding by the
students of the interactions between the strategy and its
environment. The (C) case is a truly integrative one from
a strategy viewpoint. Any individual policy decision made
at this point in time will surely affect other policy decisions. The Sea Life Park (C) case can be profitably used
as an initial case in the integrative implementation section of the course, therefore. Moreover, the (C) case is
fairly straight forward. The problems are reasonably well
defined. This makes it somewhat easier to see the interactions involved in implementing a strategy.

If the series is used as a unit, it makes a good set
of cases for swinging from the section of the course dealing with strategy formation to implementation. From the
comments above, it can be seen that the entire series can
be used to show how strategies typically are modified over
time to adapt to a changed environment. In the Sea Life
Park series, the environment does not change, really, but
the perception of the environment by Tap Pryor and his
staff changes. They become increasingly faced with the
realities of having to implement and refine a project which
started as an abstract idea and developed into a feasible
strategy faced with typical organizational problems.

The students can use all their skills developed in
the early portion of the course to help Sea Life Park become operational. As stated earlier, the organization is
small enough that the students don't get lost in problems
or organization.

The change in the objectives of Tap Pryor, and Sea
Life Park, can be traced through the series. The change
in objectives has led to a change in the priorities laid
on the actions being implemented. This set of action--
reaction relationships demonstrates at the swing segment
of the course how a decision spreads out to affect all
phases of the strategy formation process.

Key Issues

Sea Life Park (A)

1. Barriers to developing new strategic directions.

2. The need for management commitment to new strategy development is demonstrated.

3. The relationship between strategy formation and environmental trends is shown.

4. Need for consistent, appropriate information during the strategy formation process is critical.

5. Problems associated with obtaining financing from external sources for new strategic directions.

Sea Life Park (B)

1. Questions of refining strategic directions to match forecasts are critical in this case.

2. Risk analysis to provide actions consistent with external environmental factors and internal values should be presented.

3. Timing of planned actions is a critical factor in this case.

4. The interrelationship of various functional and conceptual decisions begins to be a crucial factor in this case.

Sea Life Park (C)

1. Problems of implementing a previously accepted strategy are central to this case.

2. The necessity to adapt action plans to a changed environment (if only perceptual) is demonstrated.

3. The need for contingency plans is clearly presented when plans start to go awry.

4. The effects of external factors on action plans are demonstrated.

5. The need for updated forecasts as time progresses is clearly illustrated as the case proceeds.

6. Overall, the need for a large degree of professionalism in management during implementation of strategies is clearly outlined.

Sea Life Park (A)

Analysis

The Sea Life Park, a combined oceanic research institute and marine exhibit in Hawaii, was scheduled to start
operations on January 1, 1964. It was the outcome of the
efforts of Taylor A. (Tap) Pryor, a biologist involved in
marine research.

History:

In 1957, after military duty, Pryor enrolled as a
doctoral student at the University of Hawaii. He sought
financing for a privately-owned marine exhibit catering to
tourists. He planned to negotiate for a suitable state-
owned piece of land 12 miles to the northeast of Waikiki.
It was proposed that rentals from the exhibit would under-
write research activities.

Stanford Research Institute was engaged to do the
feasibility studies for the project, paid for with $12,000
from a major broadcasting company. SRI estimated the cost
at $2.5 million and that it would operate at a loss, and
therefore that the investment was unjustifiable.

Pryor then discussed the concept with the Curator of
Marineland of the Pacific, who was also a professor of
marine biology at UCLA. He decided that, with new designs
and technology, a much better oceanarium could be built at
less cost. Pryor contacted Honolulu engineers to get cost
estimates and feasibility studies of his construction plans.

Pryor's Progress Report as of Dec., 1962:

Pryor found that a much bigger, better and more interesting exhibit would cost about $1.2 million. The broad-
casting company had decided to drop the project by this
time, however.

Therefore, as of 1960, the search for funds, or an
outside company to build the exhibit continued. In the
meantime, he formed the Oceanics Foundation to act as a
vehicle to present the plan to the state and acquire the
land. His primary interest at this time was in the research installation.

A visit to all oceanarium companies turned up negative
results -- all disagreed with the plans and designs. During the winter of 1960-61, a businessman who reviewed all
the information decided to work on the project with Tap
Pryor. They decided that they would have to form their
own company and raise all the necessary capital themselves.

In January 1962, Sea Life Incorporated was formed.
$1.00 par stock was issued for $50,000 of seed money. The
land was acquired and actual contractors' estimates were
gathered for what was projected to be the world's largest
oceanarium. The maximum cost was placed at $1.2 million.

SRI reviewed the new proposal. They felt that with a
$1.7 million investment, ROI would be 8% for the first
year.

Pryor found out that both government and industry
interest in marine research was on the upsurge at this
time. He also discovered that marine research desired by
these groups would require highly sophisticated electronic
equipment and concepts.

With industry's interest marked, Pryor began considering making the Oceanics Institute a separate project with
its own facilities. This would greatly benefit the exhibit,
though forecasting research facility utilization and income
is problematical.

The oceanarium will have some exciting innovations.
Tanks designed for specific purposes; a park divided into
marine life and man's role in it; an opii roof; a 16 foot
glass spiralling descent into the ocean floor; and a lava
flow, with oceanic topographical formations, are to be key
innovations. The descent will give visitors a replica of
the experience of a tropical reef dive. The descent exits
at a shark pool with an optical illusion of sharks joining
the visitor! Long range plans (3 yrs. - 7 yrs.) call for
a deeper descent (18,000 ft) and an exhibit of the Great
Barrier Reef of Australia.

The other half of the park will have an ocean science
theatre with seats offering simultaneous views of below and
above the water. The porpoises will be the center of attraction -- demonstrating their echo-sounding abilities and
their intelligence through crowd pleasing performances.

This part of the park will lead to the oceanographic
terrace where refreshments will be sold. The terrace will
open out to the park's climax -- the big whaler's cove with
a replica of a Lahaina whaler, the "Essex". There will be
an amphitheatre to show whale chases and other performances.

The climax of the show will be electronically cued
spinning porpoises flipping into action. The whales will
sink the boat and the men will swim into the welcoming
hands of a Hawaiian maiden.

The park will also have a gift shop (Sea Chest) and a
restaurant (the Ocean Lanai) overlooking the park and ocean.
There will also be an office and a building for trainers
and their equipment.

The research area will be developed in the future and is projected to be the best in the world. The research area will be developed at a lower cost because of the clear natural water off the Hawaiian coast. Deep diving gear will be launched off Makapuu point (down to about 18,000 feet).

The Oceanics Foundation will hold lease to the land. The Oceanic Institute will operate the research facility as a non-profit organization.

Sea Life will build and operate the park, paying 12% of gross income as rental payments to the Goundation. This will go to support the foundation be reducing overhead costs. It will also generate creative ideas and help with commercialization of oceanographic opportunities.

Admission rates are scheduled at $2.30 for adults, $1.15 for children and a season (whole year) ticket for $4 (local people will use this most).

Patrons will be brought to the Park by two bus companies, and 14 tour and travel wholesalers. It is projected that Sea Life will thus be advertised in some 3 million free folders in 1964. The Park is expected to draw 50% of the tourists visiting Oahu. 10% of the local population is also expected to visit the Park in any given year.

Questions

1. Has Tap Pryor performed a reasonable amount of feasibility study for the entire project?

2. Evaluate the concept of a combined tourist park and research institute.

3. How realistic are the attendance projections for the first year? For the long run?

4. What alternate sources of financing could Tap have approached to generate additional funds and increase chances of success?

5. What changes should Tap Pryor make in his strategy?

Responses

1. Pryor has developed much more in the way of feasibility studies than most entrepreneurs with a pet project. What is shown from the conflicting reports generated by S.R.I. and the later conversations with the University professor is the difficulty in getting accurate forecasts for new strategies. Tap is accepting all optimistic reports at face value, but discounting anything that is negative. He is not attempting to generate any contingency plans. He also has not tired to place any sensitivity

limits on his projections.

Forecasts are not set in stone. They are not guaranteed results. They may vary over time. They are affected
by a host of external factors such as the economy, societal
values, etc. Tap Pryor has not really attempted to integrate all these factors into his initial plans. The timing
aspects of his projections are vague. He seems to feel
that reactions by the tour industry will be immediate. He
has very little in the way of advance commitments by this
group to the exhibition park. Neither has he tried to
develop advance commitments for his research institute.
Both these problems could come back to haunt him as he
attempts to develop and implement his strategy.

2. The concept of a comgined exhibition park and research
institute is initially quite appealing. Problems occur
when attempts are made at evaluating potential methods of
implementing the idea.

One would have to wonder how investors in the for-
profit park feel about having to pay a large percentage of
revenues to the non-profit foundation. This large bite
comes right off the top. Also, the fate of the foundation
is inextricably tied to the park. Without its revenues,
the research portion will probably be in serious trouble.

Tap has made it clear he is primarily interested in the
institute. He is the prime mover behind the park, however. Discussion should center on his priorities and how
they would affect the success of both projects. It is not
clearly known that he can manage both at once successfully.
If he cannot, then more staff will have to be included in
the plan. This will add to the expense of the project.

The two projects are potentially mutually beneficial,
however. What is learned through research can be applied
at the park to maintain its innovative status. The park
can be used as a showplace for research carried on at the
institute. The sharing of overhead potentially reduces
overhead for both projects.

There are pluses and minuses for this combination.
Unfortunately, only the positive aspects have been explored.

3. The attendance figures appear extremely optimistic.
They are based on the park completed and opened on schedule.
Any person who has had any experience with a construction
project, if only an addition to a house, would know how
imporbable that would be.

Also, Tap is expecting the tour industry to sell Sea
Life Park to their clients sight unseen. All the promotional literature will have to be based on architects'
drawings. The tour operators aren't even sure that Tap can
complete his financing plans. They are bound to be quite
skeptical and cautious towards committing themselves to

such a project. Since a large proportion of tourists come
on pre-packaged tours, this could cut deeply into projected attendance. Also, the distance from the major transportation center of Waikiki (12 miles) could cut into
attendance, at least initially.

On the other hand his projections for local attendance
seem to be quite conservative. The fee structure for group
and season passes appears quite generous. With the combined
emphasis on Hawaiian lore and entertainment, this would
seem to be an ideal drawing card for the local population.
Unfortunately, most of his promotional efforts seem to be
aimed at the tourists in both the long and the short run.

If the Park can survive the critical short run problems,
attendance should pick up significantly. If they can show
to the tour operators that the park is capable of being
entertaining, while producing profits for all involved, they
will undoubtedly include it in their tours. The long run
attendance figures may turn out to be higher than projected.
The long run has to be reached first, however.

4.   It appears that, in his quest for financing, Tap has
placed primary emphasis on mainland corporations. Local
sources of financing would be advantageous from a couple of
points of view.

First, the state government and the local population
would be less likely to look upon the project and its
managers as interlopers or "carpetbaggers." This kind of
acceptance could greatly assist the project's ability to
get land leases and services from various state agencies.
It could also help to generate attentance and sales at the
park, especially during the critical first period just
after opening. The local population would feel that they
have a stake in the project -- that is, a truly local
enterprise, and therefore deserving of added local support.

Another potential source of financial support would be
the tour industry itself. If Tap could find a tour oper-
ator or packager who wants to integrate forward, this
would provide an excellent opportunity. The support could
be from either the mainland or, in line with the comments
above, from Hawaii. This would have the added benefit of
providing more expertise in the tourist industry, which
Tap lacks.

Finally, Tap might also look for increased support
for the research institute. If the institute could be
self-supporting from the start, the probability of success
of both ventures would be increased considerably. Support
could be solicited from the government, foundations, and
private industry, all interested in marine research.

5.   The changes at this stage would be rather tentative.
He is primarily at the idea generation and formulation
stage of strategic planning. His first effort should be to
clearly define his objectives. They should be broken down
to note what are primary and what are secondary objectives.
Priorities have to be assigned to his various objectives and
projected actions. A clear-cut distinction has to be developed between the park and the research institute. The
timing of development of each should be explored to be consistent with the resources available to the total organization, both personal and financial.

Tap has to include in his strategy a clear cut commitment of his own efforts. It is unclear that he has really
thought through the time and effort required to operate
both projects. If he analyzes this effort, he will probably see, quite forcibly, that he will have to place his
own primary emphasis on one or the other of the projects.
If so, he will have to hire someone to run the other
project.

The interrelation of the financing, promotion, construction, resource gathering, etc., of the park must be
clarified. Tap, at this time, appears to view them as
separate and discrete functions. Decisions made in one
area are going to affect the others. These interactions
must be openly explored if the overall strategy is to have
a chance at success.

Also, the sensitivity of the strategy to changes must
be explored. Tap has to start asking what-if types of
questions concerning actions and forecasts. This will
lead to a set of contingency plans to set into operation
if his optimistic set of projections do not hold up once
the strategy is implemented. These would include promotional efforts as well as decreased scale of operations if the
tourist flood does not materialize. It should also include
means to expand operations if the tour packages take to his
project enthusiastically. This could prove to be a long
run disaster for the project. The last thing Tap needs is
to turn away tourists, or to have tourists and tour operators leaving the park with a bad feeling about the park
and its management.

Sea Life Park (B)

Analysis

After Tap had concepts well developed, financing became the major task. In 1961, $50,000 high risk capital had been raised with $1.00 par shares.

To finance construction and operations would probably require $1.6 million of additional capital. This would be raised by the sale of 5½% 12 year non-convertible debentures and more shares of $2.00 par common stock. A five year loan of $400,000 from Hawaiian banks would provide the remainder of the capital. In addition, 200,000 authorized shares were reserved for current management options and 100,000 shares were reserved for future management options. With the options exercised, management and the original investors would hold control of 50% of the common stock.

By the Fall of 1963, financing was almost complete. Due to extra construction costs and added requirements, the loan had risen to $550,000 and the bank had indicated it was about the maximum that would be lent.

The needed $1.2 million was sold in units of $50,000 each., A unit and a half permitted Tap to keep the number of investors under 24. This enabled the offering to be classed as a private placement requiring no SEC clearance.

Private placement is best done, however, by contacting small business investment companies, presidents, and board chairmen of large corporations.

The placement (stocks and debentures) began in January. By Christmas, all of these stock and debentures were sold, although $73,000 had not yet been received. The oceanarium was 4/5 completed and the opening was now scheduled for January 28. The delays and increased costs had all but eliminated the financial cushion built into the budgets.

Construction progressed as funds became available. Porpoise training was begun a year ahead of opening, to give a captivating opening show. It was also used to attract investors. Later, capital was raised with better presentations to potential investors. Tap was able to show the progress being made on construction of facilities as well as training of animals.

The decision was made to start construction on tanks and exhibits when 3/4 of the required capital was raised. By May 1963, with only $800,000 raised, construction contracts were signed. The project began to move rapidly, and relatively smoothly, from this point on.

The organizational structure finds the corporate staff (Pryor and an accountant) at the top; two assistants, one

3 0

for public relations, park and plant operations, the other for marketing and sales and the park staff.

Future growth in both revenues and organization is expected to come from industrial oceanography (to follow from the oceanics division). One assistant, a graduate of Stanford, is highly interested in industrial oceanics.

What worried Tap at this point was whether sufficient sales would be generated to cover immediate expenses. There was still no solid assurance that the tour industry was going to provide customers, and the opening was less than one month away. Local support had been enthusiastic, however.

Questions

1. What critical lessons can be learned on the timing aspects of strategy from the Sea Life Park (B) case?

2. What factors should Tap have considered in making the decision to begin construction before financing was completed?

3. How has Tap Pryor refined his strategy in the Sea Life Park (B) case?

4. What contingency plans should Tap Pryor now develop to overcome the worries that plague him at the end of the Sea Life Park (B) case?

Responses

1. Tap has continued to ignore the potential problems that might develop if something happens to further delay the opening of the park. He has clung to the belief that anything that goes wrong can be rectified immediately. Only at the end of the case does he start to have second thoughts about what has happened to date.

Tap has shown, at times, an appreciation for planning, by allowing different phases of the strategy to progress concurrently. He starts on construction and animal train-ing before financing is completed. Since he is not needed for the first two areas, there are no physical reasons why all these actons must occur sequentially instead of simultaneously. This point has been forcefully brought home to students through the use of various management science approaches discussed in the text. What is inter-esting is that Tap has arrived at these decisions with little business training or exposure to such concepts or tools as PERT pr CPM. He apparently feels that this approach just makes sense and is in line with his personal values relating to risk.

3 1

2. Tap made the decision to go ahead with construction, primarily because he wanted to get on with the project. Impatience, rather than hard analysis, led him to the decision. The students should be asked to provide the analysis that is lacking at this point.

The factors that should have been brought out include trade-offs between timing and risk of failure. The benefits of proceeding early include the ability to meet the tourist season at its outset. This would potentially bring in greater revenues at the early stages of the park spending. It must be remembered that Oahu is primarily a winter vacation area in 1964.

Starting construction also provides a better selling point to the remaining investors. There is something solid to show the investors instead of just some architect's drawings and one man's dreams for the future. Also, the state of Hawaii and interested local people can be shown that Sea Life Park is committed to Oahu and the entire project.

Tour operators can also be shown that the park really does exist. They would be more confident of including the park in their tours if they can see something solid to assure them it will be operating by the time their clients (tourists) arrive on Oahu.

There may also be cost benefits as well. Even though inflation was hardly the factor in 1963 that it is now, costs of delaying construction could eat into the reserve allowed for in the initial budgets.

There are risks in this type of strategy, however. This is where Tap falls down in his planning. As mentioned above, his timetable for completion is extremely tight. He is scheduled for completion just prior to the tourist season. If anything goes wrong, he may not only lose initial sales, but also the trust and confidence of the tour operators.

Also, once started, he may find it difficult to delay construction if necessary. If the remaining funds had not been available on time, the banks might have been forced to foreclose on the construction loans. He could have been left with a costly piece of partly finished construction that would eat up his slender reserves, if he could stop construction, as well.

This kind of strategy requires that momentum be maintained if it is to succeed. It is much like a juggler trying to keep a lot of balls in the air. As long as he is knowledgeable, confident, and lucky, he succeeds. If he loses confidence or luck, the balls come crashing down on him. A slowing in the pace of progress on the Sea Life Park project could have caused many of the parties to lose confidence. This could have had disasterous effects. So

far, Tap's willingness to accept risk has been appropriate.
Also, so far, he has been lucky.

3.   Tap is now having to reappraise his commitment to the
various parts of the project. Investors' questions have
led him to better define his own interest in the two projects. While his interests still clearly lay with the
research institute, he now has made a commitment to make
the exhibition park a profitable success.

The organization of the projects has similarly become
better defined. Responsibility for operating the park has
been delegated to assistants. Tap appears at this stage
to have defined his role as the coordinator for the two
projects, seeker of funds, and director of the research institute.

The key development in the strategy was the decision
to stay with the original, although not well-defined,
timing plan despite some minor difficulty in obtaining
financing. Tap Pryor made the decision to increase the
risk of the project by starting construction in the belief
that the remainder of the financing was forthcoming.

Tap has been forced to postpone the opening of the
park despite this decision, however. He has also been
forced, paradoxically, to schedule the opening before it
is expected to be fully ready for operations. Tight capital has forced this decision on Tap Pryor. Future decisions may be just as much affected by cash flow requirements as by other factors, personal or otherwise.

4.   Key areas that have to be considered at this point
center around survival in the short run and provision for
long run success. Tap has to realistically assess projected
attendance figures. The tour industry has made no moves
toward including Sea Life Park in its current packaged
tours. This brings the SRI attendance figures into question. The tour industry is probably accustomed to optimistic projections and promises.

Based on this reappraisal, Tap and his subordinates
should draw up a new cash flow chart for the next year,
on a monthly basis. It is unlikely the tour industry will
be able to shift gears until that time.

The Sea Life Park is already feeling the financial
pinch due to the delayed opening. It has to ensure a positive cash flow over the short term to be able to live for
the long term. These projections should then be used to
secure the funds necessary for the short term. Based on
the enthusiastic response from local sources to date, this
aspect shouldn't prove too difficult. Tap could consider
approaching the local population for even greater sales.
Approximately 80% of the 600,000 people living in the state
are found on the island of Oahu. This provides a large,
captive audience for the Park.

Next, Tap should set up methods of getting people to the Park. Since the tour industry isn't providing service, at least for the first year of operation, there seems to be little worry about competing with the industry. Without transportation to the park, there is little chance of getting what few tourists are likely to come without them having to get to the Park by rented car. This also means that the car rental agencies have to be given strong incentive to promote the Park.

Finally, Tap has to make sure that everything goes well during the opening weeks of the Park. Initial impressions will carry a great deal of weight with the local clientele. It will also provide added incentive for the other groups who will be able to supply customers to see that this is a worthwhile endeavor.

In the longer run, Tap and his subordinates have to place a great deal of emphasis on encouraging the tour industry to include the Park in their packages for the following year. This should be held off until the Park is opened and operating well.

Tap has to set priorities for his own actions and plans. He has to realize that he can't do everything he wants at once or by himself. He has to delegate responsibility for operating the Park to subordinates. His strengths lie in the area of public relations for the venture and raising capital. He has to concentrate his efforts here, at least for the short run. Thoughts of developing the Oceanics Institute must be delayed for the time being. The payoffs to be derived from this part of the venture are too long-term to be considered at present. After the park is operating, efforts can be channeled in this direction. The Park is designed to fund the Institute at the initial stage. The Park, therefore, is the key to the success of the entire venture. Its long term success must not be endangered by spreading resources too thin.

Sea Life Park (C)

Analysis

Sea Life Park publicly opened February 11, 1964, instead of January 1 as scheduled. This added $50,288 to unbudgeted costs while construction had a $40,000 cost over-run. Due to an active publicity campaign, the park opened with about $7,500 cash from advance ticket sales, however.

The Sea Life Collecting Crew, assisted by local skin divers, brought in fish. The "Essex" was installed and the spinning porpoise moved into the lagoon.

On February 9, a preview of the opening was held for members of the press and their families, friends of the designing, building, supplying, and financing companies, as well as members of the tour industry.

Through Tap's announcements, the audience was emotionally involved so as to overlook shortcomings or mistakes.

The opening day's attendance was fairly good and encouraging (600), bringing in $2,213. The first week grossed 6,329 visitors, total revenue $22,465. The second week was better but in the third week it nosedived. The following comments are drawn from memoranda and letters:

March 6 (Tom): Operations have to be shifted from local to tourist patronage. Attendance trend is in this direction. Cooperation of the tour industry is vital here. For the next thirty operating days, two to three groups have been booked.

The Outstanding Accomplishment of the Year Award will go to Sea Life Park on the 19th of March.

March 11 (Tom): Radio and TV exposure to capture Easter crowds -- 10% discount ticket sales to be offered those not qualifying as wholesalers. A meeting was held with Honolulu Rapid Transit to provide non-competing transportation (with the tour people).

March 20 (Tap): Attendance is good. Easter and May through June will be high attendance, moving into the summer boost when 20% of the tourists visit Waikiki, and the Sea Life Park target is 60%.

March 31 (Bob): Governor Brown of California visited the Whalers' Cove. The holiday week was good.

April 16 (Tom): Kaena, the false killer whale really plays with the porpoises. She consumes 65 lbs. of mackerel a day. A search for a mate is proceeding.

Two rare porpoises -- sterno rostrotus, have been added. One porpoise, caught in a separating net, drowned. Sales are good, but could be made better.

April 21 (Bob): Gift shop opens this week. Tour industry is still showing reluctance to schedule Sea Life Park. Kaena is giving rides on its head.

April 28 (Tap): The Park is the greatest hit in Honolulu. It's the talk of the town. Consequently, 20,000 annual passes have been sold and the trend is expected to continue. For past Sunday, all shows had only standing room; therefore more seating is being added.

The sales program has been sound and effective. The restaurant is operating in the black with no forseeable problems.

The gift shop will meet expected standards. The back will have an art gallery and book store. Tom's introduction of a 'red flag' system allows for easy analysis of the financial situation.

Bob is doing marvelously well. Publicity has been phenomenally good lately and handlers (Tap and Bob) are considering slowing it up a little.

Karen, Tap's wife, is now a full time curator of the exhibits and is doing well.

A new animal (Tursiops) was added to the glass porpoise exhibit, and a spinning porpoise has replaced the drowned one.

The major problem now is parking; and a new lot will open before June. Most Sunday visitors are pass holders. The pass volume will be reduced by raising the price next year. Some night operations will start this summer.

May 14 (Tap): Operating results have not reached the peak as projected in 1961, therefore revenue forecasts have been adjusted downward. Actual gross revenue was $74,000.

June 16 (Bob):   It appears that the summer upswing has begun.

June 16 (Tap):   Operations are running three times the normal average. Oceanic tour for next year is being prepared by us, with tour industry cooperation. In addition to what Sea Life has to show, local mythology will be incorporated. A tour presentation will be made to the industry on June 30th.

June 22 (Bob): Expenses are going down and expected to continue. June on the whole brought a good summer beginning.

July 7 (Bob): 1965 Oceanic tour is ready. The
actual sales of $16,600 was below expected $18-20,00/week
for July and August.

July 24 (Tom): For June, July and August, Sea Life is
trying to establish itself in the tour industry for 1965.
Oceanic Sea Life tour is being packaged with the help of
consultatns. All wholesalers have agreed to include this
as part of their 1965 program; their promotion will be
boosted by our $54,000 advertisement budget. Sea Life now
gets 12% of the tourists.

August 5 (Bob): Still revenues are below forecasts;
therefore projections are being revised downward. A
revision of bank loan to us has been requested.

August 14 (Tap's letter to stockholders): Expenses
have been sliding every month, staff members are controlling their functions very well, community support mounts
daily, and will continue. Tour industry cooperation is
excellent -- for 1965.

Total revenue and admissions forecasts are not being
met. Resident attendance has been higher than expected.

The "Little Circle Island Tour" will bring in tourists by the thousands. Presentations on the mainland are
being enthusiastically accepted by tour wholesalers.
1965 projections (Exhibit 11) will be met. Since costs
don't rise with volume, profits will increase.

Season ticket sales have 35,000 outstanding and this
can be doubled. Sea Life will continue to grow with the
growth of marine life and will be the best marine exhibit
in the world.

August 24 (Bob): Revenues have been on the rise each
week ($2000 above last week which was $2400 above the
previous one). August revenue forecast will probably be
exceeded by $5000.

September 2 (Bob): Total revenue and attendance
fell. August's profitability was expected to be the best.
Bank approved loan repayment revision.

September 2 (Tap): Tap is going back to complete his
Ph. D., and will spend four half-days at Makapuu. Will
attend staff meetings and read reports, weekly inspections,
and handle the important correspondence.

Tap's absence will temper the others' handling of the
company. Later they will go into industrial oceanics.

September 9 (Bob): 50,000 to 75,000 new tourists
claimed by the mainland presentation. Cash flow is still
tight from pre-opening over-run. The September off-season
decline further hurt the weak cash position ($19000 lost).

October 6 (Tap): The expenses will be whittled down
by $8,500. The sales force is being expanded and will go
after special segments -- military, groups, pineapple
workers,etc. Remunerations will be on a small base salary
plus commission.

Sea Life newsletter will soon be released. It will
help annual pass sales as will a guest booklet. With the
exhibits' high standard, personnel can handle more responsibility without adverse effects.

The Oceanic - Sea Life Park tour is expected to bring
in 100,000 new visitors. The National Geographic and
Time will both being doing articles on Sea Life Park.

October 7 (Bob): Cash flow forecasts being revised
due to low ($8,400/week) revenues since Labor Day.

October 10 (Tap): The post Labor Day slump was completely unexpected. To avoid a repetition, future forecasts
will be based on the first eight months of operations.

A bad weather contingency deflationary factor of 10-20%
will apply. Monthly revenue will range from $45,000 to
$89,000 (summer). Sea Life's tourist market share is pro-
jected to be 37%; annual pass revenue at 60%, and new pass
sales at $2500 per month.

These forecasts are taken as conservative.

The Oceanics Institute completed some significant
projects during the year:
  i) a decompression chamber converted to an underwater
  permanent residency for researchers.
  ii) a trained porposed for offshore testing and
  research.

Some other research proposals were sent to government
and other bodies; with a high probability of two or three
being accepted -- brackish water fish pond culture and an
underwater laboratory and living quarters.

Questions

1. What problems can be seen through analysis of the
various statements and communications presented in the
(C) case?

2. Why is the share of the tourist market so low?

3. How can the number of tourists be increased in the
next few years?

4. How would you evaluate Tap Pryor's decision to return
to school on a full-time basis?

5.   What recommendatkons would you make to the management
of Sea Life Park to assure its long term viability and
success?

Responses

1.   The information presented in the Sea Life Park (C)
case points up the problems associated with a lack of
planning for contingencies. Tap has based all his actions
on the assumption that everything will proceed smoothly.
He hasn't verified the projections made by the various
outside agencies (SRI, etc.). He has already seen that
some of the projections are incorrect, such as the initial
building costs expectations.

The key problem is that Tap did not try to evaluate
his strategy for weak points. He has not worked through,
in advance, the timing of his action plan. Failure to
note the critical points in the strategy has forced him
into the position of having to react to the external environment, instead of being able to plan for it.

The comments in the (C) case show Tap and his organization trying to cut costs instead of controlling them.
There is the feeling throughout the comments that they
may be trimming muscle along with the fat.

It is clear that the tour industry has not produced
the expected customers projected by Tap and others. The
customer base is completely different from that which was
expected. Instead of adapting to this change, Tap tries
to fight it, at least initially. It is only after the
change is clear does he finally try to adapt. This re-
inforces the view that Tap is not really considering the
underlying reasons for some of his problems, particularly
in the area of marketing.

Until Tap looks at the basis for his problems, instead
of simply the symptoms of those problems, he is unlikely to
arrive at any long term solutions. He still feels that he
can spread his own talents over many areas and still serve
all areas well.

2.   Sea Life Park has opened at a particularly poor time
for the Hawaiian tourist season. The season has already
started. For the Park to have gained a large tourist
audience, it would have had to be included in a substantial proportion of the packaged tours before they were sold
to the public.

The tour industry is, by necessity, wary of promised
attractions. It has seen, too often, that bright promises
turn out to be nothing but that -- promises. The tour
agents rely on repeat business for their continued success.
If the agents sell a tour that includes a real dud or, even

worse, a program that has not even been completed, then they are unlikely to gain that repeat business.

The tour agents are unlikely, therefore, to include an attraction that they have not seen, let alone that has not been completed. This all-important group has to be shown that Sea Life Park will be a going, and lively, concern before they will include it in their packaged tours. This usually means that there will be at least a one year time lag period before heavy tourist response (except for big names such as Disney). This is particularly true where pre-packaged tours constitute such an overwhelmingly large percentage of tour bookings. Most people who arrive in the islands have bought a pre-packaged tour. The remainder would have to be approached after they arrive in Oahu.

Tap Pryor and his subordinates have placed all their efforts on the organized tour industry, however. They have made relatively little effort to reach the uncommitted tourist. They have also made little effort to reach the large number of military rest and recreation personnel coming in from the SoutheastPacific region.

Basically, Tap and his management team have not considered the total market involved in the tourist business. They have also not considered the timing involved in implementing their marketing objectives and action plan. This has led them to misjudge their short run consumer base.

3.   Tap has to take a much broader view of his projected market. He also has to realize that selling the Park to a few, large, tour packagers will not insure the overall success of his venture. This marketing strategy, if successful, would only provide a marginal return. Tap has to provide for a broader consumer base to present the parent firm with enough funds to support the Institute.

A concentrated, well rounded sales program must be developed to attract all the segments of the tourist industry. The primary emphasis must be placed on the packaged tour promoters. They must be brought to Oahu and shown that Sea Life Park does indeed live up to all expectations. They must also be given the incentive, if necessary, to insure inclusion of Sea Life Park in the pre-packaged tours. This incentive will cost nothing in advance since it will merely be a reduction in revenues.

The cost will come from transporting key tour agents to Oahu and showing them the benefits of Sea Life Park. Tap could arrange to share this cost with other travel-based attractions (hotels, airlines, etc.) in Hawaii. Development of borchures and promotions to the independent tour agents would comprise the remainder of the costs.

The remainder of the program should revolve around the military and independent tourist groups. The military provides a market that is readily accessible. All personnel have to check in at a central location. Discounts are traditionally granted to them when they check in.

The majority of tourists who arrive without a professionally packaged tour all come in through the same airport. They also can be reached through the hotel travel desks (available in all the better hotels). They also can be approached through the car rental agencies. Most of these uncommitted tourists eventually rent one of the many rental cars available on Oahu. (It should be noted that Hawaii has more rental cars per capita than any other state.)

4.   This seems to be an inappropriate time for Tap to be returning to school on a full-time basis. From the comments above, it would seem that his efforts will be required to guide the management team in the implementation of these proposed actions.

Similarly, from the statements issued to stockholders, it would seem that Sea Life Park is not yet out of the woods regarding its various internal problems. The loss of the key "salesman" of the overall project could lead to loss of momentum at a critical period in the growth of the project.

Others, however, have felt that Tap's departure at this time may be the best thing to happen to Sea Life Park. His absence would break down the barriers to changing any part, or all, of the strategy for the venture. Moreover, his return to college, and, hopefully, his completion of his dissertation and studies would add prestige to the Oceanics Institute. This could also siphon his energies towards the Institute, even after Tap returns to the project.

The trade-off between loss of top management guidance and ability to change strategies should be seriously considered at this point. The decision by Tap to leave, accompanied by need for increased cash flow and tourist acceptance should be used as a lead in to this discussion. This is one of the few instances where a dynamic, entrepreneurial manager has voluntarily absented himself from the active operation of a going concern that he has formed.

This provides the strategy analyst with a unique opportunity to propose changes that might otherwise not be acceptable to top management.

5.   A key recommendation for Sea Life Park is to expand its management staff. It has now demonstrated that it can operate successfully on a shoestring. Now it must make the transition to an efficiently run organization.

Tap has expressed the desire, from the outset, that the Park provide the inside funding for the Oceanic Institute. For this to be feasible, it must be a professionally managed operation. Tap's entrepreneurial spirit should either be channeled towards the long term increase in the attractions of the Park, or towards the improvement in the activity of the Oceanic Institute.

Contingency plans should be set up to contend with the short run cash flow problems. Also, better cost accounting systems should be instituted to insure long term profitability of the overall project. Management cannot rely on their "gut feel" appraisal of the success of the various parts of the operation to evaluate implementation of objectives and actions.

The management of Sea Life Park must be made to realize that they cannot do everything. They must expand the employees if they are going to be able to accomodate the large numbers of visitors expected in the future. They cannot continue to shift personnel back and forth between exhibits the way they do now, although this is presently efficient. As capacity of the Park and the Institute are reached, a more effective approach to management has to be considered.

Similarly, personnel will have to be segregated between the Park and the Institute. The requirements for success for the two ventures are different. One venture requires a showman atmosphere. The other segment requires a professional, research-oriented, approach to the customer. The first requires pleasing a large number of diverse customers. The second requires selling a service to very small groups of customers, typically the government. Personnel, marketing, financing, management all have to be planned for the future. Moreover, future actions and objectives should be planned in the event the entire project should succeed. The question that might be considered here is what should the firm do once the objectives of Park and Institute success are achieved?

THE ORGANIZATION AND ITS ENVIRONMENT

This section deals with the interface between the organization and its external environment. The two case series presented show how two companies have had to adapt their decision making processes to a changing social, legal and economic environment. Although both firms, Pacific Gas and Electric Company and Southern Pacific Company, are highly regulated, they retain enough flexibility in decision criteria to consider alternate strategies.

The questions that are raised in these cases can be used to demonstrate the issues raised in the text in Chapters 2 and 4, dealing with the external environment. Particularly, the trade-off between economic and social objectives can be clearly demonstrated in the decisions confronting managements at both organizations.

External environmental forces have become increasingly important in the strategic decision process. Unfortunately, most strategic decisions are still made based on internal decision criteria. Management in all types of organizations has to be convinced of the importance of political and social factors affecting their ability to make strategic decisions.

The cases in the following section should be used to enhance the analytical skills of strategy analysts when relating to the external environment. The cases also will provide the analyst with the opportunity to explore and incorporate the value system and objectives of external constituencies in the strategy formation process. Questions relating to the impact of social and political trends; whose values should be considered; how to adapt to changing environmental factors; and how to include these forces in the strategy formation process should all be included in the analysis and discussion of these cases.

Pacific Gas and Electric Company

Purpose

The PG&E case series clearly demonstrates the interaction between the internal decision-making process and the
external environment. The necessity for forecasting and
evaluating trends in the external environment should be a
prime focus when discussing both of these cases.

The PG&E (A) case should be used to demonstrate how
an organization has been forced to change its structure,
objectives and actions based on a changing environment.
The case shows that what had traditionally been a purely
intellectual decision in the past (site selection of a power
plant) has turned into a social and political decision as
well. Previously, PG&E would present a technically competent proposal to the various regulatory agencies involved
with approval of sites for power plants. The data presented
would almost always be sufficient to overcome any opposition
that might be generated.

The change in social values has introduced a new el-
ement into the decision making process. Environmental
froups are now being given the opportunity to challenge the
site selection process on non-technical and non-economic
grounds. PG&E has not fully adapted to this change in the
environment. Part of the discussion should focus on the
effect that these social and environmental changes are having on different levels of the organization.

Upper levels of the organization have become annoyed
by these changes. Lower levels of the organization feel
that requirements to answer to environmental demands are a
threat to their technical competence.

Also, the (A) case provides the opportunity to discuss
the trade-offs between economic and social returns from
business decisions. PG&E feels that the Nipomo Dunes area
provides the best (most economical) site for future nuclear
power sites. The Sierra Club wants the area saved for environmental purposes. The Sierra Club is willing to accept
a higher economic cost to save what it feels is a valuable
part of the ecology. Questions concerning who should make
these decisions, and how far these trends are likely to go
could be pursued at this point.

Finally, structural changes brought on by these external changes should be discussed in conjunction with this
case. The students should trace how the organization has
changed up to this point. Further, they should provide
solutions for further change in the decision process relating to site selection.

44

The PG&E (B) case is designed to show how an organization actually adapted to environmental opposition. It shows how co-optation was carried out by PG&E on the Sierra Club. It also shows, however, that you can't please everyone all of the time.

Specific questions refereing to future actions and decisions on site selection are inherent in discussions of the (B) case. Students can test their proposed changes presented as a result of the discussion of the (A) case. They also can present methods for limiting controversy by the minority group within the Sierra Club.

Basically, the PG&E (B) case should be used to evaluate the effectiveness of implementation of environmental strategies. In addition, the students are asked to decide between two alternative nuclear power sites based on a combination of economic and environmental objectives. The decision should be made consistent with projected environmental, economic, and social trends and organizational objectives.

Position in the Course

The two cases can be used either separately or as a series in that segment of the course devoted to external forces. The social/environmental issues are clearly pre-eminent in these cases. These areas are usually discussed at the middle or latter segments of the Business Policy course.

The analysis of the external environment typically comes after the internal analysis. Typically, students have a better background in the internal area of analysis. Accounting, financial, management, quantitative methods of analysis, are often internally oriented.

There is frequently little emphasis given to developing methods for analyzing external trends. Moreover, within the external environment, social and political trends are given even less emphasis. For this reason, external environmental analysis is the last of the problems to be discussed in the strategy formation stage of the course.

Alternatively, the PG&E (B) case could be used as a lead in case for the implementation phase of the course. The issues are relatively clear and narrowly focused. The organization is highly regulated. It is, essentially, a monopoly. This allows the class to ease into the problems of implementing strategic changes in an organization.

Key Issues

P. G. & E. (A)

1. Social responsibility of a profit oriented organization.

2. Trade offs between profit and social/environmental objectives.

3. Organizational changes brought about in response to environmental changes.

4. Relative degree of social responsibility of a "public" (regulated) versus a "private" firm.

5. Degree of public participation in organization discussions affecting the environment.

P. G.& E. (B)

1. Co-optation of environmental opposition.

2. Combination of social and profit objectives.

3. Implementing strategic decisions affecting the environment.

4. De-fusing external opposition to strategic decisions.

5. Interaction between regulated organizations and their governmental regulators.

Pacific Gas & Electric (A)

Analysis

The PG&E (A) case traces the decision process for
site selection of nuclear power plants by a large public
utility. PG&E is one of the largest public utilities in
the country. It services much of Northern California.
This area is growing rapidly. It has been estimated that,
at the time of the case, population for this region was
growing at the rate of 1500 people per day. This factor
alone requires considerable long range planning by a company such as PG&E. Added to the population growth is the
increase in usage per capita of electrical energy.

PG&E, therefore, is faced in the (A) case with a rapidly expanding demand for their product. Paradoxically,
they are also faced with repidly declining alternatives
for supplying that demand.

Many of the best sites for locating any type of power
plant have already been used. Some of the remaining
sites which are technically acceptable to PG&E are being
opposed by environmental groups, moreover. PG&E had just
lost a long and costly battle to place a nuclear power plant
at Bodega Bay, north of San Francisco, as of the time of
this case. Their public image had been badly tarnished
due to the method by which they had tried to gain approval
of the Bodega Bay power station.

PG&E set up an environmental study group as a result
of the Bodega Bay site problems. The group apparently is
purely advisory, however. This can be implied from the
fact that most of the data presented in the case relate to
economic and technical factors affecting the Nipomo Dunes
site. PG&E still is not consulting with environmental
groups during the selection process. The internal environmental group is to be used to "sell" the idea after site
selection has been accepted within the organization.

The Nipomo Dunes site that has finally been selected
lies in a scenic, ocean front setting on the middle section
of the Pacific Ocean coastline. The Dunes have been described as a unique ecological formation. The Sierra Club,
once it discovered that PG&E had purchased the site, filed
protests to its use for any type of power plant. It would
only be acceptable to the Sierra Club if the plant were
set back at least 5000 feet from the ocean.

PG&E technicians have stated that this set-back arrangement is technically feasible. They also state, however,
that a setback of only 500 feet would be far superior.
Financial analysis performed by PG&E staff shows that a
5000 foot set back would drastically increase construction

costs. These costs would have to be passed on to the consumer by way of increased electricity rates. Utilization
of the site for multiple plants would increase the cost/
technical problems with the 5000 foot set back. An alternative of a 1700 foot set back has been explored within the
company. PG&E feels that this would, at best, provide a
compromise position. Sierra Club officials have made no
show of being willing to compromise on the set back, however.

No effort has been made to educate the public as to
the overall need for increased generating capacity as of
this time. All efforts are still directed towards the
regulatory agencies involved, of which there are many.
What external efforts are made are directed to the Sierra
Club. These efforts are primarily economic and technical
in nature.

The Sierra Club is responding with environmental and
emotional arguements. The arguements presented by the
Sierra Club are, essentially, being ignored.

In the past, moreover, the Sierra Club has had to wait
until PG&E had purchased land before it could mount opposition. It was not until then that anyone outside PG&E
knew what sites were actively being considered. This has
all changed since the presentation by PG&E of its "Super
System".

The "Super System" is designed to show the future
growth pattern of generating capacity for the next 15 years.
Company officials felt that this form of long range planning
made eminent sense. Unfortunately, this plan also presented
to the Sierra Club a detailed outline of all potential
power plant sites, nuclear and otherwise, for the future.
This means that they can organize opposition to undesireable
sites well in advance of any proposed construction.

PG&E had based its "Super System" sites and generating
capacity on forecasts of population growth and projections
of power usage by its largest commercial users. In the
past, these projections had been relatively accurate. The
organization always included ample excess capacity to insure
that brown-outs would not occur, however. This necessitated
that the entire system would always have excess capacity.

Questions

1.   What is the mission of PG&E?

2.   Should PG&E pursue the application for a nuclear power
      plant at Nipomo? If so what set-back should be
      applied for?

3.   What alternative course of action should be pursued?

48

Solutions

1.   PG&E is a utility and as such it presents, beyond the normal set of problems, an entire set of additional "special" problems.

We encounter the first "special" problem in trying to determine our mission and set out objectives. Stating "To fulfil the power demands of our service area" is quite obviously insufficient. Anyone of the three sites would accomplish this snd.

In order to make the above sufficient, we must add two riders: 1) In a manner acceptable to the population of the area, and 2) As efficiently as possible (because of the lag in rate changes).

When we do this, however, we see that we have created a dichotomy. The least expensive is also the least acceptable and vice versa. As things now stand, the customer can only lose, either through high rates for power or an environmental loss. It is our task to minimize his loss.

2.   In order to pursue the application, a massive education of the public is necessary. For an optimal decision to be made the public should be working with facts. To this point they are using half-information and emotion in their protest. To best quell this current wave of protest, a 2 stage education program should be undertaken.

First, general information should be disseminated on the tremendous growth in the need for power. An ad agency can be retained to generate a primary demand for power. Next there should be a presentation as factual as is possible of the various alternatives and their costs, both in money and environmental consequences.

The second stage starts with an information search by a reputable research firm. It would be their job to determine the misgivings of the population obout a nuclear generator (our choice). Once this is determined, psychologists and ad men together can determine the best manner to elicit public backing of the 1700 foot choice (our choice).

As for "compromise", it might well be best to argue for the 500 foot site and "compromise" with the 1700 foot one.

3.   Some potential strategies the organization might follow are listed below:

a. Generate new alternate sites.

b. Start work on an existing alternate site.

c. Compromise among existing alternate sites.

The sites under consideration, currently, were all chosen by in-house experts. These men are convinced that their list is exhaustive. However, by soliciting the aid of the protesting groups new alternatives may be generated. Using a site thus chosen could gain PG&E a powerful ally.

If new alternate sites are added to the "Super System", the environmental action group organized within the organization should play an active part in the site selection process. Approval of new power plant sites is no longer simply an intellectual process. Political and social factors now play an important part in the approval process. The engineers and financial specialists who prepared all the material for previous presentations clearly did not consider these aspects. Their reactions to environmental opposition has been one of disappointment. Their perception that this technical competence is being questioned must be overcome by the internal environmental action group.

Another alternative course of action might be to speed up work on one of the other sites on the list. This would show what kind of opposition could be expected from the rest of the "Super System". The internal environmental action group would confer with the Sierra Club to determine which of the sites is most acceptable.

Finally, the organization could determine if any compromises are available to the sites set forth in the "Super System". For those sites that are initially objectionable, procedures might be developed to overcome the opposition of groups like the Sierra Club. As with the Nipomo site, the firm's site selection staff might generate compromises on the placement of plants within a general area (i.e. -- different set backs).

Regardless of what set of strategic alternatives are selected, PG&E has to expand participation in the site selection process. The external environment has changed. Managers at PG&E have to forecast what changes in the environment will be and how they will affect their ability to make decisions.

Pacific Gas & Electric Company (B)

Analysis

The decision by PG&E managers on the Nipomo Dunes
issue raised in the (A) case was to seek a compromise with
the Sierra Club. A broad based, management committee was
formed to seek a compromise.

The firm first determined that the opposition agreed
to the need for a new power plant for the region. The committee then sought the help of the Sierra Club in seeking
a new site.

The Sierra Club officers then proceeded to find an
acceptable site. The site offered had previously been re-
jected by PG&E because they felt they couldn't purchase it
without a costly, and lengthy court battle.

The final site offered was on an old, Spanish land
grant. The property, Diablo Canyon, had been in the same
family for many years. The present owner agreed to relinquish control of the site, when approached by the Sierra
Club. The factor that lead him to entertain an offer, however, was his need for cash to develop other parts of his
property.

Diablo Canyon was not without its faults from a technical point of view. The terrain was uneven. Parts were
exposed to the sea. It was totally undeveloped, thereby
requiring intensive development work simply to prepare the
site for construction. The major problem was a financial
one, however. The owner still refused to sell the property
outright. He stated he would agree to let PG&E use the
land, without cost, if they would agree to co-sign notes
for him at a bank. The notes would at no time exceed the
value of the land. If the land appreciated in value, however, the notes could be increased up to a maximum level
starting at just over 6 million dollars and reaching 20
million dollars. If the owner defaulted on the loans,
PG&E would be required to pay them. Ownership of the land
would be turned over to PG&E in that eventuality, however.

Cost estimates were more uncertain for the Diablo
Canyon site for reasons other than the unique financing
plan, however. Becuase the site is so desolate, little is
known about geological conditions, except that it does not
lie over any known earthquake fault line.

A complete analysis of comparative costs between
the Nipomo Dunes and Diablo Canyon sites appears in the
case on page 431 of the text. Various factors considered
include the need for an advanced water circulation system,
a breakwater and other incidental costs associated with

construction of either one or four units. A similar analysis is included for the Nipomo Dunes site.

If PG&E has to accept the farthest set-back available for Nipomo, Diablo Canyon provides the most economical site if a harbor does not have to be constructed, if only one plant is built. If a harbor does have to be built, Nipomo is far superior economically for one plant.

If four plants are built, the Diablo Canyon site is far superior, however, to any set-back alternative for Nipomo Dunes, without a harbor. If a harbor is constructed, only the 500 foot set-back is economically superior to the Diablo Canyon site.

All of the analyses are based on zero costs for the primary land at Diablo Canyon. The only land costs involve sure access routes. The analyses also do not take into account costs of fighting opposition to the Nipomo site or any effects to their image as a result of pressure for one site over another.

Before PG&E management could arrive at a decision, a split occurred within the Sierra Club. A dissident group started opposition to either site on the basis that the Sierra Club should oppose <u>all</u> nuclear power plants. Also, the group argued that the club would lose credibility if it supported PG&E to the extent it has.

The Sierra Club officers, with the support of the majority of its members replied that its main goal was to rid the environment of air pollution. Nuclear power plants could help to achieve this objective. The plants had to be placed so as not to disturb the rest of the environment, however.

A listing of the differences between the two groups within the Sierra Club follows:

<u>Points of difference between the Club and SSPC's opinions</u>

SSPC	CLUB
1. Dunes agreement not binding on PG&E.	The company's image is at stake. This is shown by its willingness to cooperate with conservation groups.
	The club, with help from other groups, could lobby so that money could be available to the Park department for purchase of the "Dunes".

5 2

2. Even with PG&E's cooperation, the "Dunes" still might be destroyed by Collier Coke plans.

Sierra's full impact could be mounted if such a situation should arise.

Also, as a park, Collier's plans would be void.

3. Alternatives have not been studied. An either/or situation does not exist.

The site was chosen only after the company canvassed more than 100 community and conservation groups, and examined other sites.

4. The "Dunes deserve no more protection than the Canyon.

This arguement denies the need for increased energy and is thus contrary to the club's desire for eventual electric travel.

The damage to the Canyon site is not comparable to what would happen if the site had been the "Dunes".

5. The club should battle all development on the coast.

This view is unrealistic, both from a financial and social viewpoint. The financial implications are obvious. From a social point of view, as the need for energy increased and the supply fell, social opinion of ecological priorities relative to energy would fall. Our credibility would lose out as the demand for energy rose.

6. Membership and respect for the Club will fall if adherence to principles is not followed.

Respect from whom? Industries have increased their cooperation with the club with each passing month: PG&E is a prime example. Membership has increased, not decreased.

Our principles are not even questionable. We compromised for two reasons: recognition of the energy need, and salvation of the historical and scenic dunes. We have not stopped our battle for preservation of the coastline, only allowed for a vital service to continue for our ultimate benefit.

Furthermore, compromises related to any other industry,
other than power (carefully
planned and with our ecological
supervision) aren't contem-
plated.

Questions

1.   Evaluate the feasibility of Nipomo Dunes and Diablo
     Canyon for selection as a site for a nuclear power
     plant site.

2.   How should the unique financing plan for Diablo
     Canyon be figured into cost calculations?

3.   What effect should environmental opposition to both
     sites have on the site selection process and decision?

4.   What recommendations would you make to PG&E management
     concerning future site selection?

Solutions

1.   As discussed earlier, much depends on whether PG&E
can gain acceptance for the 500 foot set-back for the Nipomo
Dunes site. If this can be achieved, at a low cost to the
organization in terms of money and image, the Nipomo site
should be chosen. This is highly unlikely, however, from
material presented in the case and newspaper accounts at
the time of the case.

     If PG&E need not build the harbor, Daiblo Canyon,
even with all its uncertainties, is an excellent choice.
Even with the harbor, which is by no means a certainty, it
is a good choice for the construction of multiple plants.
It should be noted at this point that part of the Super
System described in the (A) case included plans for at
least four plants at the Nipomo site. Since PG&E management has already committed itself to multiple plants at all
future sites, then the discussion should center around
costs for the four plant alternative. The discussion at
this point should shift to the next question.

2.   PG&E is a public utility. Similar to other utilities,
it utilizes large amounts of debt in its financing plans.
It has maintained high bond ratings because of relatively
good returns and management, however. These ratings could,
potentially, be jeopardized if they accept this relatively
open-ended financing arrangement.

Also, the cost basis for the Diablo Canyon site suffers considerably if the full 20 million dollar figure is added. The lower 6 million dollar figure makes far less impact. Clarly, however, if the owner never defaults on his loans, there is no impact for land costs.

Discussion of the potential land aquisition costs could include use of quantitative decision theory techniques. Bayesian estimates of probable costs could be generated by the class. These could include estimates of not only the amount of costs, but also estimates of the timing of a possible default. This would require some concept of the net present value of the estimated costs associated with the land costs. In any event, the students should be required to make some estimate of potential costs of the land at Diablo Canyon.

3. The management has to be made to understand that social costs have to be considered in its decision making process. The external environment is changing. The public is now willing to accept higher economic costs to retain environmental benefits.

PG&E has already suffered a loss of image because of its actions at Bodega Bay. Given the political environment in California and the need for regulatory approval of all aspects of the actions of the organization, it must consider the social implications of its decisions.

The past method of arriving at decisions by PG&E managers will be difficult to overcome. Initial decisions and site selection strategies will be severely questioned. Only after it builds up credibility will it be able to ease up in this area.

Symptomatic of this latter problem is the issue raised by the dissident group opposing the Diablo Canyon site. The group attacked the advertising expenses incurred by PG&E to increase electricity use. The group was able to determine that PG&E spent more for advertising than for research and development. Basically, they claimed that the main reason new plants were required was because the company induced demand. These kinds of decisions have to be given much more thought than is currently being done.

4. The decision making process at PG&E has to be revised. The organization must come to realize that it is to its best business interest if it cooperates with civic and conservation groups. The organization must accept the social responsibilities that go along with its role as a public service organization. It possesses a legal monopoly granted by the state.

The organization must also do a much better job of educating the various public groups concerning costs of environmental protection. Perhaps the advertising expenses

5 5

could best be utilized for all concerned by demonstrating the need for more electric power. The trade-offs between added electric rates and environmental protection should also be stressed. At the same time, the lower overall costs of nuclear power could then be presented. Construction costs may be greater, but operating costs are lower, even at the time of the case. In current terms, the difference is even more startling, in terms of operating costs.

In any event, management must go outside the organization during all stages of its strategic planning process. External groups should be given inputs into the formulation process. Strategies have to be sold to the public once they are formulated. Without an understanding of this social and political process, all the efforts in and by PG&E in site selection and power generation will result in a great deal of wasted resources.

Assignment: Evaluate the decision process being used to
select an appropriate site in the P.G.&E. (B) case. Which
site should be selected?

Student Report
Pacific Gas and Electric (B)

Pacific Gas and Electric Company, prior to the Bodega
Head incident, had a proven successful method in the selection of future electrical generating plant sites. The
procedure involved seven technical criteria relating specifically to the economics of the future sites. The eighth
criterion, the need for local support, did not present any
unusual problems to PG&E prior to the Bodega Head experience.

The Bodega Head incident was a novel experience for
PG&E. Prior to the withdrawal by PG&E of its plans to
build a nuclear generating plant at Bodega Head it had
experienced no unusual difficulty in obtaining the necessary regulatory approval to build new generating capacity
where it was felt to be most economical.

The general environment at PG&E, when it was in the
process of touching base with all the required regulatory
agencies, was that it operated in a professional atmosphere where engineering logic and economic theory prevailed.
The Bodega Head controversy caused PG&E to re-evaluate the
process by which it determines future plant sites. The
new facet that became an additional criterion that had to
be recognized and evaluated in plant site decisions was the
amount of opposition that environmental groups, such as the
Sierra Club, would present at regulatory hearings.

Any opposition prior to 1964 to plant sites was overcome by PG&E, becuase, in its application to the regulatory
agencies, PG&E did its homework and there was typically no
technical basis for a serious challenge.

In 1964, the general environment prevailing at rate
hearings had changed significantly and a new criterion
had to be recognized. This criterion was the environmental effect of future plant site construction and plant
operation. There is no doubt that the construction phase
of a new generating facility causes far reaching changes
in the affected ecology.

PG&E experienced the effects of the environmental
movement and its increasing strength when much to its
surprise it had to withdraw its application for a plant
site at Bodega Head. PG&E assumed it would prevail in its
application to build this plant becuase it had answered in
its historically highly competent manner all technical and
economic areas concerning its application. PG&E did not

5 7

properly consider the influence of environmental groups, such as the Sierra Club, that could be asserted against its application. Failure to face the facet of the application process, albeit a novel facet, caused PG&E to experience its first significant failure in the living memory of its present technical staff.

The management of PG&E, namely, Mr. Gerdes, when he became company president in 1964, recognized that the environment had changed. Mr. Gerdes elevated the Political and Government Relation Group to an advisory group reporting directly to him. This action by Mr. Gerdes was very beneficial to PG&E because it recognized that the historical clean-cut professional process of seeking site approval had become wrapped up in emotional and political decisions because of the environmental aspects of the decision.

The new members of the Political and Government Relations Group that now hold the title of executive representative have a two-fold mission. The first is to evaluate and anticipate the environmental groups' reactions to future plant site applications. The second is to provide top management with its findings and recommendations in this area so that it could be properly considered in the decision to proceed with a plant site application or seek an alternate site.

The group can only evaluate the environmental hurdles PG&E will face and make appropriate recommendations if it understands the environmental movement. To do this, the group must establish a line of communications with the significant groups that it will face in any plant site application proceedings. The line of communication between PG&E and the environmental groups is important because compromise situations or solutions cannot be determined unless one is aware of the other's objectives. The environmental groups are aware of PG&E's problems; namely locating suitable plant sites. Is PG&E aware of the goals of the environmental groups?

The environmental group that is of significance to PG&E is the Sierra Club. PG&E should be able to determine the club's objectives from two sources. The sources are direct face-to-face discussions, and secondly, public media-oriented statements.

Proper use of these sources would disclose that the Sierra Club is aware of PG&E's need for additional generating sites. The club also recognizes that it has several general goals. The main goal is reducing or eliminating the most harmful effect on California's environment, automobile emissions. The club envisions the resolution of this problem with the advent of the electric car. Common usage of an electric car could not be feasible without sufficient sources of electricity. The Sierra Club (the majority) is willing to accept compromise plant sites to assure a needed commodity, electricity, provided a reasonable compromise was accepted by PG&E.

In the same reference frame, the Political and Government Relation Group should properly evaluate a splinter group within the Sierra Club that is adamantly opposed to any compromise doctrine. The group has a responsibility to alert top management of PG&E about the relative strength of the splinter group and advise management that all important decisions regarding plant sites must be reviewed with the thought in mind, "Will it enhance the splinter group's position?"

The Group has demonstrated that it can communicate with the Sierra Club and make objective reports to PG&E's top management.

The situation that PG&E must address itself to, then, is what to do with the Nipomo site application. PG&E made a progressive decision when it allowed the Group to seek out from the opposition recommendations for compromise sites. PG&E top management did not let history repeat itself and allow it to become the victim of another Bodega Head situation. Instead, it heeded the Group's recommendation: unless a 4,000 to 5,000 foot set-back was agreed to at the Nipomo site a serious confrontation would take place. The engineering and economic findings were tempered with the reality of the impact the opposition, environmental groups, could generate. PG&E management took a bold step when it sought out the assistance of environmental groups in locating a suitable site in the general area. PG&E did not unduly surrender its right to operate the utility in the most economical manner, but, instead, it attempted to co-exist with the environmental groups that had demonstrated they could exert considerable influence on the regulatory agencies PG&E must deal with. It would almost border on gross negligence to pursue site approval at great cost only to risk significant defeat when an acceptable compromise was possible.

The Sierra Club did suggest an alternative site in the Wild Cherry Canyon area. PG&E, as a result of this, determined that another site, the Diablo Canyon, was a viable alternative to the Nipomo Dunes area.

PG&E faced an important decision: to pursue the Nipomo site, using a setback less than 4,000 feet or agreeing to 4,000 feet or using the Diablo Canyon site. It is apparent that it would be grossly incompetant on the part of PG&E top management to pursue the Nipomo site with a set-back of less than 4,000 feet. Once this was decided, the decision could then be removed from the spectrum of environmental confrontations of significance and left to proper technical and economic consideration. It is true that the 4,000 feet set-back at Nipomo or the Diablo Canyon would cost more than the original proposals, but this is a small price to pay to maintain harmonious rela-

relations with its customers and stockholders, and the regulatory agencies it deals with.

In conclusion: PG&E demonstrated that it could and did adopt its most important policy decisions to conform with a changing environment that it operates in. In effect, top management of PG&E gave due consideration to all necessary factors that affect its decision-making process: internal technical aspects, the economics of the situation, and the effect of the decision on the outside environment. Most importantly, giving the proper weight to the effect on the outside environment and the necessity to use less than optimal plant sites to remain in harmony with its surrounding environment through reasonable compromise.

Southern Pacific Land Company

Purpose

The Southern Pacific Land Company cases present the development of an organization from a one-service firm (transportation) to a multi-service concept. The specific segment of the company dealt with in these cases, land development and management, has brought the company into more direct contact with local elements in the geographic region it serves.

The cases, therefore, should be used to demonstrate the differing social and political factors that an organization has to consider when developing new strategies. Particularly, the consistency between internal values and external trends should be considered with these two cases.

Southern Pacific Company wants to maintain a good image with the localities it serves. It is highly regulated, but profitable in the transportation end of its operations. It feels that it must protect itself by maintaining a socially aware image in the rest of its operations.

Also, the top management has expressed pride in being the largest, private land owner in the state of California. This ownership, and pride, has placed constraints on the use of their internal resources, however (their land holdings).

The Southern Pacific Land Company (A) case should be used to test the consistency of internal actions with external constraints. The discussion should start with an exposition of the objectives of the parent firm in setting up this division. The organization structure designed to achieve these objectives could then be explored to see if it makes sense from the point of view of consistency and feasibility. Also, internal company policies could be discussed to see if they do, in fact, match the various internal and external value system being imposed on the organization.

The Southern Pacific Land Company (A) case also could be used to trace the development of a new strategic mission within an ongoing organization. Previous cases have shown how strategies are formed for an entirely new organization (Sea Life Park). Here we see an organization that has expanded its mission out of its traditional area of expertise. The problems associated with that shift in emphasis could be explored with this case.

The Southern Pacific Land Company (B) case demonstrates problems associated with implementing a new strategy relative to a particular decision. Having developed the strategy in the (A) case, students should now be expected to

6 1

discuss how it matches the various problems associated with the development of the Donner Lake property owned by the parent and managed by the subsidiary.

With this particular decision, students can be shown how conflicting policies have to be reconciled when implementing strategies. Questions concerning what objectives are pre-eminent in any given situation appear in this case. The students should be placed in the position of a top manager of the Southern Pacific Land Company. They then have to develop a strategy for developing the Donner Lake property which is consistent with the various internal and external constraints and opportunities inherent with that property.

Position in the Course

This series is designed to be used in the middle to latter section of the course. The student has to be able to test both the internal and external environments to be able to formulate, evaluate, and implement strategic decisions for either or both cases.

The problems in the cases are confined enough that students need not have the experience of the entire course before tackling them. Also, specific problems, such as the social issues implied in land development can be used to provide the central focus for case discussion.

The cases, particularly the (B) case, provide an excellent forum for discussions during that segment of the course devoted to information gathering. Questions concerning real estate management and development can be assigned to individual groups to research.

Other areas of the course dealing with the interaction between values and objectives and organizational structure can be usefully explored through assignment of the (A) case. Once again, these areas are typically covered during the middle section of the course.

Key Issues

Southern Pacific Land Company (A)

1. Effect of external social values and trends on organizational strategies and policies.

2. Development of new organizational mission to adapt to a changing environment.

3. Organizational structure and its role in the development of strategic change.

4. The interaction of the organization and its political/legal environment.

5. Trade-offs between social and profit objectives in a corporate setting.

Southern Pacific Land Company (B)

1. Application of organizational strategies and policies to land development.

2. Interaction with environmental and political groups in implementing organizational strategies.

3. Environmental impact of organizational policies and its effect on the decision-making process.

Southern Pacific Land Company (A)

Analysis

In July, 1972, the President of Southern Pacific Land Company was concerned about the company's lands in the north and east of California. The major reason was the fact that land management problems had proliferated and were expected to continue in that direction.

Company history: The S.P. Land Company is a wholly owned subsidiary of the Southern Pacific Company. It was organized to manage and develop its extensive land holdings in California, Nevada, and Utah. The land company was reorganized March 1, 1970, creating an operations unit with three divisions:

i) Industrial Development Division: seeks and assists the development of industries along Southern Pacific lines; installs industrial tracks; sells rail and other track materials. It also recommends property acquisitions, sale and lease of company property.

ii) Real Estate Division: this division managed, specifically, company holdings along the railroad. Division objective is to emphasize commercial development and best utilization of company properties.

iii) Natural Resources Division: is responsible for the management and supervision of the company's outlying lands and mineral rights.

There was, in addition, a special projects group reporting directly to the President, specializing in "project management" involving office buildings, hotels, shopping centers, etc.

Subsequent to the reorganization, a policy was formulated that the S.P. Land Company only engages in management and investment of S.P. lands. The S.P. Development Company was formed (100% owned subsidiary) to own and develop properties for investment and act as "dealer in real estate".

History of Southern Pacific Lands: The Federal government made "land grants" as incentive to western railroads to expand. In return the railroads gave the government reduced rates. Originally Southern Pacific got about 27 million acres of land. Roughly 3 million acres was returned to the government in 1916. By 1949 only 3.8 million acres were left and the company decided to manage them for "long term income and appreciation".

Present Lands: These holdings are classified into:

6 4

i) operating property (for railroad and transportation uses).

ii) outlying land (includes prime timber land which is on sustained yield program).

iii) industrial and commercial properties.

The company administers its outlying lands on the multiple use concept of forestry.

Agricultural lands are utilized by granting long term developmental leases to large scale operators and joint ventures in specific high-profit or potentially high-profit situations, e.g. grape vineyard. Suitable desert and grazing lands are leased to sheep and cattlemen. These lands are currently operating at a loss. Mineral developments are the sole responsibility of lesees.

Land development policy: Company lands are managed on a flexible long range plan for sustained optimal utilization and profits. Current policy of the parent firm is not to sell any land holdings.

The problem facing S.P. Land Co.: The major problem is that expenses (property taxes) are rising rapidly. This trend is projected to continue while income has levelled off and is projected to decline. Income will meet the tax costs within five years. In line with company policy and objectives, it is working with resource consultants for the exact determination of the sustained yeild cuts on its timber lands. This policy is a significant factor in the levelling of income from land resources.

Possible Land Management Alternatives and Problems: Since most lands from the land grant act are alternating square miles, company development plans may conflict with that of alternate owners.

The major problem here is that taxes are assessed at market value based on the highest and best use of the land. This has led to speculative land development in California.

Consequently, the Williamson Act was passed to stop the speculation, protect agricultural land, and prevent premature land development. The advantage of the act is that it provides for the retention of land under continuous agricultural use without higher taxes. Its disadvantage is that it ties up the land for the contract period and it shifts the tax base within counties.

Land Exchange: This could be one exit for the company from its problems. "Primative" designated land, inaccessible land, alternating lands and subdivisible lands can be exchanged for better ones. The glaring problem with this program is its extreme slowness (sometimes takes the government 20 years!)

6 5

Other Alternatives Considered: were bulk sales of
surplus lands (contrary to policy), subdivision, and
defaulting on taxes for 5 years and letting the sheriff
sell off the land to recover the back taxes.

The major decisions to be taken by the President involve:
    i) a detailed management action plan for the forrested
and mountainous lands, and
    ii) the organizational structure (centralized? de-
centralized?).

Questions

1.   Evaluate Mr. Linde's view of his problems as reflected
      by his statement of key decisions presented on p. 445
      of the text.

2.   Discuss the relevant threats and opportunities facing
      the Southern Pacific Land Company.

3.   What alternative policies and actions are open to the
      Southern Pacific Land Company in its use of its prop-
      erties?

4.   What organizational structure should the firm assume
      to implement these policies?

Solutions

1.   This case is considerably less complicated than might
originally be perceived. A careful reading of the text con-
firms that a good deal of the information given, while
nice to have, is not entirely relevant.

The questions in the case give the impression that
SP.L.C. is powerless to influence its own fate. In order
for the questions to be answered adequately, several preliminary steps must be undertaken.

Our first task, then, lies in defining the problem.
Mr. Linde is only interested, at present, with the company's
forrested lands, as is indicated by the question in the
case. According to the case, this is only 728,000 acres
of a total 3,777,160. Therefore, we are only considering
about 19% of the company's holdings. A certain portion of
this is classified as "inaccessable".

Therefore, for purposes of this case, the problem is
not what to do with 3.8 million acres, but rather what to
do with .72 million acres.

2.   The company is faced, however, with two external problems. First, rising taxes, aggrevated by assessments not
covered by the Williamson Act, are increasing costs.

Anticipated dropping revenues from sustained-level timber
cutting is rapidly reaching a point where expenses may soon
exceed revenues for these lands. These problems are exac-
erbated by the alternately patched nature of land distribution.

In the most general sense opportunities are limited to
only 3. First, maintain status quo; i.e. harvest timber.
Secondly, develop the land for other uses. Or third,
sell or rent the land.

The company has several strengths to be considered.
First, it is somewhat of a utility and as such has considerable legal leverage. Second, it is the largest landowner
in California and as such it has considerable leverage.
Third, its size gives it flexibility. Fourth, its vast
holdings give it bargaining power. Fifth, its industrial
development section represents a special strength.

3.   The alternatives are numerous and will become evident
in the solution.

An overall action plan is not really feasible. Each
parcel of land must be considered on its own merits.
Linde must determine the current and anticipated "near
future" development and use of land in the area and corres-
ponding tax situation. Where feasible present holdings
should be maintained for timber harvest and alternating
patches should be acquired through purchase or barter.
Much of this land could be protected by the Williamson Act.
Where tract housing is impending and threatens to raise
taxes, SPLC can threaten industrialization of adjoining
land and in this manner coerce owners to sell or barter.

Where no bargain can be struck, the land should be
assigned to the Industrial Development Division for consideration. Where feasible, the land can be developed
into industrial parks either for rent or outright sale.
Finally, with the current premium on housing, SPLC could
consider subdivision and sale for houses. This however
is a last resort for it violates the company's policy
(although once again, barter seems feasible).

4.   The information needed above should be obtained by a
team of real estate men whose sole purpose is to manage
the 700,000 acres in question. They should be competent
and qualified in all aspects of real estste.

The main set-up of the company should be centralized
but because of the wide-spread geographic area, there
should be on-site representation from the different functional areas. The overall land could be divided into
manageable segments and teams assigned.

In the event that land development is the logical
alternative, it is feasible for SPLC to enter jointly with
developers and real estate people.

The greatest opportunity here is flexibility and the biggest problem would be developing the necessary expertise. Right now, SPLC owns some fantastically valuable assets. Proper management of these assets can only occur when the top management divests itself of its current myopic viewpoints. Some of their ideas are good, but very constraining. If SPLC does not become more aggressive, it could easily become overwhelmed by progress.

Southern Pacific Land Company (B)

Analysis

Donner Lake Property

For the location of the property see exhibits 1 & 2 in the case. This piece of land is 377 acres with a current market value of $197,000, approximately.

The average elevation is 6100 feet a.s.l. and snow-covered for five months of the year. It has no timber (commercially) and therefore was transferred to the Company Real Estate Dealer subsidiary. The land has a small stream, a meadow and scenic views of the lake.

The company is purchasing an acre of lake front property to provide a beach for landing facilities and access to the lake. The property is easily reached by land and air transportation.

History of the Donner Lake Area: Old U.S. 40 ran through the property and the northern shore of the lake. Small businesses flourished.

In 1962, the completion of Interstate 80 bypassed this area and resulted in an "economic dryout" of the area; property values declined. With the scarcity of recreational land around Tahoe, land values here are once again appreciating.

Problems concerning development of the Property:
i)   Former decisions did not anticipate the future uses for the land. Consequently, criss-crossing above ground and underground utilities have been granted easements. Relocation expenses must be borne by the developer.

ii) Presently zoned as forest recreation, therefore unsuitable for large scale residential development.

iii) To rezone, it must connect with Truckee district sewer system which needs final authorization from the Federal Environmental Protection Agency.

iv) Developer must bear all the connection and modification costs involved in linking with the Truckee sewage system.

v)   The whole property is visible from the scenic overlook on Interstate 80, therefore conservationists and ecologists will oppose scenic destruction.

vi) The five months of snow will increase development costs for utilities and maintainance.

Development Alternatives: The major alternatives open are condominiums, single family dwellings and creation of an integrated resort.

Development considerations must be preceeded by market segmentation of the area. The identified segment will be constrained by the availability of recreational facilities.

Although the market value of the property is stated at $190,000, we cannot be sure of the potential of this land. If the history of the property prices in this area is similar to that of other regions, then outright sale of the property could be a great mistake.

The land seems best suited for leisure activities. Recreational activity in this area can occur virtually all year round. It should be noted that the "leisure" industry is perhaps the fastest growing industry in the country, with more and more emphasis being placed on shorter hours (4 day work week?)

Sports, such as skiing and camping, once the domain of the well to do are now open to the average citizen and his family through relatively less expensive areas adjacent to the more expensive resort areas. These "new arrivals" to the good life are more willing to settle for less elaborate accomodations, a bit farther from the slopes.

For a relatively small outlay, Southern Pacific could develop this sort of area in the short run. In the longer run, plans could be made for a more elaborate recreational area. In the interim, the land is appreciating.

Questions

Basically, the questions asked at the end of the (B) case, on p. 461 of the text, provide a good point for discussion. They are:

1. What should Southern Pacific do with the Donner property?

2. Should Southern Pacific consider joint ventures, and if so under what terms?

3. What sales policies on a development should be established: sell units and land; rent units and land; or sell units and lease land?

4. Should Southern Pacific get involved in the overall development of the Donner areaor just be concerned with

its own land?

5.   Considering the present pressures from various conservation groups, should the property be developed for
recreation vehicle and camping site use?

Solutions

1.   This appears to be one of the special situations described in the case where a joint venture is called for.
Southern Pacific Land Company does not appear to have the
expertise to develop the property efficiently, yet.

Given the Donner Lake site's proximity to major recreation facilities and transportation routes, it appears
ideally suited for development. To take best advantage of
the zoning requirements and the problems associated with
easements on the land, the site seems best suited for a
resort or condominium type of development. This would also
be consistent with the policy of the parent of not selling
land if it does not have to. A condominium development
would be based on a long term lease of the land with the
joint venture managing the operation.

2.   The firm should contact several other organizations
having experience with these kinds of developments. Initially S. P. should merely seek advice concerning which
of the alternatives appears most feasible. Only if necessary should they pay for the advice. In all liklihood,
the other organizations would provide the advice free in
hopes of being selected for the joint venture.

Southern Pacific has a valuable piece of land to offer
to the joint venture. It also has solid financial backing
for any development project. The firm is basically looking
for assistance in developing and managing the project.
Ideally, the joint venture partner should also be able to
teach personnel within Southern Pacific Land how to develop
and manage similar projects in the future. They will have
the expertise within the organization.

3.   The project should be based on the venture maintaining control of the land. The policy of the parent is not
to sell land.

The organization is proud of its position as the largest private land holder in the state. It is also cognizant of its vulnerability to regulatory agencies if it
developes an image as a poor corporate citizen.

Losing control of the land could leave the firm open
to charges of exploiting this natural resource. Also, if
the firm sells the land, it will not be able to receive
the advantage of future appreciation of this property.
Southern Pacific has the financial resources to carry the

property for the short term to gain these long term advantages.

4.   Once again, given the concern of Southern Pacific management for its image, it should become concerned with the overall development of the area. Also, since it will be holding onto the land for long term gains, Southern Pacific has to protect its investment. The Disney organization learned this lesson with Disney Land in California.

Disney did not control development of nearby properties. The adjacent areas have developed helter-skelter, detracting from the Park. In Florida, at Walt Disney World, they controlled the development of all the adjacent areas. As a result, the worth of their project has not deteriorated due to commercialization of nearby areas.

Overall, it is to the best interest of Southern Pacific to take an active part in the development of nearby properties. Its image and investment are at stake.

5.   Southern Pacific has to consider environmental considerations if it is to maintain its credibility with the public. The question to be resolved is whether the public has strong feelings concerning use of this property.

Although recreation vehicles may damage the ecology to some extent, many conservationists participate in this form of recreation. The key consideration should be whether this form of use is consistent with planned development of the total area. This would be in line with the previous discussion concerning participation in the development of the entire area.

In any event, Southern Pacific Land managers must evaluate preferences of various public groups when formulating development plans. Once those plans are developed, management must communicate that decision to the public as well as the reasoning and need for this form of development.

Too often, at this period, land development firms have gained bad press because of their policies. Southern Pacific Land Company cannot afford this kind of image. This is true not so much for itself as for its parent whose name it holds. The parent is a highly regulated firm. It relies on the good will of the public, through various regulatory agencies, for its continued, profitable existence.

Management of both the parent and the subsidiary have demonstrated that they are cognizant of their social responsibility. Their policies show that they realize the external factors affecting their decision-making process. The question now revolves around their ability to implement these policies in a consistent manner.

NON PROFIT/PUBLIC ORGANIZATIONS.

The case studies included in this section present problems encountered in managing organizations where profit maximization is not a
primary objective. Courses in Policy and Strategy frequently neglect
organizations that operate in the public or non profit areas. Many
business school graduates find their way into these types of organizations as managers.

The public sector is growing faster than any other. The need for
managers qualified to make decisions for these organizations is growing
just as rapidly. The policy analyst accustomed to making decisions
within the context of profit oriented organizations frequently finds
the different objectives and constraints operating in this new environment overwhelming.

Primary objectives associated with non profit and public organizations typically include quality or quantity of the product or service
supplied. The external environment frequently plays a far greater role
in the decision making process in these organizations. The political
factors influencing strategic decisions frequently take precedence over
factors of efficiency or effectiveness.

Two of the cases, Metropolitan Tulsa Transit Authority and the
Pennsylvania State University are public oriented. They receive most
of their funding from various governmental agencies. As such, they
must consider the effect of their decisions on their ability to continue to receive funding.

The other two cases, St. John's Hospital and Illinois Masonic
Medical Center (E) trace the decision process where simply breaking
even is sufficient. Consideration of quality and quantity of service
are at least as important. Also, various external groups present constraints on the decisions made by policy analysts. Values and objectives for these groups frequently clash. It is the function of the
manager to weigh the relative benefits and costs involved in these
types of confrontations to the best long term interests of the organization.

ST. JOHN'S HOSPITAL

PURPOSE:

The St. John's Hospital case is designed to present students with a situation requiring analysis of the total environment in a policy decision. The organization's goals include quality of health care for a specific geographic region. The hospital merely has to break even to insure its long term viability.

The values of the individuals operating the hospital are relatively clean. This makes it easier for students to place emphasis on community needs and the effectiveness of the operations at St. John's.

Political factors are relatively minor in this situation; the organization is operating in a relatively isolated region of the country. It is also relatively autonomous from the central headquarters of the parent organization (the Mother Parish.)

The main focus of the case is to design a strategy for operation of the hospital for the long run. The top manager at St. John's, Sister Marvina Ryan, has been given free rein to do what she feels is best for the hospital, the community and the parent order. One strategic alternative is to close the operation entirely, and sell off all its assets.

This latter alternative is one that is rarely presented to a policy analyst. It should be discussed not only relative to St. John's but to any organization. It can lead to a broader discussion of the effects of ceasing operations of any organization.

Our society has become conditional to equating cessation of operations with failure. Frequently, however, going out of business, especially for a public service organization means that it has succeeded in its objectives. Keeping public, or non profit operations going after they have reached their objectives or are no longer needed can be counter-productive to the aims of the entire community.

Similarly, an analogy can be made to an organization in the private sector. A profit oriented firm that finds demand for its product is no longer available should consider when and how to change its strategy. The St. John's case can be used to make this point, since there are other alternative uses for the facilities employed by the hospital.

The key focus should be matching resource utilization of the hospital with environmental needs. To do this, a fairly rigorous, and realistic analysis of community needs, resources and values has to be presented.

POSITION IN THE COURSE:

Clearly, this case could be used in that section of the course dealing with non profit organizations. It can be used at other points in the course, as well, however.

The students should already have the ability to realistically evaluate the external environment facing an organization. They should then be able to match that environment with the resources provided by St. John's. This, typically means that the St. John's case will be used at the latter end of the course.

Many of the problems presented by the St. John's case involve implementation of strategies as well as development of strategies. The structure, personnel, public relations and other factors involved in developing methods of change should be clear in the minds of the students.

The case, since it does eliminate some of the value oriented problems of change, could be used as the lead case for the implementation section. It could also be used at the end of this section, as well, since it does present the option of closing the organization. The peculiar problem presented with ceasing operations can be discussed with this case. That is best left, however to the latter stages of the course. If not, it may confound and confuse analysis of later cases. The "easy" way out of simply ceasing operations in an environment where value systems are not as flexible as at St. John's may lead students to propose an unacceptable strategy.

KEY ISSUES:

1. Development and implementation of strategic change.
2. Matching community needs with organizational resources.
3. Decision concerning cessation of operations for an organization.
4. Provision of quality health care.
5. Operation and decisions within a non profit oriented organization.

ST. JOHN'S HOSPITAL

Analysis

HISTORY:

St. John's Hospital is located in Helena Montana. It was founded
in 1870 as the first private hospital in Montana Territory. It has always served Helena, the state capitol, and the surrounding counties,
providing health care to all socio-economic classes.

The present physical facility was first built in 1939. It has
been added to twice, in 1958 and 1965. There are ancillary buildings
for housing, heating and garage purposes. It provides nearly full
hospital services. It does not provide maternity services, having
closed that department in 1968. All maternity services are now provided by St. Peter's Community Hospital also located in Helena. This was
accomplished to create efficiencies in health service provisions in the
Helena area.

St. John's Hospital is run by the Sisters of Charity of Leaven-
worth Kansas, a Roman Catholic order. St. Peter's is non-denomination.
Shodair, Crippled Children's Hospital is also located in Helena. Outside Helena, there is a Veteran's Administration Hospital filled large-
ly by patients from outside the community.

Patient population at the three Helena hospitals is relatively
low. Although St. John's consistently breaks even every year, their
percentage occupancy is below that considered economical by national
health groups. Shodair is used at an extremely low rate due to the
elimination of Polio as a critical health problem. Since moving into
new quarters in 1968, St. Peter's has seen its occupancy rate climb
slowly. It also, however, is below national standards.

CURRENT PROBLEMS:

Sister Marvina Ryan, the current administrator at St. John's, is
faced with the necessity of determining the future of the hospital.
The most pressing problem was the need to renovate the main building to
conform to new, state, fire standards. The required charge would be
extremely expensive.

Another area for concern involved the outmoded, but still useable
emergency room. It was no longer efficient to utilize this area for
both emergency patients and the growing number of outpatient visits.
Outpatient visits, both locally and nationally, had been experiencing
a sharp increase as hospital costs and charges had increased. The
combination of the fire protection requirements and change in type of
service offered made the two problems more difficult to handle than if
only one were present.

Other questions facing Sister Marvina involved the disposition of

excess land and buildings. She was not sure whether she should sell
the holdings and use the funds (up to $125,000) to renovate the present
facilities or to hold on to them and use them for expansion. This was
further compounded by the knowledge that there was excess health care
capacity within Helena.

CONSULTANT'S STUDY:

Sister Marvina contracted with Medical Planning Associates (MPA)
to help her arrive at decisions concerning these problems. Their primary task was to survey the health care needs for the Helena area.

Some of the alternatives being considered are listed below.

1. Elimination of services duplicated unnecessarily by other
area hospitals.

2. Expand services not covered by other facilities. Adequately
(i.e. extended care.)

3. Transform St. John's into a specialty center (i.e. burn
center, cardiac center.)

4. Cease operations and turn patients over to St. Peter's and
Shodair.

Vital considerations for any of these alternatives concerned the
health needs of the community and availability of adequate resources.
Medical staff, especially specialty staff, was limited in Helena. Also, the physicians currently using St. Peter's and St. John's enjoyed
the ability to take advantage of the two facilities. They could trade
off resources. The two competing facilities also gave them more leverage.

Financially, St. John's was considered sound. Over the last
several years operating costs had run very close to operating revenues.
Charitable contributions are negligible. The recent wage-price freeze
had necessitated some belt tightening, however. St. John's had been on
the verge of increasing charges when the freeze was put into effect.
This could critically hamper its ability to pay for any extensive renovations.

Political factors also confronted Sister Marvina. National health
planning could limit her ability to expand if she waited too long. Already, regional health planning placed some constraints in this area.

Helena was growing at a modest 3 per cent per year. It is the
fourth largest city in Montana. It was the state capital, however,
this meant there were minor fluctuations in population when the legislature was in session. Population in Montana is spread over a large
geographic area.

A shortage of general practitioners was developing in the Helena

area, as it was nationally. Nursing personnel were in even shorter
supply, relative to demand. The nursing shortage had become exaggera-
ted since St. John's had closed its own nursing school program in 1968.
The program was closed because of the increasing complexity of nursing
and its education. This had lead to increased costs.

Whatever decision was made regarding St. John's would have to be
acceptable to the Mother House in Kansas. To a great degree, however,
the Mother House would accept Sister Marvine's recommendations, particularly if they were based on several MPA analysis. That analysis
should be based on the long range needs of the total environment.

FINANCIAL ANALYSIS:

The following presents a synopsis of the financial information
provided in the case.

	1967	1968	1969	1970	1971	1972
Total Revenues (000)	1,279	1,543	1,744	1,836	2,076	2,282
Total Expenses (000)	1,240	1,607	1,774	1,918	2,062	2,259
Net Revenues (plus interest) (000)	39	(59)	(25)	(63)	20	30
Current Assets (000)	480	502	577	485	521	589
Fixed Assets (000)	1,403	1,517	1,562	1,617	1,554	1,476
Improvement Funds (000)	98	147	65	104	122	194
Current Liabilities (000)	98	105	141	190	180	214
Long Term Debt (to Mother House) (000)	516	492	484	485	438	404

QUESTIONS:

1. What are the objectives of St. John's Hospital?

2. Evaluate the alternatives open to Sister Marvina for
St. John's Hospital.

3. What effects would there be on the community of St. John's
ceased operations?

4. What key environmental factors should be considered when
deciding the long run strategy for St. John's?

SOLUTIONS:

1. There are several tiers of objectives operating at St. John's
Hospital. The primary objective is to provide quality health care for
the Helena and surrounding community. Particular emphasis is placed
providing health care needs required by a significant portion of the
community, but not available nearby. Quality service is only constrained by the need to break even, over the long run, financially.

Another secondary objective is to provide health care services
consistent with the best use of resources for the total community.
Similarly, funds provided by the Mother House should be protected, and
if at all possible, be repaid to be used elsewhere.

Finally, all decisions concerning the Hospital should be consistent with the long term goals and needs of the community.

2. Any alternative selected by Sister Marvina will have to be
coordinated with the other hospitals in the area. Elimination or
expansion of services will affect the demand for services at these
hospitals. They must have time to prepare for these changes in demand.

It is unlikely, given the influence of the Helena physicians, that
any of the normal services have not been accounted for in the community. Any expansion of these normal areas would probably just increase
the duplication of efforts. Moreover, given the financial constraints,
expansion in one area will require a cut back in another area.

If Sister Marvina decides to selectively cut areas of operations,
she has to consider the effects on the community as well as St. John's.
The physician may decide that it is no longer worthwhile to use St.
John's due to the restricted services offered. Also, St. Peter's or
Shodair will have to be willing to accept the added demand for the
service. Elimination of selected services will probably not increase
capacity utilization at St. John's. It may enable the organization to
close those areas of the facility requiring extensive renovations, however.

Use of the St. John's as a specialty center for burn or cardiac
treatment is not too feasible. Transportation to Helena is not very
good. These services require the ability to reach the center rapidly
and safely. St. John's could be used as an extended care or nursing
facility. There is not a great need for those services in Helena,
however. Study of extended care facilities shows a rough balance
between supply and demand for these services in the Helena area.

Closing of the facility would actually require the most planning.
Services relinquished by St. John's would have to be provided for at
St. Peter's or Shodair. Since Shodair itself is a specialty operation,
most of the slack would have to be taken up at St. Peter's.

This would require fund raising by St. Peter's. They would have
to increase capacity by approximately 30 beds in the near future. St.
Peter's would also be forced to become a total, full service hospital

as well. They might not increase capacity utilization for this reason.

Plans would have to be made for placing personnel in other positions. Plans would also have to be made for disposition of St. John's building and property. Equipment could be disposed of at other hospitals in the Order or in Helena. The Mother House would like to have its initial investment returned. This may not be possible if the assets are liquidated. After all, there are limited uses for hospital buildings.

3. There could probably be a lessening of total services to the community if St. John's closed. Choice of services would be limited. Competition would be decreased.

Costs, however, would also probably be decreased. St. Peter's should be able to operate more efficiently. The physicians would not be able to require costly duplication of resources. This might lead to a loss of specialist physicians in the community, however.

Clearly, St. Peter's would have to expand. This would force all the health services to plan for the future in a coordinated manner.

A side benefit for the community might be an addition to the tax rolls. If the St. John's rite were not taken over by a charitable or public organization, the owner would have to pay property taxes. Given the probable valuation of the property, this could prove to be a decided plus for the community.

The Mother House, moreover, could free up assets to be used elsewhere. These assets would include the Sisters on the staff as well as the equipment and funds from sale of buildings and property. This might be especially useful since the Sisters of Charity were considering placing more emphasis on center city areas of large metropolitan areas.

Initially, there will be a loss in employment in the community. From information in the case, this would be fairly small. Most of the employees could probably be placed at one of the other medical facilities. Unfortunately, the employees to be hit hardest would be the unskilled laborers. They might find it difficult to find new work. Given the objectives and value system of the Sister of Charity. This might have some effect on their decision.

4. The future growth patterns in the Helena area are of great importance to any decision made in this situation. The area is not growing rapidly. It is unlikely that the area will require the number of hospital beds available for sometime. Also, the population in the surrounding area is not great enough to require the services of a specialty health care facility.

The older age segment of the population is growing, however. This would speak in favor of an extended care nursing facility. Also, this older age group apparently prefers St. John's over St. Peter's. There is no facility providing complete extended care services for the elderly in Helena at the present time. There are plenty of nursing homes, however. The questions to be resolved involve the demand for such a facility and the determination if this would be the best use of the current land and buildings.

Clearly, the long term needs of the total community have to be considered, not just the desires of one or a few special interest groups. Sister Marvina must contact St. Peter's management, however. Any decision she makes must be coordinated with the people at St. Peter's. It must be clear that St. Peter's is willing as well as able to take up any slack caused by actions taken at St. John's.

<u>Sample Case Report</u>

Assignment: Evaluate the alternatives open to Sister
Macrina Ryan. Which do you recommend?

Student Report
St. John's Hospital

The mission of the voluntary community hospital is to
provide quality patient care. The hospital has a minimum
of two pricing mechanisms: charges (similar to retail
pricing policy) for self-paying patients and commercial in-
surers, and costs (wholesale pricing policy) for Medicare,
Medicaid, and Blue Cross reimbursement. Often the institution is not reimbursed for free care and must then dip into
its depreciation fund to maintain an operating balance.
The hospital is a labor-intensive business with 70% of its
expense dollar going to labor. Whereas industry decreases
its labor input as technology expands, the hospital increases its manpower. Personnel range from the unskilled
housekeeper to the highly-trained nurse; with a minimum of
upward mobility. Turnover is high, even among profession-
als; registered nurses, who must devote at least three
years to an accredited nursing program, last approximately
2.5 years in the field. The physician, who does not pay
for the use or misuse of the institution, obtains the bulk
of his income directly and indirectly from the hospital.
The hospital is controlled or regulated by no less than 143
public and private agencies, and operates in an environment
of financial uncertainty, with its revenue increasingly
controlled by outside sources.

We have assumed the role of the MPA consultants to
St. John's Hospital, which has been asked by the Regional
Comprehensive Planning Agency (CHP) to disclose their in-
tent for long-range planning (1973-1977) affecting both
St. John's and the surrounding community. It is incumbant
upon the hospital to take the initiative in major decision-
making matters because of the growing influence of RCHP and
its growing role as regional decision-maker for all health
activities, expecially hospitals. RCHP, created by federal legislation in the mid-1960's, has a mandatory voting
membership of 51% consumers, and has the legal authority to
make decisions that will affect the Helena area whether
the hospitals are in agreement or not.

Lewis and Clark County is presently overbedded. While
there is a growing demand for outpatient services, the absence of hospital-based ambulatory services has contributed
to the overbedding problem. The need for both pediatric
and maternity care has been declining with the drop in the
birth rate. Nursing homes and extended care facilities
(ECF), which provide less expensive and less skilled
nursing care, have expanded over the last decade.

The two general hospitals in the Helena area have a capacity of 223 beds. There are three long-term facilities with 240 beds. Our projected general hospital bed needs, based on the national average of 3.5 beds per 1000 population are as follows:

1973	1975	1980
126	134	151

The long-term care bed requirements, based upon the RCHP guideline of 10 beds per 1000 geriatric population, will expand from 35 beds in 1973 to 45 beds in 1980. While 700 long-term care beds are currently needed for the entire state, 240 beds, or 34%, are located in Lewis and Clark County, which has less than 5% of the geriatric population of Montana.

Although the data for St. John's Hospital show a drop in occupancy for one year only, admissions for the area have risen. Therefore, it would seem appropriate to assume that the utilization of St. John's Hospital is dropping, for various political reasons.

The Sisters of Charity, who operate St. John's Hospital, have recently been reevaluating many of their social commitments, and are now questioning the role of and need for this institution in the Helena community. Despite the financial stability of the hospital, Sister Macrina's "brilliance", and goodwill from the community, the costs to the community of empty beds and unnecessary duplication of services cannot be ignored. Admissions, average daily census, and percentage of occupancy have been declining to alarming levels from the keen competition at St. Peter's Hospital. St. John's and St. Peter's are within two miles of each other, and most physicians, who have admitting privileges at both institutions, apparently prefer to admit their patients to St. Peter's, the most modern medical facility.

We selected and evaluated the following alternative directions for St. John's Hospital:

1. To remain an acute general hospital.
2. To convert to a rehabilitation or other specialty hospital.
3. To convert to an outpatient facility.
4. To convert to a long-term care facility, i.e. a nursing home or ECF.
5. To close operations and terminate the institution.

We feel that a 20 bed addition to St. Peter's would meet the present patient load at St. John's. The additional beds would raise St. Peter's capacity to 131 beds, which compares favorably to our projected bed needs of 126 in 1973 and 134 in 1975 (for the Helena area). Although the MPA-Engineering Division has determined that the fire

prevention measures can be met for under $25,000, we feel
that this is not a sufficient reason for continuing to
burden the community with the unnecessary duplication of
facilities, services, and costs from an institution which
is operating at less than 60% occupancy. Per diem costs
have risen at St. John's from $67.16 in 1971 to $95.22 in
1972, and have increased at St. Peter's from $103.57 to
$107.38 over the same period. In the absence of St. John's
Hospital, and with a capacity of 131 beds, the per diem
cost at St. Peter's could have been as low as $82.00 in
1972, assuming a rise in occupancy to 85% (by accomodating
an average of 40 medical-surgical patients from St. John's)
and increased operating expenditures of $504,000. The
1972 operating cost savings to the Helena community and to
the Sisters of Charity would have approximated $1,750,000.
Accordingly, we feel that St. John's Hospital cannot justify continuing its existence as an acute general hospital.

The conversion of St. John's to a rehabilitation or
other specialty hospital would necessitate outlays in the
range of $125,000-$175,000 for changing facility design
and the purchasing of special equipment. Because physical
therapy is already provided by the other Helena hospitals,
there is little evidence to indicate a need for this type
of specialty hospital. There is currently a minimum of
community support for a specialty facility, and the poor
weather conditions during the winter months do not make
Helena a suitable location for a regional center. Since
any project exceeding $100,000 must be brought to RCHP for
approval, we feel that St. John's will not be able to
justify the need for a special facility. Despite the trend
away from general practice and towards specialties, the
number of physicians per 1000 population has declined in
Helena from 1.83 in 1964 to 1.72 in 1972, since we have
strong reservations as to whether St. John's will be able
to attract a specialty medical staff to this remote community, we feel that conversion to a rehabilitation hospital
or other specialty hospital is not feasible at this time.

Demand for ambulatory services has been increasing;
with the exception of the V.A. Hospital, there are no
hospital-based outpatient departments in the Helena area.
Although the community has not specifically demanded hospital based clinics, we believe that a medical facility
will be able to reduce its inpatient load with clinics for
maintaining potential inpatients in an ambulatory state.
Since outpatient facilities require highly technical equipment, we feel that St. Peter's complete radiology department
would be an ideal base for development of a hospital-based
ambulatory facility.

As previously discussed, the Helena area is overbedded
for long-term patients. While an ECF would theoretically
reduce hospital stays pre se, the hospital (St. Peter's)
and the ECF (St. John's) would be located two miles apart.
The difficulty in providing emergency care at St. John's

and the tenuous situation of transporting both recuperative and critical patients from one facility to the other are considerations which will be difficult to resolve. Despite the high quality of care provided by St. John's, the duplication in services and costs, and the above logistical problems seem to mediate against this alternative.

The most feasible alternative is for St. John's to close its doors. Patient care would be adequately by St. Peter's, while the cost to the community would be significantly reduced by eliminating unnecessary duplication of both facilities and service. Although we forsee some serious problems associated with the closing of this facility, an orderly plan, composed of distinct yet flexible phases, would minimize the hardship and confusion which would result from an automatic mandate from RCHP with an immediate cut of reimbursement funding.

The following steps should be taken immediately:

1. Closing of all patient areas in the building which do not meet the fire and safety standards. The present census of 40 medical-surgical patients can be accomodated in the north and south wings.

2. Negotiations begun with RCHP and St. Peter's to certify and mandate St. Peter's to increase its bed capacity by 20 beds, and including a shelled-in area for an addition of beds by 1980. Barring unusual delays in the negotiations, a design-construct addition could be erected within 18 months.

3. Negotiations begun with RCHP and St. Peter's to relocate the Speech Therapy, Dental, and Social Work Departments.

4. Negotiations begun between St. John's and St. Peter's to arrange transfer of certain usable assets upon completion of the addition to St. Peter's.

At the moment of completion of the new facility, the following will take place:

1. St. John's will cease its operations: hospital patients will be transported, by ambulance if necessary, to St. Peter's. ECF patients will be transferred to the ECF facilities of Western Care, Parkside, or other area nursing homes.

2. The Sisters of Charity will sell the entire St. John's property. We feel this will be feasible because of St. John's central proximity in the capital city of the state.

3. The note payable to the Motherhood will be repaid from the proceeds of the sale, with the balance going also to the Motherhood.

Despite the benefit to the community from the elimination of duplication of services and costs, a major cost associated with the closing will be the displacement of personnel from St. John's. We feel that this cost will be minimized for the following reasons:

1. Based upon St. Peter's personnel-bed ratio of 2.2, 44 employees could be transferred to St. Peter's upon completion of the addition.

2. Normal attrition at St. Peter's over the next 18 months will open up some positions for St. John's employees.

3. The 25 Sisters of Charity who work at St. John's will return to the Motherhood for reassignment.

4. Some of the remaining St. John's employees will be eliminated through normal attrition. Hospital patient care and ECF care will be scaled down accordingly during the next 18 months; the hospital will attempt to fill only those vacated positions which are absolutely critical to the welfare of the patients.

Although the unemployment consequences affecting approximately 25 staff and the impact of the involuntary transfer of employees to St. Peter's must be considered a major drawback to the closing of the institution, the costs of not closing the institution would be to continue the burden on the community of supporting the unnecessary duplication of facilities, services, and costs. The Personnel Department of St. John's will, of course, assist in finding new employment for those employees who may be left without jobs.

We feel that St. Peter's will be amenable to their expanded role in St. John's plan. The financial stability of St. John's, and particularly the absence of "losers", such as maternity and pediatrics departments, to be transferred to St. Peter's will benefit them in terms of increased occupancy, fiscal soundness, and goodwill from the community.

We recognize the strong political implications in that the Sisters are losing a facility and goodwill, the community is losing a respected facility, the physicians will lose some of their competitive leverage, but the social and economic implications of doing otherwise will place even greater burdens on the community. We hope that the Sisters of Charity will again recognize their community responsibility as they did in 1969 when they elected not to reopen the maternity wing which was, in Sister Macrina's words, "one of the most expensive examples of duplication and under-utilization of services in Helena."

Illinois Masonic Medical Center (E)

PURPOSE:

The Illinois Masonic Medical Center (E) case is designed to illus-
trate the internal political problems associated with strategic and
tactical decision-making in a highly complex, non profit organization.
The case focuses on the capital budgeting function at IMMC. This
focus should be used to note how a diffused budgeting process can often
determine the long term strategy of an organization without any real
guidance from top management.

The IMMC case also points to the difficulty of arriving at a con-
sensus decision when faced with vastly differing value systems in this
kind of highly complex organization. Although IMMC is clearly a hospital, similar types of organizations can be seen in both the profit and
non profit sectors.

Typical problems demonstrated in this case include the interaction
between professional and administrative organizations. The medical
side of the hospital is structured loosely and very flat. The administrative side follows a more traditional, functionally oriented organization structure. The clash between differing objectives and methods
of operation of these two structures should provide focus for discussion of resolution of conflicts within organizations.

This conflict resolution process should be tied in with the whole
concept of preparing priorities for objectives and actions. IMMC, like
all organizations, has limited resources. It must allocate those
resources in a manner consistent with the best, long term results for
IMMC and the community as a whole. The focus of the case is primarily
internal, however, and shall remain so.

POSITION IN COURSE:

This case should come at the earlier stages of the course. External factors are not a key consideration in the IMMC (E) case. Organizational and values problems are key considerations.

The problems are focussed in this case. It is ideally suited for
the section of the course dealing with values of internal constituency
groups. Students could be asked to determine what the different value
systems are and how they may conflict.

The case could also be used in a section of the course dealing
with organizational structure. The effect of structure on strategy,
and vice-versa can be demonstrated by the interaction between the
various groups at IMMC. An adjunct to this includes the problems of
allocating resources between competing power groups within the organization.

Finally, the case could be used in the section of the course dealing with non profit organizations. The trade-offs between quality service and the need to meet certain budgetary constraints is presented at IMMC. This case, unlike St. John's Hospital, however, provides the opportunity for external funding of capital improvements and operations.

This case provides far less external constraints then others in this section of the text. The problems, since they are more focussed, are somewhat simplier to analyze. The internal social and political forces involved, plus the different set of objectives in this non profit organization provide a good case for discussion centering on top management resolution of organizational problems.

KEY ISSUES:

1. Capital budgeting in a non profit organization.

2. Resolution of conflicting group values.

3. Organizational structure in complex hierarchy.

4. Authority/responsibility between live and staff functions.

5. Determination of priorities in a non profit organization.

ANALYSIS:

IMMC was faced with several budgeting problems in 1972. Gerald Mungerson, the new Executive Director, felt that the short term budgeting decisions he had to make would probably determine the future of the hospital for some time to come.

Several committees and groups were responsible for the budgeting process. Only Mr. Mungerson reviewed budgets for the entire organization. This implied a rather "pecky" organization.

The organization however, was split between professional and administrative functions. The professional side of the organization included all of the physicians on the staff. Finance, Operations and Nursing were in the administrative section.

FINANCIAL POLICIES:

Until recently, all capital and operating budgets had been funded entirely with cash. Borrowing was considered taboo. Since 1967, however, mortgages had been used freely for financing purposes. At the present time, virtually all the buildings at IMMC were mortgaged.

These funds gained from this loosened financial policy had been allocated to improvement of patient care. The medical departments had been relied on for recommendations. Prior to Mr. Mungerson's arrival, most capital budgeting decisions had been made directly by the

Executive Director on an informed basis. Few details of these requests, or decisions, were available for this reason.

The current financial position is presented below.

	1967	1968	1969	1970	1971	1972
Add to fixed assets (000)	246	1,319	1,163	875	738	1,026
Secured bank loans (000)	144	144	—	—	900	
Unsecured bank loans (000)	—	240	—	—	—	
Interim Mortgage (000)	—	—	—	1,714	2,510	
L.T. contracts payable (000)	74	257	186	85	65	
Permanent fund bal. (000)	11	12	13	14	19	

A summary of the 1971-1972 capital budgets are also presented below:

	1971 Budgeted	1971 Approved	1972 Budgeted
Nursing Division	41,060	31,215	69,821
Professional Services Division	76,982	105,817	228,937
Operations Division	98,252	19,314	17,173
Finance Division	13,210	8,250	3,695
Administration	5,793	0	0
Medical Division	6,000	0	19,170
Contingencies	170,000	497,500	61,204
TOTAL	411,297	662,096	400,000

The new Stone Pavilion was being financed entirely through the Development fund. An Endowment fund had been established, but had not provided much of an increase in resources yet. The lack of coordination between departments created problems in budgeting for the Stone Pavilion.

Decisions concerning the Stone Pavilion included whether new equipment should be purchased for the facility or whether present equipment should be moved. Separate committees were formed to decide on requests from departments involved in the Stone Pavilion and regular capital requests.

8 9

CURRENT PROBLEMS:

A combination of events had lead to the need for tight budgets at IMMC. Basically, however, a delay in payments from the state and federal governments had lead to a cash flow problem. Austerity Committees were established to overcome this problem.

The Austerity Committees were supposed to oversee requests from operations and medical departments. There was only one overlapping member on these committees. Bill Blessing, Director of Professional Services performed this function.

Most of the decisions made by the various committees involved relatively small and narrowly defined requests. There was no standard format for considering requests presented to either committee.

Although neither committee refused many requests, both groups felt they served a viable function. They both felt that the mere existence of such a review committee served as a deterrent to wasteful requests.

Mr. Blessing observed, however, that the medical committee, in particular, relied on the specialists for advice on requests. This meant that the areas presenting requests frequently were called on to evaluate those requests. Specialization was so great at IMMC that no single individual felt capable, or willing, to evaluate requests from other areas. This included the Medical Director, Dr. Clarke.

Coordination of efforts of the two committees was informal. It relied on the dual role of Mr. Blessing.

One of the immediate problems involved a request by the anesthesiology department for new equipment. The department had relied on one firm for its estimates and had opted for that firm's equipment. Attempts were made to evaluate these requests by seeking outside consultation. Expected costs were cut through such recommendations. Questions involving the trade-offs between costs and the desires of the anesthesiology department had to be resolved.

Mr. Mungerson is faced with several problems at the end of the case. Among them are questions relating to structure and control of budgeting and decision-making processes. Also, the timing of any proposed changes worried the Executive Director.

QUESTIONS:

1. Should the Austerity Committee system be retained? If so, should it be modified?

2. How could IMMC's administrators exercise effective control over capital spending in medical departments without imposing laymen's "arbitrariness" on medical plans?

3. When should changes be implemented?

4. Describe the effects of the organizational structure at IMMC on the planning function.

RESPONSES:

1. The Austerity Committee system clearly plays a vital role in the overall planning process at IMMC. The Austerity Committees fulfill several different functions.

First, they apparently inhibit some requests that are difficult to justify. Peer group pressure works against individuals who try to press for petty or inconsequential expenditures. In the past, these could be buried, without anyone ever questioning them. Now, they at least have been discussed.

Also, the committees provide a forum for discussion between various groups. Professional and administrative staff are now able to see what the needs and values of others are within the IMMC organization. The committees, therefore can provide a forum for determining priorities at IMMC.

The structure and charge of the committees should probably be altered, however. There should be more formal overlap of membership on the two committees. Part of the discussion should center on who should represent which side on both committees.

The committees should also be forced to consider requests as part of a total package instead of individually, as they do now. In conjunction with this, Mr. Mungerson, the Executive Director, should incorporate the two committees into the total planning/budgeting procedure. To do this, the committees will have to determine what the long term objectives of IMMC are. They can then use those objectives as criteria for basing future budgeting decisions.

2. This has always been a problem when professional managers are faced with the task of interacting with technical specialists. Universities, research groups and high technology industries are frequently faced with this same problem.

The key factor is to involve the medical groups, through the committee system in the formal planning function. Right now, Mr. Mungerson does the planning and has others carry out his plans. Since the departments have little initial say in the formation of plans, they often feel no obligation to follow them. Moreover, they probably feel that the administrators do not understand their particular needs.

All of these requests should be presented to the medical Austerity Committee. It should develop a policy whereby any request over a specified limit will be evaluated by outside specialists. These external agents should be selected by and report to the committee, not the department originating the requests.

Naturally, this plan of action is contingent upon recommendations

contained in response (1) above. Priorities and objectives have to
first be determined by the committee and Mr. Mungerson. The committee
has to be working within the context of a total budget.

3. These changes cannot be implemented overnight. It will take time
to determine the precise composition of the various committees. The
real problem will be in developing a set of objectives and priorities
within the new structure.

For the time being, the reformulated committees will have to carry
on as they have, one decision at a time. The primary emphasis of the
committees over the next several months should be to familiarize themselves with the formal planning process. Starting with the next formal
budgeting process, the committees should take an active part from the
start.

This plan of action will cause some inconvenience on the organization. It maintains a makeshift system for the next 12 months. The
dangers of rushing in before the personnel are ready, however, are
great. This, combined with the necessity to redo all the departmental
budgets in the two months left before the end of the fiscal year probably outweighs the difficulty of living with a temporary system for
awhile. Besides, the structure of the new committee system should be
in place shortly. This will give personnel time to familiarize themselves with the structure before having to adapt to the substance of
the change.

4. The IMMC case provides an excellent forum for discussing non standard organizational structures. The organization is really a hybrid
form in a hospital.

The administrative side of the organization follows a more traditional, hierarchical, functionally oriented organizational structure.
It is highly centralized and "pecky." The medical departments are very
flat, however. Span of control in this side is very wide. Also,
typically, everyone thinks of himself as a chief. In this respect, it
is very similar to most university settings. In fact, comparisons
should be made with your own university or college structure at this
point.

This organizational structure has interesting effects on the planning and budgeting process. Typically, as at IMMC, neither side feels
that the other understands the needs and pressures facing them.

The administrators are unsure of themselves when discussing
technical issues with the medical staff. They feel that the medical
staff are prima donnas. The administrators also perceive their lack
of status relative to the medical staff as a constraint in dealing with
them.

The medical staff doesn't help this latter problem any. They are
frequently antagonistic towards the actions of the administrators. The
medical staff perceives them as hindering their ability to perform
their function effectively. They know, however, that the top adminis-

trators, eventually, have veto power over budgetary requests.

The two sides of the organization have different objectives. Given the structure as it now stands, with only Mr. Mungerson as the unifying force, all disagreements end up travelling all the way up to him to be settled. A restructuring along the lines discussed would help to alleviate these problems. The committees could be used as a lower level agency for determining priorities and settling budgetary, and other disputes.

Metropolitan Tulsa Transit Authority

Purpose

The Metropolitan Tulsa Transit Authority (MTTA) case demonstrates the difficulty of resolving conflicts between different objectives. MTTA has set forth a rather detailed set of objectives.

The students should be asked to evaluate the various objectives presented by management. The relationship between objectives as well as their interaction with the external environment should provide the focus for discussion.

Management at MTTA is faced with the necessity of balancing economic, social and political goals. Management has an economic responsibility to provide a service at a reasonable cost. It has a social goal of assisting the center city residents and businessmen. It has a political goal of staying in office. To do this, its decisions must be acceptable to the municipal authorities in Tulsa.

The MTTA case is primarily concerned with matching objectives with the external environment. The difficulties encountered by managers of a public organization working in that external organization should be discussed. What might seem to be relatively simple decisions are soon discovered to be fairly complex in nature. Greater understanding of public managers can be developed through presentation of this case.

Position in Course

The MTTA case is designed to be used in that segment of the course devoted to public organizations. It should be used at a point in the course when the students have the ability to analyze the values of diverse constituency groups.

These various groups, politicians, taxpayers, commuters, etc., all make demands on the MTTA. The students have to be able to discover the priorities of the various demands and how they can be combined to develop a strategy for the future.

The mission is fairly well defined. It is to provide a transit system for the city of Tulsa, Oklahoma. The students have to be able to refine the mission and objectives to guide further actions for the MTTA.

The problems appear relatively simple, at first. This would suggest placement at the early stages of the course. Simply increasing ridership is not the only concern of the managers at MTTA. The students must have the ability to scan the total environment, especially the political scene. For this reason, the MTTA case is also ideal for use in a segment of the course dealing with the external environment.

Typically, the problems discussed above are presented by the middle or later stages of the course. Depending on the specific problems selected, either specific or general, the case should be presented either earlier or later in the course.

Key Issues

1. Trade-offs between economic and political objectives.

2. Determining priorities of conflicting goals of different constituency groups.

3. Decreasing ridership in a public transit system.

4. Management of a public, service-oriented, organization.

Analysis

History: The Metropolitan Tulsa Transit Authority is a relatively new mass transit system. It was started in 1968 to take over the bus operations of the Missouri-Kansas-Oklahoma Transit Lines in the Tulsa vicinity.

The M-K-O Transit Lines had operated the bus system for some time prior to its takeover by the city of Tulsa. Ridership and revenues had declined precipitously between 1960 and 1969. Nearly 40 % of their loss in ridership occurred during a two month strike. The strike, during the summer of 1968, had led the M-K-O management to conclude that further operations would be unprofitable.

The MTTA trustees formed a planning commission to determine the short and long range problems of the Authority. Objectives and actions to solve these problems are also to be determined.

Rate structure: MTTA served 10 separate routes. All served the central business district. Seven of the routes made round trip loops from one end of the district to the opposite end. Frequency of trips was every 30 minutes on weekdays and every 60 minutes on Saturday. There was no service on Sundays or holidays.

Most of the riders came from the predominantly Black area of Tulsa. School riders also make up a sizeable number of customers. 90 % of all trips were made during morning and afternoon rush hours.

The Tulsa area had frequently been compared to Los Angeles. Although considerably smaller, it is spread out over a large area. It has a well-developed highway system

and people are accustomed to using personal autos for transportation needs. This geographic dispersion of potential
riders added to route scheduling problems.

The suburbs were even more spread out than the actual
Tulsa area. They were inhabited primarily by middle- and
upper-socio-economic classes. They were also predominantly
White. The Black population lived within one section of
Tulsa itself.

National trends: Ridership had been declining nationally for the past 15 years. Although revenues had increased
slightly over the last several years, they had not been
enough to offset sharply rising costs. Deficits, therefore,
had increased to close to $0.5 billion for the industry as
a whole.

Federal spending had helped to close this gap to a
small extent, however. Much of the added funds had gone to
bus and rapid transit companies. Most went to offset capital expenditures, however, not operating expenses.

Financial statistics:	1970	1969
Current Assets	$31,942	
Fixed Assets	472,270	
Total Assets	522,353	
Current Liabilities	112,902	
Long-term Liabil- ities	225,021	
Deferred Liabilities	352,255	
Surplus (Deficit)	(167,846)	
Total Liabilities and Surplus	522,353	
Total Revenues	$311,201	$349,648
Equipment Expenses	20,696	24,154
Transp. Expenses	235,003	213,905
G.S. &A. Expenses	158,123	167,482
Net Loss	(81,925)	(31,739)

Future: The top management at MTTA felt they had to
evaluate their policies set forth for public transportation.
The problems seemed to concern trade-offs between quality,
quantity, and expenses of transportation services. All
deficits had to be made up by the Metropolitan Tulsa com-
munities. Basic policies are set forth in the text on
pages 512-513.

Equipment was considered old by industry standards.
Maintenance policies were, therefore, necessarily rigid,

and expensive. There was a possibility of federal funding for new equipment for the MTTA. This would affect the operating and capital budgets of MTTA.

Many questions facing the trustees of MTTA are listed on pages 515 - 517 of the text.

Questions

1. Why has ridership dropped at MTTA?

2. Evaluate the 15 service standards referred to on pages 512 - 513 in the case.

3. Evaluate the 12 considerations presented on pages 515-517 of the text.

4. What alternatives are available to the MTTA?

Responses

1. The immediate cause of a decline in ridership was the disasterous two month strike recently settled. All data that have been collected on transit strikes show that this same result occurs as riders are forced into finding alternate forms of transportation, and may not return once the strike is over. These riders find they either didn't need to go to the Central Business District as often as they once thought, or, more often, they find they enjoy the convenience of private transportation even if it is more costly. Forty percent of MTTA riders were lost because of having to do without the system for two months. It is likely, however, that those who are left provide the hard core of passengers serviced. They are undoubtedly the ones who can get to work or shopping no other way.

Other, longer range reasons for the decline in riders have to do with the policies followed by the former owners. The buses are relatively old, averaging ten years of service. Surveys have shown that riders greatly prefer clean, efficient modes of transportation. It is probably very difficult to keep these old buses such that they appeal to the general riding public.

The route structure also presents many problems. Frequency of service during weekdays is limited to every 30 minutes. This is a long time to wait between buses. This requires a lot of planning to use the system, and virtually eliminates the impulse user.

Since there are only 10 routes, this also means that many potential riders are far from existing lines. They either have to walk excessive distances to get to a bus, or they have to make inconvenient transfers or take lengthy

bus rides going out of their way. Once again, this inconvenience leads most potential riders to seek other modes of
transportation, even if more expensive.

A final reason for the decline in ridership relates to
other policies of the various government transportation
agencies. Tulsa has grown rapidly over the recent past. A
relatively good highway system has been developed to help
the new suburbanites to get in and out of the city. While
service on the bus lines has been decaying, former passengers have found it relatively convenient and easy to use
autos to travel to and from work or shopping.

Also, like other types of suburban development, more
services are found outside of the Central Business District.
New bus routes haven't followed these shifts in rider patterns, however. These riders have been forced to use alternate methods of transportation as well.

2.   The 15 policy standards described in the case demonstrate the severe problems faced by a public transit manager.
They are, for the most part, service oriented. Only three
of the standards mention costs or price. Even here, the
fare structure is supposed to be held at a low level.

The public transit manager has many constituencies to
please. He is trying to provide adequate service while
keeping costs low.

The policy standards referred to in the case can be
likened to motherhood and apple pie. If all the standards
could be adhered to, Tulsa would have the ideal system.
Riders would be provided frequent, efficient, clean service
with a low fare. The local government would also not have
to subsidize the system.

The system is designed to operate, according to the
standards, on a break-even or better format. They provide
admirable objectives for such a system. The question that
students often overlook, and that should be forcefully
presented, is how these objectives will be met. Moreover,
since there are no priorities mentioned in the case, the
relative importance of these standards should be discussed.

An interesting exercise would involve asking the students to list their preferences, individually, and then
compare priorities. The differences brought out by this
exercise should forcefully present the problems and conflicts faced by a manager in the public sector.

3.   The 12 considerations presented in the case are a
mixture of social and economic goals and perceived constraints. Once again, they seem to present a blend of
idealism with a desire for economy.

There are clearly contradictory considerations facing
the top managers of MTTA. The primary goals presented here

are socially oriented. They are designed to improve the job and health opportunities of a sizeable minority in the city who rely on mass transit to provide access to these services.

These social objectives are counter-balanced by the lack of public funds. It is noted in the case that $400,000 is required to cover deficits for the MTTA for the past 2½ years. It is interesting to note, however, that this represents just over a single one-way trip per year for every person in the Tulsa district.

The social goals are long term in nature. Unfortunately, fiscal objectives of most governments, including Tulsa, are mainly short term in nature. This latter point is clearly brought out by the hesitance in providing funds for a professional administrator as well as funds for public relations.

Finally, the last five considerations question the place of public transit in the future of Tulsa. The question raised here is where public funds should be directed. Clearly, the public prefers the convenience of the private car. This mode of transportation is more expensive, overall, however. It is more of a pollutant, and is not available to lower economic segments of the population.

The trustees of MTTA have to present management with a clear cut set of objectives for the organization. Without firmly set, long term, priorities, the managers can only hope to adapt to short run demands and crises.

4. The range of alternative available to managers of MTTA is extremely wide. At one extreme, they include closing down the system entirely. On the other end of the spectrum, is the total commitment of resources to a well rounded mass transit system.

Given the values of the various constituency groups involved, however, it is highly unlikely that either extreme will be chosen. The people who require public transit for jobs, health care and shopping live primarily north of the Central Business District. They will resist cessation of operations. Federal influence will probably also be used to further mass transit.

The suburban dwellers who do not use the system are more likely to resist continued deficits. Typically, those who don't use the system have to pay for it. On the other hand, the mass transit riders have to live with their poverty as well as the pollution caused by the large amount of autos.

The federal government, pressured by environmental and social action groups, is beginning to divert funds to mass transit. MTTA should join these groups as a lobby as well as requesting financial aid. The $1 million request for assistance should be a beginning.

The managers and trustees have to present a public relations effort showing that money has to be spent before a
viable system can be maintained. Clearly, however, the
planning structure for the system has to be based on more
than a yearly format.

MTTA has to be incorporated into a long range plan
for the development of the entire Tulsa area. Without
taking an integrative approach to planning in this situation
a great deal of resources could be wasted. The values of
the relevant constituency groups have to be considered here.
This is a truly political question. The groups in the
public sector are usually larger and more vocal, however.
This case clearly shows that strategies are more than just
an intellectual exercies. The political and social implications, demonstrated here on a macro scale, have to be considered when determining priorities and action plans.

Pennsylvania State University

PURPOSE

The Penn State case is designed to provide the student with insight to the problems and management of a major, diversified, non-profit organiztion. One of the important aspects of the case is the need for the student to recognize the size and diversity of the organization. The impact of the diversity or management is significently greater than in the St. John's Hospital case. Concentration on only one college at Penn State (such as the College of Business) will not yield realistic recommendations. This case requires a balanced approach to both analysis and solutions.

The case is designed to show the complex political and social relationships in the policy formation area. President Oswald knows that whatever decisions he arrives at will draw criticism from one or more powerful constituencies. The students will have to analyze the values and objectives of all the power groups influencing decisions in the organization.

The case is intended to provide experience in problem identification in this type of organization. The complexity of the situation may be misleading. The case does not lend itself to simple solutions. Some students let their own values sway their judgments in this case, they can use this case to develop a better understanding that there is more than one way to look at any problem.

The case also is designed to look at the comparability of diverse programs. The university, in this sense, is similar to a diversified business organization such as Westinghouse. However, it has been suggested that diversity is also more extensive at the accountability level (state legislature, board of governors, students, faculty, community.)

Finally, their are significant people problems present in the case. Administrators are protective of their programs. Budget cuts have to be made. The President of Penn State has to make decisions based on the overall objectives of the organization. If reduction of services is required, the students have to come to grips with what is most viable for Penn State in the long run.

POSITION IN COURSE

The complexity of the problems in the Penn State case require that it be placed at the latter part of the policy course. The students have to be able to integrate fully the complex interrelationships involved in the environment facing President Oswald.

This case is similar in nature to discussing a complex, profit oriented organization. It is often interesting to schedule Penn State next to the Gulf and Western Industries case mentioned later. They both present problems of comparability of operating divisions.

The students have to be able to analyze the values of the various interest groups involved. They also have to be able to determine what effects any decisions arrived at will have on the long run potential of the organization.

The Penn State case should be presented well after the intellectual and political factors of strategy formation have been discussed. Ideally, it should be used at the latter stages of the implementation phase of the course. Any solutions have to be accepted and implemented. The Penn State case can be used to demonstrate problems in both these areas of strategy formation.

KEY ISSUES

1. Comparability of programs in a diverse organization.

2. Analysis of values in a quasi public organization.

3. Organization structure in a multi-goal institution.

4. Necessity of retrenchment in a diverse organizational setting.

5. The interaction between organization structure on strategic decisions.

6. Political factors affecting strategic decisions.

ANALYSIS

The Pennsylvania State Univeristy land grant college for Pennsylvania. It was founded in 1855 as the Farmer's High School. It evolved into a college in 1863 and was granted university status in 1953.

Penn State is a well-established institution enjoying considerable funding from the state. Legally, it is a private institution. A sizable minority of the board of governors is appointed by the State of Pennsylvania, however.

Penn State has several small campuses scattered around the state in addition to the main campus at State College, Pa. The enrollment is roughly equally divided between the main campuses and the Commonwealth campuses.

MISSION

The mission of the Penn State is to provide an instrument of self-renewal and development for the Commonwealth in the area of higher education. Plans and programs coordinated with those of other state higher education institutions should be offered to provide the most complete educational opportunity for the citizens of the Commonwealth of Pennsylvania. It is to act as an instrument of self-renewal and development for the Commonwealth.

This mission is to be implemented through a balanced offering of graduate and undergraduate programs as well as extension services of high quality. Students from all social and economic levels should be given the opportunity to learn and mature at a Penn State campus. This requires a minimization of tuition expenses and a maximization of programs and campuses consistent with the rest of the Commonwealth System of High Education (including the University of Pittsburgh and Temple University.)

ORGANIZATION

The university has a dual structure within the organization. The administration is functionally organized. The academic side is organized according colleges, type of degree, geographic area, and services. The administrative officers have relatively, various spans of control. The academic officers have extremely wide spans of control in a flat organization. Provost larson has 24 separate people reporting to him.

President Oswald is the Chief Executive Officer of the University. He reports to the Board of Trustees of the University who have ultimate responsibility for the operations and policies of the university.

FUNDS

Penn State receives funds from a variety of sources. These include the Commonwealth of Pennsylvania, the federal government, student tuition and charges, auxiliary enterprises, sales and services of educational departments, private grants and contracts and other sources. Some of the funds are restricted as to their use (i.e. land grant status provides funds for agricultural research and extension services.) It is difficult to project long term sources of funds due to the nature of government funding processes.

An analysis of the financial condition of Penn State is reproduced below.

Source of Funds (000,000)	1972	1971	1970	1969	1968
Penna	36	41	43	41	38
Students	21	20	18	17	16
Aux.Ent./Serv.	16	14	14	15	15
U.S.Govt.	15	17	3	21	23
Private	2	3	4	3	3
Sales	6	3	4	4	4
Other	3	2	-	-	-

EXPENDITURES

Much of the expenses at Penn State are incurred in resident education and research. This accounts for almost 50% of the total. The remainder is distributed between various services, provided to students and other groups or to maintain the physical and educational facilities.

Distribution of the funds to academic departments is not proportional to size. Exhibits 7,8,9, in the case provide a breakdown of size and fund allocation to these departments.

Agriculture, because of the land grant status of the University, receives a disproportionately large share of the funds. Much of this is restricted to that department by legislation however.

CURRENT PROBLEMS

President Oswald is faced with the prospect of no increase in state aid for the following year. The Governor's budget for 1973-74 holds appropriations constant for Penn State, as well as other state related institutions. President Oswald notes that this, in effect, represents a 6% cut in funds. This is due to inflationary factors and contractual obligations of the University. (The faculty is not organized, although that is the case at some other state related institutions in Pennsylvania).

The federal government has also made clear its plans to reduce aid to universities. This would drastically reduce the options available to Penn State is the appropriation bill is not changed.

Penn State is also required, by the Snyder ammendment to the previous year's appropriation, to prepare plans to improve the efficiency of the institution. A report has to be submitted annually detailing the productivity of faculty and staff. With this report is supposed to come a formula for evaluating productivity.

These financial problems come as Penn State is experiencing a decline in the growth rate of admissions. Admissions are growing primarily at the Commonwealth campuses. Student population at the main campus has remained relatively constant. This growth at the widely scattered, satellite campuses has caused problems of control within the administration as well.

President Oswald is concerned with the effect of the budget cuts on the university. He is also concerned with the increasing difficulty of controlling the complex organization.

QUESTIONS

1. Given the conditions of a declining budget and marked organizational diversity, how and/or where does the organization reduce its budgetary expenses?

2. How can the diverse programs offered by Penn State by compared for evaluation purposes?

3. What alternatives to budget cut are open to President Oswald?

REPONSES

1. President Oswald is faced with extremely difficult decision if he is forced to cut the budgets of the various departments reporting to him. The mission of the organization clearly centers

around the teaching and research functions of the university. Initial budget cuts should come from administrative functions where possible. And other departments not directly affecting the teaching and researc or other fund generating structures, should also be cut.

After all non-essential areas have been cut, efforts must be made to trim costs in the research and then the teaching functions. The implications of these kinds of decisions are severe. The long run visability of the organization may be affected.

In any event, all cuts should be planned in advance. Cuts that are instituted in the middle of an academic year could prove even more diastrous to morale and confidence, than the cut themselves. The budget cuts, therefore should be instituted as of the next fiscal year. The budget cuts should be forecast well in advance of their actual implementation.

2. If budget cuts finally have to be made in the academic segments, priorities have to be set. Care has to be taken not to endanger programs with growth potential. This presents a good situation for applying the growth/market share analysis presented in the text.

Mature programs should provide funds for the growing segments of the market. This means that whatever funds are available for promotion of programs and hiring should be funneled into the growth areas.

Analysis of growth areas should consider the long term funding requirements of any program. If a program is going to be overly expensive to maintain in the long run, the resources should not be allocated to it. Cost/benefit analysis should be provided for each of the programs, but on a future oriented basis.

The evaluation of diverse, educational programs presents the opportunity to implement management by objectives. The objectives of the various departments could then be evaluated with regard to the overall mission and future objectives of the university as a whole. This concept would have to implemented immediately if it is to be effective for the coming fiscal year, however this kind of wrenching change will take time for the faculty and staff to become accustomed to it.

3. The budgetary considerations include a considerable amount of political factors. The organization should first rally its forces to put pressure on the legislature to increase the appropriations to Penn State. There are over 50,000 students attending Penn State. Those students and their families, who are residents of Pennsylvania, should apply pressure to the legislature. Similarly, alumni should be asked to apply pressure for increased funding.

President Oswald should attempt to determine if the budget is expendable, or if any increase in his funds must come from some other budget. If it is expendable, then he should seek the assistance of the other colleges and universities to assist in the lobbying process.

In any event, Penn State should attempt to increase the amount of funds for other sources. This should include, private grants payment for university services to outside agencies, if necessary, tuition and other student charges.

This latter area should be tried last. Given the mission of the Penn State to provide education to a broad social-economic class of students, a rise of tuitions might be counter productive. The only way to overcome this problem would be to increase scholarship assistance to those absolutely requiring aid and letting those students who can afford the added charges to pay the increase. The problem that this presents is that potential students may be frightened away from applying due to the high perceived charges.

Whatever decisions are made, they must be consistent with the overall mission and objectives of the organization. If the mission and objectives are not feasible, then they must be changed to be consistent with the current environment.

EPILOG

It might be of interest to note that the three main universities (Penn State, University of Pittsburg and Temple University) coordinated their efforts to increase appropriations. They were relatively successful in this task. The combined enrollment of the three universities is in excess of 110,000 students. This, combined with alumni provides a powerful flow of support.

SAMPLE STUDENT REPORT

Assignment: Prepare a set of recommendations
for President Oswald to combat the
effects of the proposed state budget
allocation to Penn State.

THE PENN STATE CASE

Governor Shapp in his budget message called for a zero appropriations increase for Penn State University for fiscal year 1973-74. This, in effect, is a 6% cut, or approximately $4.7 million less than the appropriation requested of $83.3 million.

Penn State is battling against rising costs. The appropriations request submitted by the University was extremely austere. It provided for mandated increases such as Social Security, retirement, unemployment insurance, the additional cost of doing business because of inflation and the opening of new facilities.

In conjunction with this, Penn State is confronted by the increasing threat of unionism of its professors. Presently, there are only three public universities that are not unionized in the state. If Penn State cannot provide increases in compensation to its professors at a time when most individuals in the nation are participating in some form of income compensation related to cost, the number of non-union universities may drop to two.

There is no increased money for financial assistance to needy students planned in the forthcoming year. Therefore, the amount Penn State can raise tuition without forcing many out of school is limited. Also, students have been applying pressure to hold down costs and are no longer willing to pay for educational luxuries.

Penn State is facing a student enrollment growth rate that is increasing but at a decreasing rate. Since 1970, growth has dropped from 17% to 2% in 1972.

The importance of education is a declining priority with the state and the nation.

Federal funding is also being reduced. Only about 1.0% of the national income is appropriated for high education.

Penn State is also confronted with the requirements of the Snyder Amendment, requiring recommendations of a formula to be applied in the determination of annual appropriations to be made to the University.

The financial crunch is here. It is primarily the result of a declining rate of income growth, a general rise in academic standards, and an increase in activities considered desirable for a university to perform.

If Penn State cannot improve its performance, the national issue of governance in high education will be a critical one. This trend to abolish boards of trustees in universities, state colleges, and community colleges, and place them all under one state governing body tends to draw a happy medium among the institutions. It has been demonstrated that cost efficiencies and standardization can result from this type of rule.

Penn State has established a long-term objective as one which provides programs of instruction, research and public service at a reasonable cost to both students and the Commonwealth. In conjunction with this, Penn State must assume the mission as an "originator of new knowledge" for it is this concept which distinguishes Penn State from other public educational institutions. Penn State's strategy assumes that the ability to stimulate, and to cope with, the rampant change that occurs in modern society cannot occur by accident but must be part of its planning process as an apparatus of development and self-renewal. Because Penn State is funded by public bodies and private individuals, its objective is to provide a means of measuring success. Objectives such as programs of instruction (11 colleges), research (16.7% of funds allocated here), public service (8.8% of funds allocated here) and reasonable cost to students (tuition competitive with other state related schools in Pa.) are easily quantified and measurable. However, Penn State believes that these figures cannot measure its ultimate existence and reason for being. It must be concerned with academic excellence, knowledge, innovation and relevancy as factors which contribute to the quality and validity of its educational experience. These factors cannot be precisely quantified in terms of dollars. Yet, Penn State has an immense public responsibility to provide the state and the nation with graduates who are products of these factors.

Penn State also has the objective to maintain its present system of goverance. It believes that it should enjoy the autonomy to pursue its mission because its mission is different from other schools. Penn State wants the opportunity to make its own decisions concerning the cost and quality of its educational offering. It believes that its expertise in developing its own program will permit the University to adjust more completely to the threats and opportunities in the environment. Coordination among schools on a voluntary basis can result in cost efficiency without disturbing academic equilibrium.

Penn State needs additional funds to keep on serving the public now and in the future. Funds may be acquired from the following sources: (1) Alumni contribution; (2) from parents and guardians of the students; (3) from the state through its alumni lobby; (4) from the state legislator through its permanent lobby; (5) from the recommendation of Governor Shapp and elected officials, by using its own president's persuasion; (6) from the private corporations; (7) from the foundations; (8) from the Federal Government and its various agencies through our senators and congressmen.

Penn State does not want students to drop out due to financial difficulties. The following courses of action are planned: (1) set up a financial consultation service at the school; (2) advertise state loan programs and awards; (3) encourage needy students to apply for federal work-study programs, national defense loans, federal and guaranteed loans; (4) encourage disadvantaged students to use the Higher Education Equal Opportunity Act; (5) encourage students for summer and part-time jobs; (6) encourage veterans to use their benefits.

Areas for cost cutting: (1) capital and maintenance cost of buildings and teaching equipment; (2) teaching cost which includes equipment cost and material cost; (3) administrative expenditures; (4) library expensitures; (5) student facilities.

Other specific actions for cost cutting include: (1) new programs that can replace old and ineffective programs; (2) use of mechanical aids to instruction; (3) consolidation in curricula and reduction in small class sizes; (4) increased use of present buildings capacity; (5) expensive tools such as computers, electron microscopes will be used in moderation; (6) experimentation with different student-teacher structures.

At present, Penn State is confronted by the problem of allocating funds if a proposed budget cut comes to pass. Since this proposal is only in the recommendation stage, a committee, comprised of the Provost and the eleven collegedeans with a staff of professors and students, should be formed immediately. This group should review each college's budget and make decisions where budgets will be cut. A strict accounting and justification of all reductions is necessary. Rather than impose a budget cut of 6% on an overall basis, Penn State should concentrate on those areas which are experiencing declining enrollments to investigate how much of a cut they can absorb before imposing cuts on other schools. At this time, professors will not be considered for elimination.

In the long run, zero appropriations may be a recurring problem. Penn State must eliminate, as far as possible, program obsolesence and duplication. A permanent program and review board, consisting of the Provost, the deams and academic vice-president, a committee of faculty and students, must be developed. Consideration of the many diversified points of view is necessary. Primarily, mission and its financing, must be the focal point of departure. It will take a period of five years to analyze Penn State's curriculum. The board must judge the quality, efficiency and relevancy of a program according to its relationship with other program and according to the direction of the university at large. Considerations must be made or individual programs, the colleges in which they are located and the organizational unit.

Penn State is required by the Snyder Amendment to develop an appropriations formula. The results of this provision are located in Presentation Exhibit I.

Finally, Penn State should develop some comparative statistics which show that the school itself has assumed the private responsibility to accrue funds through its own merits. During a time when enrollment has increased by 46.2% from 1967 to 1972, Penn State has greatly outpaced both the state and Federal Government in the raising of funds to be used in accomplishing its mission. Penn State believes that it has fulfilled its public responsibility to the best of its ability.

In order to meet the threat of statewide governance, Penn State is going to have to operate efficiently while providing quality and relevancy to its programs. To help accomplish this, Penn State desires to convince the state legislature to allow more flexible management of state funds. Currently many funds are restricted where there are an over abundance of funds; such as in the School of Agriculture. These funds could be utilized more efficiently in other areas without hurting the quality of agriculture programs.

Another approach would be for the schools that have excess funds to expand their program to include an integrative approach with university schools that are in need of greater funds. Such a program could be used only between schools that relate to each other.

The Federal Government also needs to be convinced to provide for more flexible use of its funds (through the American Council of Education). One alternative to consider would be for the Federal Government to provide tax credits to individuals for gifts which they would make to schools of higher education. Their tax bill would be the total tax minus the donation (Congress would set a limit). Problems here to study would be the effect on taxes, tax deductions and changes in the amount of gifts to the schools.

Another alternative would be to lessen dependence on public funding. Efforts could be increased to obtain private gifts and grants through increasing the number of sources and convincing sources to give more. Currently there is much untapped potential lying with corporations and private foundations; increased alumni donations or other possibilities.

The University could also increase attendance of private organizations conferences using the University's facilities and programs. Providing more University services and auxiliary enterprises could provide additional income. Providing planning and engineering services to local governments (below and including the county level) would be one large potential market. Care must be taken not to arouse competing private interest.

Another long-range possibility would be to adjust the number of graduates in the various schools to fit projected employment opportunities. In addition to helping students start off on the right foot in regard to their careers, this measure would also provide one fair criteria by which to adjust the expenditures of resources between the various university colleges.

PENNSYLVANIA STATE UNIVERSITY

PRESENTATION EXHIBIT I

OPERATIONAL BREAKDOWN

CLASSROM	12.3 HRS. - 24%
RELATED INSTRUCTIONAL	27.1 HRS. - 54%
RESEARCH OR ADM.	11.2 HRS. - 22%
	50.6 HRS. - 100%

OPERATION - 40 HR. WEEK BASE

CLASSROOM	12.3 HRS. - 31%
RELATED INSTRUCTIONAL	27.1 HRS. - 68%
RESEARCH OR ADM.	11.2 HRS. - 28%
	50.6 HRS. - 127%

OPERATION - 40/50.6 = .791 SCALE DOWN FACTOR

CLASSROOM	9.73 HRS. - 24%
RELATED INSTRUCTIONAL	21.41 HRS. - 54%
RESEARCH OR ADM.	8.86 HRS. - 22%
	40.00 HRS. - 100%

PENNSYLVANIA STATE UNIVERSITY

EXHIBIT I

FACTORS REQUIRED FOR ANNUAL APPROPRIATIONS FORMULA

No. of FTE Students	31.835	students
Avg. Class Size	14.9	students
Avg. Faculty Teaching Assignment	12.3	students
Faculty Productivity	50.6	hours

    (a) Instruct   12.3 hrs. 24%

    (b) Rel. Instruct. 27.1 hrs. 54%

    (c) Research   11.2 hrs. 22%

OBSERVATIONS

(a) Average faculty work week is 27% greater than a normal 40 hour week;

(b) The breakdown of the allocation of faculty time on a per-centage basis corresponds identically with the way in which state funds are allocated (top of Presentation Exhibit 1A).

MULTI-NATIONAL ORGANIZATIONS

This section presents three cases involving operations
in one or more countries outside of the United States. Most
students find, when they are confronted with strategic problems related to multinational organizations, that policies
which proved satisfactory for purely domestic operations,
are no longer sufficient.

The cases presented in this section are designed to
explore many of the problems found in the multinational sector. Control and coordination become an even greater problem when operations are confronted with different cultural,
economic, and legal systems.

Given the increasingly international nature of organizations, exposure to these cases should provide additional
insight into this important area. The organizations discussed in this section attempt to deal with the full range
of multinational issues in various ways. They range from
a small start-up operation in a developing country to a
relatively new subsidiary in Britain, ending with a large
well-organized and integrated organization operating throughout the world.

Fluid Flow (Electronics) Ltd.

Purpose

The Fluid Flow (Electronics) Ltd. case (FF(E)) is designed to demonstrate the problems of starting a major enterprise in a foreign country. It also demonstrates the interaction between subsidiary and parent in a multinational organization.

Multinational organizations find they have to adapt policies from one foreign area to another, if they are to bu successful. FF(E) presents the changes that have to be made in starting an operation in Great Britain. While that country is often considered to be quite similar to the U.S., there are enough differences to cause problems in implementing the strategy.

The case focuses on the organizational structure of the company. In so doing, however, it presents a well-rounded discussion of all functions in an organization. In this respect, it is designed to be an integrative case.

Position in Course

This case is designed to be presented at the latter part of the course. It discusses all functional areas within the organization. It also explores the external environment. The case, therefore, can be used in the integrative segment of the course. It is extremely well suited to explore problems of implementing strategies in the international sectors. Typically, this type of discussion is also presented at the latter part of the course.

To support these recommendations, it must be pointed out that the analysis and data gathering required are rather advanced. Even though financial data are scarce, the strategy developed has to consider the effect of FF(E) operations on the parent company. Other areas are equally complex.

Key Issues

1. Effect of subsidiary operations on the operations of a multinational organization.

2. Strategy formation and implementation in an international environment.

3. Environmental analysis in a foreign society.

4. Setting objectives for a multinational, subsidiary organization.

115

Analysis

FF(E) was incorporated in Britain in 1970. Mr. Ian Richards, the Managing Director, perceived his primary objective as providing 35% return on invested capital in the long run. The firm was to reach this objective through the manufacture and sale of specialized computers for industrial process controls. These systems had to be tailored to the specific needs of a customer. The product, although costing from $4000 to $500,000, essentially required a job shop manufacturing process.

FF(E) was a wholly owned subsidiary of the Fluid Flow Company based in the U.S. FLOCO produced the same kind of product for the domestic market. FLOCO, in turn, was a wholly owned subsidiary of a billion dollar conglomerate corporation, based in the U.S. FF(E) management reported to FLOCO top executives. They received their funds from their legal parent which was another subsidiary of the major enterprise that had been incorporated in Britain.

Top management had decided to organize FF(E) at a time when demand for its product far exceeded supply in Europe. By the time the organization had been set up, other, similar firms had either set up new operations or expanded present operations. This had led to an oversupply situation in Britain. FF(E) had enough orders to maintain production for another two months.

The organization included a ten man sales force. It had not been determined yet whether the sales force should go after many small orders or try to make a big splash with a few huge orders. FF(E) relied for product development on FLOCO, for which it made royalty payments. This gave FF(E) some cost advantages. Top management wasn't sure whether it should use this advantage to cut prices or to increase its own profit margins. Nationalistic tendencies, even within the Common Market, tended to complicate pricing decisions.

All operations had been set up in a new plant in Cragmoor, located in Southwestern England. The construction finally had to be supervised by FF(E) management. It had, subsequently, been completed on time under the budgeted cost, using local labor and materials where possible. The cost was half of a similar structure in the U.S. The plant had been designed so that it could be expanded rapidly.

The production process relied on a job shop process. It also required an extensive testing program to achieve reliability. Because of the value added, and specialization of the product, inventory was kept in materials rather than finished goods.

Due to the small size of the organization, at present, the top managers had to wear several hats. Mr. Richards had hand picked all of his subordinates and held them in

116

high regard. Plant personnel came from the local labor force. The pay scale was low, but the owrkers had to go through extensive training to be able to work with the advanced technology of FF(E) products.

Mr. Richards required that any significant expenditure (over about $20) be approved by him. He, in turn, had to account for funds to the British subsidiary of Major Enterprises, as well as at FLOCO, due to the complicated legal/ responsibility structure.

Questions

1. Comment on the organizational relationships between FF(E) and its parent operations.

2. What are the strategic decisions facing Mr. Richards?

Responses

1. The present system of reporting relationships faced by Mr. Richards is, to say the least, confusing. One of the biggest problems involved reporting of financial results.

FF(E) is supposed to be responsible to FLOCO for achieving its objectives. Mr. Richards was selected by FLOCO top managers for his present position. Mr. Richards seeks funds from its legal parent, which is not FLOCO, however. Since the parent, which is a direct subsidiary of Major Enterprises, has to account for its funds, one would expect that FF(E) has to report to it on use of funds. This dual control system assures that funds won't be spent frivolously. It also means, however, that Mr. Richards probably will be spending an inordinate amount of time justifying budget requests and strategies.

More important, the dual reporting system will reduce the flexibility that Mr. Richards feels is a key strength. If he has to justify his needs twice, he will invariably lose time. Also, he will have to compromise his strategies to gain acceptance by managers at both organizations to which he reports.

Basically, the organizational system demonstrated on the chart on page 551 violates a basic principle of management. Unity of command is not present. Regardless of present statements, Mr. Richards is going to find himself reporting to top management at both parent firms. At some point, for instance, the legal parent will want FF(E) legal, labor and accounting policies to be consistent with theirs since they are both operating in Britain. The legal parent will be held responsible for FF(E) actions by the British government. What FF(E) does will reflect on the legal parent as well as FLOCO. Conflicts are inevitable.

This potentially conflicting situation should be cleared up soon, if FF(E) is to attain its optimistic objectives.

2.   There are several strategic problems facing FF(E). One is clearly the organization reporting system discussed in the response to question 1 above.

Another problem concerns the pricing policies to be adopted by FF(E). Using its cost advantages, Mr. Richards could follow a low price strategy. Mr. Richards was afraid of the effect of this strategy on the reputation and image of the firm. He also felt that, at least initially, this would reduce the return on investment. Since this is the method by which he is evaluated, this latter point holds considerable weight.

A high margin strategy, while beneficial to the ROI of FF(E) could produce negative long term effects. The experience curve strategies, presented in the text, would not be optimized by high prices. This kind of pricing is not likely to help FF(E) gain the position as market leader unless their technology is clearly superior to its major competitors. A low price strategy could allow the firm to capture rapidly a large market share. This might bring cries of protests from the British government if it negatively affects British owned firms.

The pricing decision will clearly affect their marketing strategy. If they follow a low price decision, they should probably press for the many small orders available. They will need the large quantity of orders to achieve efficient operations consistent with the low price.

If, however, FF(E) follows the high price strategy, it should also go after the few large, prestige orders. These orders require high technological expertise. They are looking for dependability and quality. Pricing, while important, is probably of secondary importance to these other factors.

Whatever decisions are finally made by Mr. Richards, they must be made as an integrated whole. They also have to be consistent with the changing environment in Europe. England has joined the Common Market on a rather tenuous basis. Support for this move, as of 1970, is not total.

Also, nationalism is still strong in Europe. The economies of Europe are finally slowing down after an extremely long period of expansion. This may explain the continued nationalism. These factors have to be included in the strategic decisions.

Meppam Land Incorporated

Purpose

The Meppam Land case presents the attempts by a large, diversified U.S. based firm to deal with its multinational operations. It should be used to demonstrate the problems of designing an effective organization where operations cross national boundaries.

Meppam Land had found that its traditional organizational format of allowing each operating division to set up separate subsidiaries in each country had become extremely unwieldy. Meppam's operations overseas had grown to become a major part of the organization. The case shows two organizational formats that are developed to cope with problems of coordinating efforts of the different subsidiaries operating in close geographic proximity.

In addition to the question of what type of organizational design best fits Meppam's operations, there are several functional problems that could be explored. The case discusses the legal, political, taxing, pricing and labor policies Meppam has found it necessary to adopt. Students should be asked to note how these different policies interact to affect the overall operations of the organization.

Finally, the problems of operating in different cultural settings should be a primary focus of the case. Although the case takes place in Western Europe, cultural differences are significant enough to create problems in implementing strategic change. Changes that might be perfectly acceptable within the confines of one society may turn out to be offensive elsewhere.

Position in Course

The problems discussed in the Meppam Land case appear, at first, to deal simply with the development of an effective organizational format. The interaction between organizational policies and other areas of operations requires a fairly high degree of analytical skill. For this reason, the case should be presented in the latter half of the course.

Also, the problems of operating in the international sector increase the complexity of environmental analysis. Political, legal, economic, as well as cultural differences compound the difficulties in forming and implementing feasible and, especially, acceptable strategies. This also suggests that the Meppam case should be placed at a latter point in the course.

The Meppam case is also well suited for a section dealing specifically with multinational organizations. Once
again, however, this type of section is placed in the latter half of a course due to the complexity of the issues
involved.

Key Issues

1. Development of an organizational format consistent
    with effective, multinational operations.

2. Analysis of external environments in a multination-
    al setting.

3. Transition of a domestic organization with for-
    eign operations to a multinational organization.

Analysis

Meppam Land, Incorporated, is a multinational company
with sales of $1.6 billion in 1969. Although operations
are based in the U.S., foreign operations in 25 countries
accounted for almost 30% of gross revenues.

In 1966, Meppam Land had a corporate reorganization of
its international operations. The purpose was to partially
centralize planning and decision making at corporate headquarters. It also was designed to bring about a partial
consolidation of operations into product division, country
subsidiaries to reduce costs and create a more substantial
corporate image among customers.

Product Lines:
Meppam Land is a highly diversified manufacturing and
sales organization. It is organized into six operating
divisions: Improvement Land for fertilizers; Improvement
Foods and Soils for grain and seeds; Uniprod for office
equipment; Meppam for ball bearings and industrial equipment; Bollins for real estate; and Bel Twenty for toilet-
ries. Prior to 1966, each of the product divisions had
operated autonomously. They had little incentive to integrate planning or provide information to other divisions
which might be of value, such as currency exchange move-
ments.

The 1966 reogranization maintained the various product
lines. The organization was restructured along functional
lines at corporate headquarters, however.

The "Umbrella" Concept:
The new, interactional structure has been referred to
as an "umbrella company". This concept placed all product
groups operations within a country within a new company
to consolidate certain administrative, financial and reporting activities. Each of the product divisions would still

120

report to the relevant product manager at corporate headquarters. The umbrella company president reported to the
staff vice president for international operations.

The umbrella company officers were selected from the
officers of the product division operations within the
country. They were expected to fulfill the functions of
the umbrella company officer in addition to their duties as
officers of the product division companies in the country.

The umbrella officers had no direct authority over
operations of the product divisions. They were supposed to
coordinate policies for the product divisions within the
country and across functions. These would include cash
flow, personnel, legal and other functional policies common
to the various product divisions. The umbrella officers,
however, are only responsible for the budget of the umbrella company, not those of the operating divisions. A complete description of the role of the President and Secretary-
Treasurer of the umbrella company is presented in Exhibit 6
of the case.

International Organization:
An international vice-president had line authority
over the umbrella officers. He acted in a staff role for
the rest of the organization, however. His function was
to coordinate efforts of the product groups at the corporate level.

By 1970, 24 umbrella companies had been organized
throughout the world in the primary countries where Meppam
Land operated. 13 of 47 presidents and treasurers of the
umbrella companies came from the Bollins division although
Bollins only accounted for 12% of gross revenues.

By 1970, all product divisions except Improvement Land
and Bel Twenty had reorganized on a functional basis for
their international operations. These functional organizations then set up regional headquarters in various areas to
provide staff assistance and coordination for international
operations. The product divisions maintained five regional
offices for European operations.

Trade observers questioned the overlap of functions between the regional product divisions and the umbrella companies. Information flows were going in two directions.
One from the regional officers to division headquarters,
the other starting with the umbrella officers and going to
internal headquarters at corporate headquarters.

The umbrella officers did not receive extra compensation for their added responsibility. Initial policy, also,
had been to rotate umbrella presidents among the various
officers within the country frequently. These factors increased the complaints about the umbrella concept.

Problems:

The most frequently stated problem involved lack of definition of authority of the umbrella officers. They had no direct authority over the product company officers. The budgets had to be approved by a myriad of superiors and committees. Funds actually were supplied by the divisions within the country.

Several committees had been set up at the umbrella level to coordinate efforts in various areas. They, typically, included general management, treasurers, personnel, advertising, purchasing, and computer systems committees. Not all umbrella companies were equally successful or coordinated, however.

Another problem involved the morale of these officers not selected to serve as umbrella officers. Some countries had a surplus of qualified officers while others were devoid of them.

In April, 1970, Mr. Burton was promoted to Vice President, International. He replaced Mr. Balm who retired early, that year. Mr. Burton's position as Vice President Staff for Administration was left vacant. Essentially, Mr. Burton was expected to fill both functions. It was at this time that Mr. Burton, although he felt everything seemed to be going well, wondered if any parts of the Meppam organizational strategy should be evaluated.

Questions

1. Evaluate the umbrella concept in use at Meppam Land.

2. What changes would you suggest in the implementation of the concept?

Responses

1. The umbrella concept is a good, first attempt at coordinating policies of international subdivisions. Meppam found itself operating multiple divisions within the same company with little, if any, coordination between them. The idea and objectives are good. The implementation leaves quite a bit to be desired.

First, the umbrella companies were organized solely within one country. There are many areas where groups of countries with similar laws and customs allow for a natural grouping on regional lines instead of by countries.

The purpose of consolidating certain administrative functions is commendable. The terminology setting up the new structure is vague. The definition of authority and responsibility of the umbrella company officers is also

122

vague and incomplete. There is little relationship between teh responsibility placed on their status and persuasive powers to gain acceptance by other product division officers within their territory. Moreover, the system of remuneration and tenure of office does little to generate total commitment to their umbrella duties.

Several key areas were left out when determining which functions should be included in the umbrella company. This detracts from the potential synergies to be gained through this reorganization. See question 2 for these key areas.

Basically, little planning was put into the implementation of the umbrella concept. The long term interaction between divisions was not well thought out. The fact that the divisions were able to restructure their own international organizations without having to consider the effects on the umbrella concept is an example of poor coordination at corporate headquarters.

2.   There are several changes that could be recommended for implementing the umbrella concept.

First, the budgets for the umbrella companies should be established by the umbrella officers in consultation with the corporate, international officers. The costs should then be allocated among the divisions according to some rational system such as sales, personnel, or some other feature. This would eliminate some overlap in authority.

The management of the umbrellas should not have to split their time, or loyalties, with product divisions. They should report only to the corporate vice president, international. The corporate staff, moreover, should be increased to absorb this added load.

The responsibility and authority of the umbrella officers should be clarified and be consistent. They should not have operational control over the product divisions. They should have control over major capital allocations, however. The umbrella should have the authority for coordination of normal corporate financial reporting, tax and legal questions, as well. The umbrella officers should also be the arbiter for all transfer pricing decisions.

Above all, however, the relationship between the umbrella companies and the new, international structure of the divisions has to be rationalized. This will require top level decisions at corporate headquarters. This will probably require the restructuring of some of the umbrellas on regional lines. It may also require the international divisions to decrease the size of some of their regions, as well.

SAMPLE STUDENT REPORT

Assignment: Evaluate the "Umbrella" comcept
              used at Meppam. What changes
              would you recommend?

MEPPAM LAND INCORPORATED

ANALYSIS OF MEPPAM

In analyzing Meppam Land Incorporated, one must review the opportunities and threats in the external environment. The international market for Meppam products and services was on the rise as evidenced by the increase in international revenues as a percent of division revenues. In all countries, with the exception of Germany, certain tax advantages were available through the use of an umbrella approach; i.e., the losses of one firm could be used to offset the gains of another. There were also, however, certain areas threatening to Meppam. In certain countries, Meppam did not employ enough nationals, resulting in a feeling by the people of that country that the United States' control was too tight and denied them adequate representation. There was also the problem of possible confusion of the part of the consumer during the transition to the umbrella system. On the financial side, the trend seemed to indicate a decrease in the number of Neppam stockholders. This could have been partially caused by the disappointing increase in revenues (less than 30% over a five (5) year period).

Any discussion of Meppam's internal strengths and weaknesses must necessarily center around the umbrella program, which as many advantages and disadvantages. Meppam's concept of the function of an umbrella was good. The proglem arose in the implementation of Meppam's objectives. The umbrella serves to present a unified corporate image to customers, the citizenry, and the government.

The consolidation of administrative, financial, and reporting activities can substantially reduce costs. By coordinating the various firms, uniformity can be achieved in the establishment and administration of policies, such as personnel policies and practices. The mere size of an umbrella leads to the realization of cost savings; i.e., leasing of automobiles and more influence at leading institutions. The increased cooperation between firms of different divisions can lead to greater achievement of corporate objectives. The umbrella serves to increase the flow of information between existing firms and provides expertise relative to local customs and practices for new firms entering a country. The umbrella serves to mediate local problems between firms. The umbrella reduces the need for staff assistance from the parent division. Recognizing the feelings of nationalism, Meppam did an excellent staffing job in France by placing nationals in all six firms' general managers' positions. On the negative side, one of Meppam's greatest weaknesses in its umbrella approach was that of communications. It appears that everyone concerned assumed that communications were flowing smoothly-- except a few people with umbrella responsibilities. Corporate policy did not come down division lines--it was left up to the umbrella to handle. The divisional presidents often-times were not aware of what was going on with their sub-units. Instead of communicating up, down, and laterally, the umbrella resulted in parties communicating with successive people all the way "around the horn" instead of to each other.

The implementation of the umbrella system was not clearly communicated to all those effected resulting in unenthusiastic acceptance by local general managers and divisional presidents. There was very poor planning involved in the implementation of the umbrellas. This resulted in overlap of functions and the duplication was a cause of conflict; i.e., regional division offices and umbrellas had overlap in their staff functions. The assumption that umbrella responsibilities could be handled on a part-time basis was shown to be erroneous in that many people were spending too much time on umbrella functions to the detriment of their divisions. This fact also caused some split royalties. Along with this resulted dual reporting relationships, in many cases two direct lines instead of a direct line and a dotted line. The umbrella manager often had responsibility without authority. The international vice president had no control over compensation of umbrella people, who were getting no more pay for additional duties (this was a source of friction among many of them). The umbrella budget was determined by revenues of the various firms. Umbrella management, however, seemed to vest in Bollins personnel. This favoritism shown Bollins people is evidenced by the flagrant violation of corporate policy in having two Bollins people run an umbrella. The selection of umbrella management was far from perfect. Fortunately, the problems of rotation were recognized, however the problems with selecting only older workers were not as easily anticipated. The drop in morale of younger management people far outweighed the easy solution of selecting the over 55 group. Looking at Meppam as a whole, the trend seems to indicate that long term debt is increasing. The other area of concern is that 1970 was the first year since prior to 1961 that a preferred dividend was not declared.

OBJECTIVES

The following objectives are proposed for the next five years:

1. Eliminate all overlap in staff functions to reduce overhead and eliminate duplication and possible conflict.

2. Establish and administer uniform policies for each umbrella.

3. Reorganize umbrella personnel in proportion to the revenue contribution of the respective divisions' operations in a country.

4. Divorce all divisional responsibilities from umbrella personnel.

5. Establish a system to provide for upward, downward, and lateral communications.

IMPLEMENTATION OF STRATEGIES

1. All umbrella personnel presently in office will be given the choice of retaining their position in the umbrella or their position with their local company. No individual will have responsibilities in both areas. Whichever position is vacated can be filled by additional people. The cost of the additional people will be covered by reduction in staff personnel where

overlaps and duplication exist.

2. All personnel functions will be determined by the appropriate committee within the umbrella framework as opposed to a divisional framework. Personnel policies and practices are more common to a geographic area than to a line of business.

3. New umbrella people will come from those firms in proportion to the firms contribution to revenue. New divisional people where possible, will be nationals. They must, however, be the most qualified for the positions.

4. No person will report directly to more than one supervisor. Dotted line relationships are permitted. Compensation of personnel will be determined by the immediate supervisor within umbrella guidelines and corporate policies.

5. A communications procedure will be established whereby upward, downward, lateral, and line-staff communications will be available.

6. Umbrella personnel will be administrative coordinators and advisors. The divisions will be the profit centers.

7. Twenty (20) percent of all cost savings from elimination of staff overlap will be allocated to reduce long term debt.

8. Through the reduction of long term debt and future cost savings, the preferred dividend will be restored.

Once the organizational problems of the umbrella - divisional relationships are eliminated, Meppam will be a more efficiently run organization.

The Marco-Lumber Company

Purpose

In the less developed countries, the success of the multinational corporation is both a source of its strength and weakness. It has proven itself to be a most efficient mechanism for deploying financial resources, technological know-how, managerial expertise, and the latest scientific organizational techniques to maximize production and profit. In the process, it has tended to disturb old cultural patterns and antiquated economic practices while bringing many benefits in the way of new industries, social infrastructure, more employment, a more skilled labor force, as well as increased taxes, revenues and exports to the host country. The adjustment process occasioned by these changes has led to frictions with indigenous economic interests and with host governments. Nationalistic tendencies have often led to an anti-foreign bias. To advocacy of quasi-socialistic development plans and to espousal of nationally-owned public sector enterprises or joint ventures where the foreigner holds a minority interest. These conflicting crosscurrents have come at a time when the possibility for developing an integrated world economy based on a more rational allocation of world resources, which the multinational corporation is uniquely equiped to bring about, run counter to the inward looking, essentially nationalistic and statist biases of many less-developed countries.

In fact, the future role of multinational corporations in assisting the development of the less-developed world hinges on the possibility of working out a "modus vivendi" between the companies and the national governments which preserves enough autonomy and profitability, for both parties. The International Company has had many problems, has played and continues to play an important part in their economic development despite these problems, if a favorable investment climate can be fostered. It is to this area that this case study is addressed.

The objectives of this case are to: 1) study and analyze a multinational firm and the typical problems it faces; 2) to create a basis for discussion of startup problems of an international operation; and 3) to identify how the firm's strategies and policies are influenced by the various constraints of the company's domestic and international environments.

Position in Course

The problems faced by management in the Marco-Lumber case are reasonably well focused. It is possible to present this case at the middle segment of the course, or even slightly earlier.

Besides the uses of this case in a segment dealing with multinational business, the case could be used in several other segments, given the problems encountered in the implementation of strategies. What sounded like a great idea at the formation stage turned into a nightmare when it came to the implementation stage. The practical problems of implementation, both forecasted and unforseen, can be demonstrated through this case. The case can also be used in the segment of the course dealing with the interaction between organizational strategy and the cultural sector of the environment.

Finally, the case can be presented in a section dealing with the reformulation of organizational strategies and policies. At the end of the case, changes clearly have to be made at Marco-Lumber. The managers are faced with several alternatives. Students can be asked to evaluate and choose between these alternatives.

Key Issues

1. The effect of cultural differences on the implementation of strategies.

2. Control of an international operation that is physically separated from corporate headquarters.

3. Formation of organizatonal strategies for a new, multinational operation.

Analysis

The Marco-Lumber Company was formed in September, 1968, to develop the forestry resources of Marcoland. The firm was owned by a group of American investors. Although all the operations occurred in Marcoland, corporate headquarters were located in the U.S.

Marcoland was a former British colony located in Africa. It was attempting to develop home based industries. It had started to develop a lumber industry several years earlier with the aid of another country. Problems had occurred and the project was abandoned. All the machanery was still intact, and in working condition, however.

The top executives at Marco hired a Canadian forestry expert as the resident manager for the new operation. All his experience had been in the Canadian lumber industry.

Various directors of the organization, meanwhile, had gained tentative commitments for the output of the operation. These agreements had been made with a large plywood firm in the U.S. for veneer and a Japanese shipbuilding company. Both agreements were contingent upon receiving acceptable samples of the firm's products. If the agreements were formalized, the success of the venture was virtually assured.

The major part of the case describes communications between Mr. Wilkins, the resident manager, and the board of directors. Mr. Wilkins describes the problems he has encountered trying to set up operations in a different cultural and economic climate.

Among these problems included dissention between workers from different tribes. Mr. Wilkins initially assigns workers to live in the same dormitory regardless of their tribal origins. Other problems are due to a lack of understanding of local conditions; workers, once trained, leave to work in higher paying jobs; monsoon rains wipe out virtually all construction efforts; differences between Wilkins' Canadian English and local English dialects; lack of modern equipment and amenities; and health problems at the isolated site. All of these problems caused him to miss the deadlines for shipments to both potential customers.

The directors ordered immediate shipment of all products. They found that when material was shipped, it was not up to specifications. It was felt that some problems were due to a misunderstanding between centimeters and inches. Mr. Wilkins complained, however, that he only sent samples. They were not supposed to be examples of finished products. One of the directors claimed that the lateness of the delivery, and the poor quality of the product, had caused him to lose considerable face with these customers.

At this point, almost $400,000 had been expended with no promise of early revenues. At a board meeting, questions of the future of the operations were considered. Mr. Wilkins management strengths were attacked. He was defended by the President on the basis of the difficulties of starting operations in a foreign environment.

The U.S. customer, after sending a research team to Marcoland, offered a proposition that changed the entire complexion of the situation, however. They found a strain of lumber required for their operations.

Based on these findings, the U.S. firm proposed a joint venture. They would put up the equivalent of the present investment by Marco-Lumber (about $650,000). They would provide physical assets and management expertise. Marco-Lumber had to consider which of their options to take, at this point in time.

Questions

1. Evaluate the environment facing Marco-Lumber.

2.   What is the root of the decision making problems at
     Marco-Lumber?

3.   Evaluate the alternatives available to Marco-Lumber.

Responses

1.   The opportunities of threats in the environment are
many. If Marco falls short of expectations of the host
government, thier temporary agreement could be revoked or
not renewed, thereby losing all expenditures to date, about
$400,000. This represents about 40% of the total capital
of the company. The host government can then give the permit to another company.

     Since they are in extractive industry (i.e. process-
ing lumber, slicing or logging lumber and veneer) the user
can take over the operations if they are not doing a good
job. The government's aim is to develop its agricultural
and forestry resources and has no time to waste with a
firm that is not progressive.

     The company is faced with the following problems:
     1.   Labor disputes
     2.   Cultural - a) custom and tradition
                      b) living pattern
                      c) political ideology
                      d) economic orientation
     3.   Language (linguistic problem)
     4.   Technological skills
     5.   Bureaucratic red tape
     6.   Management skills.

     While they face these problems, there are also oppor-
tunities available to them:
     1.   Cheap labor
     2.   Untapped forest resources
     3.   Contribution to social and economic development.
     4.   Profit potentials
     5.   Opportunities for expansion and mergers with U.S.
          Panel.

2.   Decisions have been made on a sporadic basis primarily
responding to the environment. These decisions emerged
over a period of time.

     The company has need for greater competence in lumber
business, which they lack. They apparently have competence
in coffee blending but not wood products. They have no
competence in international business. They have not been
producing any wood since the agreement was signed in 1969.
It was unwise for them to go into a business in which they
had little direct knowledge. The company does not possess
the proper management skills. They employed a technician
(forester), not a manager, and charged him with too many
responsibilities.

The company finally determined that going it alone would no longer be profitable or wise because of the many complex problems that the company is faced with. The company is in an adaptive environment. To survive, it has to respond to the environment in which it is operating.

3.   Under their limitations the following options or alternatives are open to the company:
1.   Go into partnership
2.   Sell the company
3.   Pack up and leave
4.   Continue with the present strategy.

In looking at alternative four, this would not be a wise decision. Presently, they are losing money. They have no prospects of making any money soon. Problems seem to be compounding every day with no solutions in sight. This is not a feasible solution.

To choose alternative three is to lose everything they have invested to date. (This is about 40% of their capital). This would be optimal if there were no potential for growth. But the potential for growth is still there, untapped. To pack and leave is to create an opportunity for another person or organization.

To sell the company is as bad as leaving. The potential for growth and profit are still there. They have the forester who has the technical expertise, but lacks management skills. If the buyers developed the skills that were lacking, they would surely tap the fruit of the labor of Marco-Lumber Company.

Alternative 1 is left to be considered. Using all the limitations that the company is having and the opportunities available to it, this option would be recommended. They should go into pertnership with another company that has the strength to offset their weaknesses.

U.S. Panel has successfully operated in the Congo. Marco-Lumber has the veneer products which U.S. Panel has been searching for for years. This will give Marco-Lumber a bargaining power to equalize the advanced technology and management skill that the U.S. Panel company possesses.

ORGANIZATIONAL EXPANSION

This section presents an extensive review of the strategies and policies followed by Franklin National Bank over its organizational history. Much of the information has been gathered from published sources. It is designed to demonstrate the problems peculiar to an organization whose objective is rapid and constant growth.

Barriers to growth, as described in the text, include both internal and external constraints. The key factor, for the organization, is matching its internal resources with external opportunities in an effective manner.

The lengthy, and complete, Franklin National series lends itself to analysis and presentation by student groups. The situation has been well documented so that information gathering should not be a problem. The real problem will be in getting the students to provide feasible and acceptable solutions to the organization's future instead of providing an in-depth autopsy of events that occurred after the time of the case and led to the demise of the organization.

Franklin National Corporation

Purpose

This case series is designed to trace through the expansion and development of a major, profit-oriented organization. The company involved has, as its primary asset, the Franklin National Bank of New York.

The case is derived primarily from published sources including annual reports of the parent and the subsidiary. Statements made in interviews with top managers give additional insight into the values of the key people involved with developing strategies and policies for this influential organization, however.

The case series should present the students with the ability to trace the changes in strategy for this organization. The organization started from a small base with a limited degree of competition. The changes required in adapting to an environment of increased competition should be a primary focus of any discussion of the case series.

Similarly, the transition from an entrepreneurial, highly centralized organization, as described in Chapters 6 and 8 of the text should be emphasized. The firm has expanded its role from the traditional small town country bank to one of an international, truly full service financial institution. This has required a change to a decentralized, professional style of management. The problems developed as a result of these changes should be another focus of the case series.

The series is designed to be used either as a unit or on as individual units. The units, moreover, can be combined in various ways to fulfill different objectives for a policy oriented course. The organizational implications of the case are classic. Reference can be made to Chandler's "Strategy and Structure" analysis presented in the text. The organization has evolved from a functionally structured, centralized position to a relatively decentralized, product (service) oriented, profit center approach. At the end of the series this transition is still in progress. Questions could be asked concerning the willingness of top management to continue this trend.

The case series also presents the opportunity to trace and evaluate the changes in specific policies of the organization over time. The firm has been characterized as aggressive. This aggressiveness can be traced through its various policies such as loans, branch placement, organization structure, personnel, merger and acquisitions, etc.

The Franklin (A-1) case is primarily designed to show how an entrepreneurial type, Arthur Roth, devised a strategy to bring a small bank to the brink of greatness. There is a large amount of quantitative data to be analyzed in this case. This should present the basis for comparison with other rapid growth situations. It also should be used as the basis for developing alternative strategies for a firm being faced with severe competition in a regulated industry.

The (A-2) case shows how one organization reacts to the acquisition of another organization of significant size. Both banks were developed by entrepreneurs. Both needed each other, for different reasons. Students should be presented with the task of showing what problems ensued from the merger and how they might have been overcome. In this age of offensive and defensive mergers, this should be a valuable exercies.

The (A-3) case presents an ideal situation for analyzing the personal thoughts and values of a top manager. Mr. Gleason, the hand-picked successor of Mr. Roth, gives his views on the direction and objectives of Franklin National Bank as of 1973. The students should, at this point, be asked to note how the values of the top manager can affect the strategy of an organization.

The future problems of the organization should not be dwelled on at this stage of the analysis. Everyone knows what finally happened to Franklin National. Much of the future results were due to a lack of analysis of the total environment. If students feel it necessary to bring up the forced dissolution and sale of the Franklin National Bank in 1974, they should be asked to devise a strategy to overcome this problem.

The (B) series in the Franklin provides the opportunity to analyze specific function and policies within the organization as of 1973. The (A) series provides an overall view of the total organization.

The (B-1) case looks at bank loan policy through the managers and structures of various operating divisions. The Domestic, National, and International Groups should be analyzed to determine how they interact and affect the bottom line operations.

The (B-2) case looks at non-lending, financial groups. Comparisons should be made with other international banks. Interesting comparisons could well be made with banks such as Morgan Guarantee (the largest trust operations) and the First National City Bank which had recently passed Chase Manhatten in size of deposits. These areas are closely watched by industry observers as a means of evaluating the aggressiveness of a banking operation.

The (B-3) case is designed to show how the Franklin National Bank has followed the industry in expanding out of traditional banking services. Much has been made of this expansion in recent years. Analysis of the effects of this kind of diversification is a primary purpose of this

135

section. Once again, this is a place where discussion may stray to the failure of Franklin National. Diversification isn't necessarily the evil, however. The methods with which this diversification is carried out should be the key issue in this section of the case.

The remainder of the material presented in the case series should be viewed in the form of an extensive note. Banking regulations, demographics, competitive analysis and other pertinent data are presented in this extensive note. This is a situation where the student will find it difficult to state that initial information is impossible to secure. The purpose of this data is to allow the student to test his analytical skills. Students should be required to compare this information with present and future (projected) results of Franklin National.

Position in Course

The Franklin National Series is designed primarily to be used at the latter stages of the policy course. If used at this stage of the course, it should be used as a total package. Even if each of the individual case segments is not discussed in class, they all provide informational value to the students for analysis.

For the students to be able to do a credible job of analyzing and solving, they will need the cumulative experience of the whole course. The problems presented in the Franklin National series are truly integrative and complex in nature.

Internally, the firm is faced with all the functional problems presented in a standard business program. The firm has also to provide solutions to various behavioral and organizational questions as well.

Externally, the students have to be able to analyze a full panoply of issues to provide for continued growth. Not only are the usual problems of competition, customers, and the economy facing the firm, but top management has to continually react to potential and actual regulatory changes.

The combination of internal and external problems facing the students requires a relatively sophisticated analysis by the students. To provide this type of advanced analysis, the series can be assigned as a group assignment at the end of the course. In this manner, the groups can benefit from the expertise of students with different academic majors and backgrounds.

Individual cases in the series can also be used to highlight specific types of strategic problems. The following comments demonstrate how the six cases can be used individually or in smaller groups.

The (A-1) case can be used at the early stages of a
course to demonstrate the growth of an entrepreneurially
oriented organization. This case provides a good summary
of the growth, particularly at the crucial middle stage, of
Franklin National Bank. The students can explore the manner in which a dynamic and dominant top manager interacts
with his environment to maintain growth.

The (A-1) case also presents the students with an
opportunity to trace the development of an organizational
strategy over time. Of particular interest would be the
later part of the (A-1) case where the managers at
Franklin have presented tentative merger criteria. Students
can also be required to evaluate the present strategy and
make recommendations for the future.

The (A-2) case traces the difficulty of continuing
growth in a large organization. The strategy for growth is
simpler to implement in the smaller organization presented
in the (A-1) case. Due to the added difficulty of evaluating and creating a growth strategy for a relatively
large organization, this case should probably be presented
at the middle portion of the course, or later.

The (A-3) case presents the views of the top manager
of the organization. This provides an excellent opportunity to explore the impact of top management values on
structure and strategy. Mr. Gleason's comments and values
should be compared by the students for consistency and feasibility. This type of analysis should be presented relatively early in the course.

The B cases are designed to be used as a unit, or as
backup information for the series as a whole or the (A)
series individually. The (B) cases provide an in-depth
analysis of the organization structure and internal policies of Franklin National. On their own, the (B) cases
should be presented at the early or middle stages of the
course. The students can evaluate the internal policies
relevant to external constraints and opportunities.

Students should also be required to analyze the priorities associated with the various financial and non-financial divisions mentioned in the series. Moreover, the
effect of the divisions on each other and the organization
as a whole can be studied.

Key Issues

Franklin National (A-1)

1.   Growth of an entrepreneurial organization.

2.   Innovative development in a conservative industry.

3. Effect of a dominant manager on organizational strategy and policy.

4. Development of merger and acquisition criteria.

5. Problems of entrance into a highly competitive market dominated by much larger firms.

Franklin National (A-2)

1. Problems of assimilation of a large acquisition.

2. Transfer of power from a dominant leader.

3. Decentralization of a formerly centralized organization.

4. Social responsibility of a regulated onganization.

Franklin National (A-3)

1. Impact of top management values on organizational strategy and policy.

2. Consistency of strategy and environment.

Franklin National (B-1)

1. Control of financial policies and actions in a banking institution.

2. Interaction of widely dispersed, geographic markets with organizational strategy.

3. Effect of diversified operations on organizational strategy and structure.

Franklin National (B-2)

1. Effects of non-lending financial policies on total strategy of a bank holding company.

2. Marketing strategies of a financial institution.

3. Public relations in an organization competing in a regulated industry.

Franklin National (B-3)

1. Effects of service group operations on organizational strategy.

2.   Control of operations of a diversified and decen-
      tralized organization.

Analysis

Franklin National (Introduction)

In a 1971 national survey of the 22 largest commercial
banks and holding companies, Franklin showed the best
record: As of the end of the third quarter of 1971:

Franklin   Industry (22 companies)
                                          Median

Five year return on equity:
    15.5% [1]   11.5%

Five year growth in annual per share earnings:
    15.1% [2]   10.0%

Five year return on total capital:
    11.7% [3]   10.4%

Five year growth in annual sales:
    16.0% [4]   14.2%

Latest 12-month Period Covered Profitability:
Return on Equity:
    13.7% [4]   12.6%
Return on Total Capital:
    11.6% [5]   11.4%

Detailed bank rankings by performance are found in
Franklin New York Corporation (C).

In spite of Franklin's record, it is not rated as one
of the prestigious banks. It is viewed by some as a "Maverick". Outside of the New York metropolitan area and
Long Island, its name was not publicly known.

By the late 1960's and early 1970; Franklin was admitted to the New York Clearing House Association -- the
banking elite, and was no longer considered "the country
bank" by the industry.

This case gives the company's history, detailing
1961-1970, and is meant as a basis for readers to formulate Franklin's objectives, strategies and tactics for the
1970's.

---

1. Highest   2. Second highest   3. Third highest
4. sixth highest   5. Ninth highest

Franklin National Bank (A-1)

Analysis

History: Franklin National Bank opened on Nov. 1, 1926
-- a storefront facility at Franklin Square, in a semi-rural
community. Deposits for the year were approximately
$100,000. In 1940, deposits were $3.4 million and ranked
1,231st. Ten years later it ranked 35th, with $71.0 mil-
lion is deposits. By 1967, depositys had reached $2.2 bil-
lion and 18th in rank.

In 1970 the bank had 91 branches: 64 on Long Island,
and 27 in New York City.

Mr. Arthur T. Roth who dominated the bank first joined
as cashier in 1934, became president in 1946, and chairman
in 1959. His leadership was committed to growth and profitability. He was highly innovative, very dedicated to the
bank, and had almost no interests outside the bank.

In a booming local economy, the bank expanded rapidly
through 1964. In 1960, the omnibus banking act knocked
out the branching limits of the 1934 act and allowed branch
banking across state banking districts.

As a result, in 1964 Franklin opened three New York
City branches. In 1967 it merged with Federation Bank of
New York City ($281 million in deposits). These started as
defensive moves against the branching of the big New York
City banks.

Rapid growth in the 1960's centered on internal expansion which failed to build a solid base for expansion
through the holding company. The Company chose a one-bank
holding company in 1969 but did not in fact significantly
diversify.

Financial Statements: Introduction: Exhibits 1a -
4b in the case show the consolidated statements of conditions and earnings, per share earnings, yields and ratios,
1961-1967. Loans and deposits are given for 1965-1967.

Consolidated Statement of Condition

	1961	1967
Loans	$530.8 million	$1.25 billion
(% of resources)	(58.7%)	(96.7%)
Federal Funds sold & Purchased to resell	$14.5 million*	$71.8 million
(% of resources)	(0.8%)	(2.7%)
Deposits	$821.9 million	$2.18 billion
(% of liabilities)	(90.8%)	(82.7%)
Demand Deposits	$419.4 million**	$850 million
Time Deposits	$624.5 million	$1.32 billion

*1965 figure   **1962 figure

140

Despite growth (57.5%) in 1962 of time deposits, volatile demand deposit growth for the period exceeded the national rate. Federal funds purchased later in the decade became an important source of funds.

Consolidated Statement of Earnings

	1961	1967
Total Operating Income	$40.4 mil.	$120.7 mil.
	66.5%	65.5%
Interest & Dividents on Investment	15.4%	13.4%
Other Operating Income	14.1%	7.3%
Net Income Applicable to Common Stock	$ 9.0 mil.	$ 9.5 mil.
Net Income as % of Operating Income	22.3%	7.9%

Lowering profits are due to higher expenditures for federal funds, borrowed money and exceptionally high loan charge-off -- in the mid-60's. Improvements in 1966-1967 are due to normalization of the loan charge-offs while staff expenses steadily rose in 1966-1967.

Yields and Ratios: Return on average common equity persistently decreased from a 1961 high of 17.10% to a low of 7.37% in 1966, while return on year end common equity slipped from $16.28% to 6.14% in 1966.

Return on average assets: 1961=1.66%; 1966=0.28%.

Return on year-end assets: 1961=0.99%; 1966=0.25%.

Factors and Decisions for Growth, 1926-1967: Introduction: Franklin's phenomenal growth can be attributed to innovation, mergers, aggressive lending, publicity, high morale and a booming Long Island economy.

Innovativeness: This was generally targeted to the retail banking market. E.G., i)active participation in FHA mortgage program, ii) improved banking convenience such as being first to provide customer parking space, iii) first to open drive-in windows, iv) open late on pay days, v) cash checks of any known business, vi) offer minimum-balance checking accounts, vii) consumer certificates of deposit, viii) offered modern bank credit card system.

Mergers: Expansion through opening branch offices for new business and forestalling falling profits were substantial in the 1950's. However, a good part of its growth and geographical extension came through mergers, acquisitions, and assimilation, as described in the case.

Loan Policy: The aggressiveness of this policy is due to Mr. Roth's desire to quickly increase the size of the loan portfolio. Most of the loans fell in the high risk, rapid growth areas: "entrepreneurs, early conglomerates, and real estate developers."

141

Since 1945, loans outstanding roughly doubled every five years. The result of this policy was an abnormally high loan-charge-off rate (one major factor being deteriorating real estate market--restrictive zoning laws, low rents, sharp decline in values).

To reduce the high charge-offs, real estate lending was centralized, loan officers became more specialized, and a special department was set up to collect as much of the charge-offs as possible.

Publicity and Community Relations: One reason for Franklin's growth is its president's belief that a bank should be socially responsible. This is the bank's perceived role.

The bank also embarked on pure publicity programs (see Franklin B): i) World War II display of durable goods to encourage savings, ii) Fanfare opening of new branches, iii) Flower bouquet invitation to new homeowners to save with them, and iv) Giving lollypops to children ("lollypop bank" image).

Entrance into New York City, 1961-1967: On May 8, 1964, three branches were set up in New York City. This is the beginning of the implementation of geographical extension and deliberate, ambitious design to compete with the sophisticated City banks, for both retail market and commercial banking in local, national, and international markets.

This move was the result of a definite concensus of bank officers, as well as the passage of the omnibus bank act (even though Franklin had opposed the bill all along). Also important is the fact that Franklin had outgrown its Long Island market.

Objectives: Franklin entered New York City with these goals: set up 25 offices by 1970, deposits to reach $2 bil. by 1970, become the 18th largest bank by 1970, and a 20% earning on capital stock, surplus and retained earnings.

Actions: To meet competition, Franklin offered a full range of banking facilities while shunning areas it had no chance of gaining a significant share of the business.

In seeking the loan business, Franklin used the following methods: i)unsolicited visits to potential clients, ii)contacting firms here (NY) who had dealt with them on Long Island, iii)seeking the not-too-attractive companies, those in turnaround situations, iv)utilizing Franklin's "newness" to get business, v)seeking the dissatisfied customers of other banks.

Before New York City operations were started, about 5% of the deposits came from outside Long Island. Three years

after the entrance into the New York City market, 33 1/3%
came from outside of Long Island. This rose to over 50%
after the Federation Bank and Trust merger.

Management and Structure, 1964-1967: Just before the
New York extension, Franklin was reorganized into four
geographically-based semi-autonomous divisions, each with
a president and a division board of directors.

Each division was responsible "for all administration,
growth and other activities." These were:
1. Metropolitan Division: was responsible"For loans and
other banking services, including branch operations, for
both businesses and individuals in New York City."
2. National-International Division: this division took
charge of large corporate accounts, administration and development of correspondent banking network, while the international gave banking services and correspondents to
customers in international markets.
3. Nassau Division: at Franklin Square, was mainly for
branch banking in Nassau county. This was largest of the
four divisions (had 36 out of a total 52 branches).
4. Suffolk Division: had 16 offices and committed to rapid
growth through branch expansion, especially into potential
industrial areas.

Operations that remained centralized were: investment
portfolio management, corporate trust, operations and control, as well as business development.

In anticipation of its expansion, Franklin revised the
divisional structure in 1966 by forming a Long Island
Division out of the Nassau and Suffolk divisions.

Federation Bank and Trust Company Merger, 1961-1967:
Early Approaches, 1961-1964. Federation Bank and Trust
Company, based in New York City with $221 million in assets
and $200 million in deposits, was approached by Franklin in
the spring of 1961 about a possible merger.

The merger did not materialize at this time because of
price and the fact that neither of the two presidents would
take a second position at a merged bank. Franklin tried
again in 1964 in order to get Federation's 13 New York
branches. Again it flopped because of the personality conflict of the officers and because no cash was offered.

Agreement in Principle and Merger, 1966-1967: In
November, 1966, with a new president, Federation reached
agreement with Franklin to merge to "realize added balance and depth in manpower, management and locations which
will give added support to (Franklin's) New York City operations".

The agreement was for an exchange of stock on a share-
for-share basis. 801,000 Federation shares were outstanding. The merger announcement caused Federation's over-the-

counter price to rise from $28 to $33 per share of stock.
Franklin's stock price did not change.

Assimilation, 1967: Franklin assimilates its acquisitions. In 1967 Federation had 13 branches and because of
highly specialized officers was dominant in specialized
businesses, eg. taxicab operations, furs, women.'s dresses,
and construction.

Questions

1.   Why has Franklin National Bank been accorded big bank
     status despite its performance?

2.   Evaluate the maverick image of Franklin National.

3.   What do you consider are the major factors in Franklin
     National Bank's growth to date?

4.   Evaluate Franklin National's growth strategy.

Responses

1.   Although Franklin's growth has been nothing short of
phenomenal since Arthur Roth took over direction of the
bank, there are several disturbing elements. First, the
banking industry is extremely conservative. The maverick
image generated by Franklin National is counter to this
conservatism. Regulatory agencies still have a depression
psychosis. Aggressive policies are frowned on in this
light.

All of the statistics are not bright, however. Franklin is having to absorb relatively high loan charge-offs.
This means that some of the high risk loans it is giving
are rather shakey. Also, its recent twelve-month performance is now coming down to the median industry performance.

Performance and growth above the industry average, by
itself, would not be bad however. The problem is that
Franklin is having to compete in the areas traditionally
the strongholds of the older, major New York City banks.
These banks are also moving onto Long Island where Franklin
has been generating high case flow to finance its expansion. In terms of the matrix developed by the Boston Consulting Group discussed in the text, Franklin's stronghold
in quadrant III is being threatened. This is occurring at
the same time that it is trying to break into high growth
banking areas that are already dominated by the large competitors.

2.   Franklin feels that the only way it can successfully
compete in the intense New York City market is to present
the image of an innovative, aggressive, service-oriented
 organization. Unfortunately, these are deemed to be

maverick tendencies in the banking industry. It should be noted that some of the most successful of the regional banks also have that image.

The traits that have made the organization a maverick have worked reasonably well in a boom economy. What worries the analysts, and regulators, is what might happen in a poor economy. This is where the historical fears of the depression still weigh against banks like Franklin.

3.   Franklin National has been fortunate in many respects. During its formative years, it was protected from competition from the major New York City banks. State law prohibited the Manhatten banks from crossing to Long Island and vice versa. This allowed Franklin to pursue its aggressive policies in competition with very conservative rural banks.

It must be stated, however, that management at Franklin set as its policy, service to the customer. It attempted to offer a full line of services to potential clients. It actively sought out new clients instead of waiting for them to come to the bank.

Franklin was also fortunate in that it was located in a high growth area. Population and income were both growing very fast. People had to keep their money somewhere and Franklin National was out to see that it got more than its share.

Franklin also learned from the industries that an effective method of growth is acquisition and merger. This provides ready made growth in assets, deposits, and income.

Finally, during the period of Franklin's most dynamic growth, the 1960's, the economy was in a prolonged period of growth. It was difficult for an aggressive bank not to grow during this period.

4.   Franklin's strategy for growth is extremely aggressive as outlined in the previous responses. The objectives of growth in deposits, assets and earnings are high in the face of a faltering economy facing high inflation.

The actions being taken by Franklin management are risky, especially for the banking industry. If they succeed, Franklin could move into the really big time. The strategy requires sufficient management talent and controls to oversee this type of strategy.

If the strategy fails, it could seriously affect the firm's ability to survive. Moreover, given the size of Franklin, failure of the bank could also have serious implications for the entire economy.

Basically, Franklin management has to pay attention to internal and external details affecting the strategy. Timing and the economy will be crucial. The loans and services pursued by Franklin have potentially high returns. The risks associated with these returns are equally high. Control has to be the keywork here. This means that Franklin should probably go a little slower with adding branches or making mergers. This should be a time for the organization to regroup and consolidate its considerable gains.

Analysis

Technically, the merger with Federation Bank and Trust
was a success. Total assimilation, however, was prevented
by conflict of personalities and operating philosophies.
(For divisional level problems, see Franklin B cases).
Mr. DeSantis of Federation soon quit.

The Franklin New York Corporation, 1965-1970: Franklin
recognized bank expansion potential through a holding com-
panypany format. It was as yet unsuccessful in exploiting
this device. These attempts informally began in 1960. On
June 7, 1965 Franklin announced the establishment of a
statewide holding company projected to have $3 billion
in assets by 1970.

The company would be formed with a maximum of three
small upstate banks. This would stand better chances of
regulatory approval.

By 1966 no company had been formed and the Federation
merger pushed plans further back.

In January 1968 a formal plan for a multi-bank holding
company was announced. It was to be called Franklin New
York Corporation. The major importance of this to Franklin
was to assure its continuous expansion.

This plan failed. It did not get federal approval due
to unresolved "legal problems". Franklin said it was because of the interim bank device they tried to use.

In June 1969 Franklin put out plans for a one-bank
holding company with the former proposed name. This would
help serve "broad and changing" customer needs as well as
diversified financial services. Franklin still showed
interest in a multi-bank holding company.

Even though Franklin was the largest non-New York City
bank, its bargaining power was low due to low share price,
and low price/earnings ratio (the latter averaging 10.6,
9.6, 7.1 in 1968 through 1970).

Expected areas of diversification were financing, fac-
toring, EDP and Insurance.

In 1970 the 1956 Bank Holding Company Act was amended.
This brought all bank holding companies under the Federal
Reserve and restricted activities to those very closely
related to banking.

In 1971 Franklin indicated that talks were in progress
on the formation of the multi-bank holding company.

Managerial Changes, 1967: During the summer of 1967,
Mr. Roth, 62, Chairman and chief executive, handpicked
48 year old Mr. Gleason, Divisional President of Long
Island, to become President of Franklin National. Mr.
Gleason was to take over in December 1967, at Mr. P. E.
Prosswimmer's mandatory retirement. Many disgruntled
officers quit for being passed over.

Managerial Changes, 1968: In July 1968, Mr. Roth continued as chairman of the board while Mr. Gleason added
the chief executive position to the presidency. Several
directors' dissatisfaction occasioned this quick move on
Roth's part.

Reorganization, 1969: In 1969, as a result of an independent consulting firm's recommendation, the 4 division
structure was replaced by a functional group structure.

The new organization called for weekly top management
meetings "to review policies and long-range plans." This
was to facilitate a "greater degree of diffusion of responsibility and development " of better financial potential
and specialized services to more customers.

Attitudes and personnel: The bank's fantastic Long
Island boom, New York City entrance, successes of its programs, and continued growth were Franklin's golden era and
resulted in employee cohesiveness, esprit de corps, and a
sense of destiny.

Many officers realized in the late 1960's that some of
this closeness was gone due to mergers, too rapid expansion, high specialization, and people growing into positions
they had not been prepared for. New York entry made them
think as managers.

Managerial Changes in 1970: In early March 1970, Mr.
Roth, now 65, decided not to seek reelection. In October,
Mr. Gleason was elected chairman of the board while keeping
the chief executive position. Mr. James G. Smith was
elected Bank President.

At the 1970 annual meeting Mr. Lawrence A. Tisch,
chariman and chief executive of Loew's Theatres, Inc. (which
owned 15% of Franklin stock as an investment!) was elected
as director of both Franklin New York Corporation and the
Franklin National Bank.

An interview with Gleason elicited "Communication,
coordination and motivation" as the chief executive's
major responsibilities. Concerning social responsibilities
he stated that as the size of the bank increases, its social responsibilities get closer to that of a government.
On the changing structure of banking, he saw an approaching "banking revolution" requiring more innovativeness to
cope with it.

On the bank's growth, the chief executive viewed
Franklin's expansion as "conservative" and profitability
was expected to rise.

Questions

1.   Evaluate Franklin's merger policy in relation to the
     Federation merger.

2.   Comment on the efforts to set up a bank holding com-
     pany at Franklin.

3.   Evaluate Mr. Gleason's comments concerning the future
     of bank operations and competition.

Responses

1.   Franklin National had one basic objective in following
its merger and aquisition strategy. That objective was
growth in assets and deposits. It hoped to move into geographic regions with higher growth potential through this
means.

     The management at Franklin felt that it was far easier,
faster and less expensive, in the long run, to aquire existing branches than to start their own. Existing management problems at the aquired organization could be overcome. Also, the synergy of the merged operations would be
beneficial to everyone. This synergism was felt to be
strong enough to overcome any potential problems.

     With Federation, the problems inherent in this growth
policy via merger came to the fore. Although the merger
provided Franklin with an immediate entree to Manhatten, it
did so at a cost.

     Overhead costs shot up considerably. More important,
however, the close comaraderie of the earlier years at
Franklin was disrupted. There was a definite clash of personalities between the two organizations. Both top managers were highly independent and entrepreneurial in style.
This specific clash led to the resignation of Mr. DeSantis,
former president of Federation Bank and Trust.

     The breakdown in the esprit de corps of the officers
at Franklin conditioned by the Federation merger, was not
simply due to personality clashes, however. The added
size of the merger lead to a greater degree of impersonal
treatment in the ranks. Also, there were more people vie-
ing for a limited number of higher management positions.
There was a great deal of duplication at lower levels of
the organization.

     The Federation merger demonstrated the organizational
pitfalls inherent in rapid and large mergers. Economically,

149

the merger was relatively successful. Organizationally, and behaviorally, the merger was not nearly as successful. Lack of attention to proper planning and clear cut objectives and criteria for mergers and acquisitions are at fault. These objectives were not clearly enough defined.

2.   The many attempts at setting up a bank holding company are significant more as a symptom than an actual problem. Lack of planning and attention to details killed all early attempts at forming a bank holding company.

Also, many other banks were hesitant about joining with a maverick like Franklin in a multi-bank holding company format. This factor, together with the desire to enter the New York City market in force, necessitated further delays.

Franklin finally settled on a one-bank holding company format to allow it to expand into other financial operations. This advantage was shortly denied by new federal legislation. This type of response had been predicted for some time, however, and should have been expected at Franklin.

Overall, the efforts at expansion via the holding company route had been mostly unsuccessful. These efforts had drained resources from the organization. They had been poorly planned. They also had lead to a degree of confusion on the part of officers as to the future plans of Franklin top managers. Even after the formation of the one-bank holding company, top managers were still discussing a change to a multi-bank holding company format.

3.   Mr. Gleason's comments at the end of the (A-2) case seem to demonstrate an awareness of the proper function of the top manager. He views his role as that of the planner and problem spotter.

Mr. Gleason also sees his job as leading the organization in its social objectives and actions. He realizes that, particularly with a regulated industry, management has to be concerned with the objectives of the government and society as a whole.

He still feels that an aggressive and innovative posture is necessary to compete in a rapidly changing environment. He seems cognizant of these changes.

The problems arise in analyzing some of this other comments. He states a desire to meet with and understand his junior officers. While this may be commendable for a top manager, it is highly unrealistic, given the increasingly large scale of operations at Franklin. This kind of personal approach would draw valuable time from the more important task of planning for the future.

Moreover, Mr. Gleason states that expansion policies to date have been conservative. He would get a great deal of arguement on that point. His very last statements show that he is still willing to pursue what, to many, is a high risk strategy at Franklin National.

Franklin National Bank (A-3)

Analysis

This case presents an interview with Mr. Gleason in February 1973. In answer to a question on the bank's size and profitability of the lending divisions, he gave the statistics presented on the first page of the (A-3) case.

On Franklin's objectives and strategies, he produced a 5-year plan with eight parts:
i) corporate development,
ii) investments,
iii) international banking with $3 billion in assets as a 5-year goal,
iv) loan policy to adapt to changes in the banking industry,
v) retail banking: 66% increase in personal credit, 250% increase in A/R, 100% in industrial credit,
vi) real estate: statewide construction loans,
vii) national banking: "large buyer and seller of funds" especially spread loans,
viii) metropolitan banking: get high calibre sophisticated professional bankers to handle acquisitions, tender offers, etc.

For over-all growth, Mr. Gleason projected 10%/year in assets with deposits and earnings tracking this rate.

In a closing remark, in reference to the entrance into New York, Mr. Gleason said that Franklin was "now a microcosm of the major multi-facet, multi-national bank."

Questions

1. Comment on Mr. Gleason's objectives of becoming an international bank within five years.

2. Evaluate Franklin's management requirements and organization as discussed by Mr. Gleason.

Responses

1. This is an extremely ambitious project. Mr. Gleason is correct in noting the change in emphasis to multinational corporate status by large business organizations. Gleason reasons that if the bank is to capture this business, it must follow the lead of its large, potential customers into the international sphere of operations.

Franklin has little direct knowledge of operations in this area, however. It has primarily been a domestic, and even regional, bank to this time. What experience it does have has been generated through joint ventures with experienced, international banks. This is certainly a viable method of expanding in this area.

Basically, Franklin will probably be forced into an expansion strategy in the international area similar to that followed in its domestic expansion. It will probably have to take on the smaller, newer companies as customers in the immediate future. It will have to compete with large, sophisticated foreign as well as domestic organizations. Many of the foreign competitors, moreover, are actively supported by their governments, if not subsidized by them.

This kind of competition is going to require a great deal of talent in the Franklin organization. It is also going to require close coordination and control in areas new to the organization. Without this kind of control, the high risks required of this kind of rapid expansion could overwhelm Franklin.

Also, the effects of inflation and economic instability are magnified when considered on a world-wide basis. Franklin's lack of experience with nationalism and international economic interaction add to the problems faced by Franklin in its efforts at growth via the international sector.

2.   Mr. Gleason readily admits that the Franklin organization will require a rapid infusion of sophisticated new managers. He also admits that they will probably have to be considerably younger than current managers. These new managers will have to be technical specialists in quantitative methods of investment and control. Many will have to be knowledgeable in the areas of international finance discussed above.

New management expertise will also be required in the operations area. There will have to be a partial shift in emphasis from the traditional lending functions to those of marketing and control. This could lead to severe problems with the morale of the organization.

Mr. Gleason notes that top managers are now meeting daily. He feels that this helps control and coordination. He also notes that junior officers do not meet all that often. Since it is likely that the new managers will be brought in at junior levels, this lack of coordination at the crucial levels could lead to inefficiencies of operation in the future.

Basically, the strains placed on the organization by the need to assimilate a large number of new, technically proficient managers could be overwhelming. Not only will new managers be required to make the kinds of sophisticated decisions implied by Mr. Gleason's stated objectives, but someone is going to be found who can control, coordinate

and evaluate their performance. This last factor may prove
to be the most difficult for the organization.

Franklin National Bank (B-1)

Analysis

Introduction: Mr. Lewis together with several commit-tes evolved the bank's loan policy.

Through the late 1960's and in 1970, he noted the loan officer's dilemma caused by tight Federal Reserve mon-etary policies.

Loan Policy: Despite tight money conditions, personal loans and loans to small businesses will continue as usual. Large commercial loans will be on a more selective basis to maintain control over the loan portfolio.

Loan Review and Approval: This function was performed by the Loan Control Committee which met biweekly to consider loans above a specified limit. Anything below the limit could be approved at local levels.

A loan proposal was often referred to one member for a detailed review. His recommendations were frequently accepted.

Loan Supervision: All loans made by the bank were mon-itored. Loans that appear to be uncertain of repayment are referred to a special loan committee (see Franklin A) to protect the bank's interest.

Domestic Banking Group: The group president observed in 1970 that his group had made good progress in growth and sophistication but still trailed other banks in many service areas.

He added that the tight money situation had its effect on loanable funds. Therefore, loans were made on a selec-tive basis.

Metropolitan Division: This division handled the large domestic corporate accounts which, in 1969, increased by 9%, accounting for 21% of the bank's commercial loans.

Much of the business went to medium-sized or emerging growth companies. Business solicitation, however, was tar-geted on New York City-based Fortune 500 companies.

Larger total volume and larger accounts merited larger staff, but Franklin maintains a traditionally low personnel/bank size ratio.

A senior officer noted the division's growth could be 20% per annum.

National Division: This division operated nationwide, except for New York City and Long Island. Correspondent banking, negligible in 1961, grew dramatically through the decade, through the efforts of the division.

Branch Divisions: Branches totalled 91 in 1970. The lull in branch expansion in 1967 was followed by accelerated expansion in 1970. The immediate goal was to reach 100 branches.

Long Island West Division: This division with excess deposits provided most of the bank's loanable funds to back up the aggressive lending policies.

Within a mature economy in 1970, expansion in this region slowed considerably.

Long Island East Division: This is the smallest lending division. It is on the verge of expansion in expectation of local economic growth (see demographics in Franklin E: A statisitical description of Long Island).

The restraints here were i) the home office control, and ii) possible competition from large New York City banks.

New York City Branch Division: This division accounted for about 17% of the bank's commercial loans. Its New York offices had reached 27 by the close of 1970. Further expansion will depend on cost and "when"; Franklin's ready to follow competition in locating branches.

International Group: Established in 1963, but its lending activities were hurt by the Federal Government's voluntary credit controls begun early in 1965.

Rapid growth was achieved mainly by financing import-export businesses. In 1969 a representative office was opened in London (for Eurodollar borrowings). Branches were located in Nassau, the Bahamas.

Franklin International (1967 with capital $3 mil.) acquired American-Swiss Co. Ltd., a Canadian company, to facilitate short- and medium-term international financing (maturity 75-80% within one year). It also gave Franklin access to direct European borrowing.

In 1969, Franklin took a 15% interest in Banque Commerciale de Paris to give it a foothold in the Common Market. In 1970, Franklin acquired a 10% interest in Sterling Industrial Securities, Ltd., a new small merchant banking organization. It also had an established, extensive, correspondent banking relationship.

This division also joined other banks in international financing ventures, organized banking syndicates, and took shares in the Private Export Finance Corp. The international division was also considering participation in the Ivory Coast Development Bank, the World Bank, the EXIM Bank and the Asian Development Bank.

This division contributed 12% of the bank's earnings. Its five year goal is to increase this figure to 25%.

Real Estate Group: This division, in consonance with changing business environment, deemphasized residential business and stressed industrial and commercial accounts. Tight money, high costs and zoning problems caused residential construction to decline. Industrial construction and expansion is projected to continue unabated, however.

Specialized Lending Group:
A/R Division: This provided alternate financing to borrowers who fail to meet regular standards and yet needed funds to bail out or provide a turn-around position for the firm. These loans were approved and controlled with very close supervision.

Industrial Credit Division: "financial equipment and machinery for dealers and manufacturers of all types of products" as well as equipment leasing. Most loans were due in 5 years.

Master Charge Division: This division franchised the Franklin National Bank charge plan initially. Low profitability caused many banks and retail outlets to drop the plan. Franklin continued it, expecting general public acceptance and eventual profits imporvement.

After rejecting many alternatives, Franklin joined, in June 1969, the Eastern State Bankers Association and adopted the Master Charge. Volume grew greatly and profits were expected within three years.

Personal Credit Division: Handled all personal loans (autos, boats, student, medical, etc.) and the credit phase of full service checking accounts.

Final approval for these loans was this division's responsibility.

Questions

1. Evaluate the loan policies of the Domestic Banking Group.

2. How does the loan policy of the National Group relate to the policies of the Domestic Group?

3. How are economic conditions affecting overall operations of the banking groups?

Responses

1. Franklin National's Domestic Loans policy is committed to funding new, aggressive, small businesses. It also

intends to continue to actively seek personal loans. Large
commercial loans are supposed to be solicited on a more selective basis.

The Domestic Group encountered problems in this regard,
however. Top officers of this division admitted that their
loan officer lacked the sophistication of their large competitors. This decreased their ability to be selective in
analyzing loan applications.

The traditional personnel policy at Franklin of maintaining a low staff size relative to bank size also works
against proper controls. The Domestic Group is committed
to keeping up the rapid growth of loan and asset expansion.

The personnel weakness was heightened by other policies
of the group. The stated objective was to increase the
number of branches from 91 to 100 within the foreseeable
future. This, connected with the policy of allowing local
loan officers a fair degree of autonomy in decision making,
could add to the coordination and control problems at
Franklin.

Basically, a combination of rapid expansion, lack of
mamagement depth, and internal policies could increase
Franklin's loan charge offs. This, combined with a tight
economic situation could put a serious squeeze on cash
flow and profits.

2. The National Division sought loan arrangements with
correspondent banks and syndicates on a national basis.
This required Franklin to evaluate and, occasionally lead,
the solicitation of loans for large organizations.

When acting in concert with the correspondent banks,
Franklin was relied on for the purpose of soliciting, evaluating and setting up financing plans. The correspondent
banks typically are smaller local banks that rely on the
large, big city banks to utilize their funds efficiently.
The big city banks, on the other hand, needed the surplus
funds of the smaller banks to fund the big loans they frequently put together. This was a symbiotic relationship.
The small banks, however, had a great deal to lose if many
of the syndicated loans went sour.

When acting in concert with other large banks, Franklin, in turn, relied on the syndicate leader for guidance.
It did have to consider how these large loans might affect
its overall loan portfolio, however.

Once again, it can be seen that lack of management
depth could lead to a compounding of errors. The statements
of Mr. Gleason and other top managers in all divisions
could lead loan officers to accept an unduly large number
of high risk loans at both the domestic and national
levels. A serious imbalance in the loan portfolio could
result. Given the lack of coordination, except at the very

top levels, decisions in one group could be compounded, instead of offset, by another division.

3. The economy, in 1970, is experiencing high inflation and economic stagnation. The Federal Reserve has instituted a tight money policy. This makes it difficult, and costly, for banks like Franklin to secure loanable funds.

The economic slowdown is making more difficult the process of finding good loans in the traditional areas of industry, however. The firms that need the loans worst are those that are in the weakest financial conditions. Franklin already has enough of these loans outstanding. It does not really need more of them. These organizations have provided Franklin's traditional areas of growth, however. If Franklin deserts these organizations in bad times, they are not likely to return to it in good times. Franklin is in a difficult position. Loanable funds are expensive to get. Once it finds them, it is called on to loan them to firms it doesn't want to pursue in the short run, but can't afford to ignore in the long run.

Analysis

Non-Lending Groups:
Trust Group: It had three divisions--i) corporate
trust, ii)personal trust, and iii) investment advisory.

Corporate Trust Division: Few banks offer this service.
At Franklin, it is one of the fastest growing areas. The
"bread and butter" activity here is stock transfers which
began with the move to Hanover Square. (Other activities
included registrarship, auditing, bond paying agency, con-
versions, redemptions, etc.) Franklin gained a reputation
for quick (48 hrs.), quality service.

Personal Trust Division: In addition to trusteeship
of living trusts, employee benefits, and welfare plans and
customer securities, it also was executor for many estates,
handled probate requirements, "inventorying handling
assets, appraisals, claims, taxes, accounting and distribution." 1969 trust assets exceeded $600 million.

Investment Advisory Division: It gave investment management "services for securities owned by individuals, corporations, partnerships and other organizations".

Investment Group: This group was mainly in charge of
the bank's investment portfolio ($940.2 million in 1970).
Securities trading in 1970 netted record short term profits
in three areas.

Portfolio Division: This division was responsible
for maximizing investment earnings, while providing adequate liquidity for fluctuations in deposits and loan demand and "a cushion for contingencies."

A Government instruments portfolio was held only for
liquidity. Therefore, only short term notes were included.
Municipals were held for yield and were, therefore, long
term.

Municipal Finance Division/Municipal Bond Division:
This division handled underwriting, distribution, trading
of short-term municipal obligations, and advising munic-
ipalities in their investments.

To maintain Franklin's reputation, it felt it had to
bid on every municipal bond issue on Long Island. Large
New York City banks had underbid Franklin in recent times,
however.

Future plans centered on development of the municipals
market.

Money Market Center: This division was responsible
for managing Franklin's money position and servicing of customer needs in short-term money market instruments.   It kept
trading accounts in government securities and advised correspondent banks and corporate customers regarding money management and portfolio affairs.

Marketing Group:
This group's functions were i) offer bank customers the
widest possible services and ii) generate new business
through continuous promotional campaigns.   The Central Development Division for all practical purposes was was the
group.

Consumer Banking Department: This department handled
the majority of the Central Development Division's role.
It supported overall bank sales efforts.

Expansion of this formerly undefined department occurred
with an increased budget and was staffed with marketing
specialists.

The department conducted many programs to attract more
retail business, eg. merchandise awards to non-officer employees, give away programs for new residents (75% - 80%
bank close to home) and employees of new companies (20%-
25% retail banking customers bank close to work) and a
flatware and china distribution.   These were notably successful though would not be repeated any time soon so as not to
tarnish the bank's image.

Also, the department initiated a pilot program in 1970.
Consumer service representatives were available to let customers know what services were available.

Advertising: The ad budget fluctuated between 1960 and
1970.   Advertising was to be used on an as-needed basis.

To reach a wider audience on entering New York City,
TV advertising was also utilized.   Though some advertising
ideas originated with the marketing group, much of the
creative ideas came from the Advertising Agency -- Duncan
Brooks.   Media selection followed standard advertising
principles.

Public Relations/Community Relations Department: This
department coordinated representation of the bank "in a
very wide range of businesses, civic, charitable activities,
and conducting certain training programs for contact personnel".

Programmed Customer Services: On a limited scale the
bank offered customers computer services in Payroll, Account
Reconcilliation, Income Tax Computation and Lockbox Bill
Payment programs.   The major reason for these services is
to meet competition.

Questions

1. How does the existence of non-lending groups affect total operations of the organization?

2. What potential conflicts could arise between policies of the lending and non-lending financial groups?

3. How is the formation of the marketing group affecting future growth of Franklin National?

Responses

1. The various trust groups provided an added service to lure large organizations to Franklin National. Franklin can truly promote itself as a full service organization to a complete range of clients.

This list of clients is not limited to business corportions, however. Organizations such as unions, pension funds, charitable foundations, as well as individuals with excess funds, are also the target of large banks such as Franklin.

Few banks can afford to offer the services of a complete trust and investment advisory group. This type of service, however, is quite expensive to maintain. The results experienced by these groups also reflect on the image of the total organization. If the financial service groups provide poor advice, on investment decisions, potential and present clients could view this as a negative factor in using Franklin's total services.

The operation of the non-lending groups have an even more direct effect on operations. The results of the investment group directly affect the profitability of any large bank. These groups account for almost 25% of the earnings of the organization.

The investment group has the responsibility for investing the excess funds of the organization. Its results could lead to wide fluctuations in the earnings of Franklin.

The Municipal Finance/Bond division has a dual effect on operations. Directly, if it fails to make realistic bids on municipal bond issues, it will lose money. Indirectly, if it fails to make an effort to bid on a large spectrum of municipal issues, Franklin's reputation as a Long Island based bank could deteriorate. This would negatively affect the cash producing areas of Franklin's operations.

2. Depending on the relative importance of the various groups, pressure could be brought to bear on group policies. If one group was having difficulty attracting business, other groups could be influenced to alter policies to change

demand.

An example of this type of action would be where the municipal bond division was pressured to submit low bids on particular issues so that the banking groups could hold or gain funds. Other examples would include conflicts between lending and trust division policies.

Franklin proclaims its social responsibility. What would happen if one of the organizations it is lending funds to, and in which it is investing trust funds, looks like it is in trouble? The loan group would probably find out first. Should it tell the trust division first to allow it to bail out? Or should it make its information public knowledge to everyone at the same time? This kind of conflict faces all institutions of this type.

3. The formation of a strong marketing group at Franklin demonstrates how banks are becoming more similar to other kinds of service and production organizations. Formerly, banks waited for customers to come to them. The loan officers ruled the roost. Bank officers frequently operated as if they were doing their customers a favor by offering bank services.

Intense competition has altered this view, however. Particularly at Franklin, the marketing group is pushing the aggressive, innovative image. This has lead to the traditional conflicts between marketing and operations. The marketing group would like to offer maximum services at minimum cost to consumers. Operating groups want to offer only the most profitable services at lowest cost to Franklin National.

The traditional banking groups still cherish their relatively conservative image and method of operations. The style of the marketing group often belies this image, however. Promotional campaigns centering on chinaware and dog biscuits hardly seemed suitable to some of the traditionalists. This undoubtedly caused friction with some of the managers of the smaller, acquired banks.

Franklin National Bank (B-3)

Analysis

Service Groups:
Travel Department: This is a fully licensed travel
agency, offering the normal services of a travel agency.

Corporate Group: This groug included the legal department. It also maintains Franklin's records, stockholder
records, issues notices for both Director and stockholder
meetings as well as the execution of corporate documents.

Administration Group: It has responsibility for EDP,
financial services, and personnel.

Central Operations Division: Top management attitudes
made Franklin a late comer to computers and this division
was responsible for implementing EDP operations.

As noted by a senior officer, EDP expansion in 1960's
had been haphazard, "quick and dirty".

1967 EDP problems: personnel attrition, underutiliza-
tion of computers (using 1400 programs on an IBM 360-30).

By 1970, the division was staffed by bankers and
highly qualified technicians who "computerized virtually
every banking application."

The future of EDP was to include heavy investment at
Franklin with proper systems design to effect change and
action. The results were to be measured by correlating
this to change in Franklin's income.

Financial Division: This division included audit,
general accounting, insurance and management services departments and the budget planning department.

Standards for actual monthly performance were set by
this division. Variances occurred in the controllable
expenses.

The budget officer was considering the adoption of a
computerized econometric model to be used in conjunction
with the bank's own economic forecasts and money market
surveys for a better budget forecast and for other banking
operations.

Questions

1. What effects could the formation of non-financial oper-
    ating groups have on Franklin National?

2.   How will the various staff groups affect the operation
      of Franklin National?

Responses

1.   The formation of non-financial operating groups potentially has at least two effects on Franklin National. The
primary objective in setting up these non-banking operations is to diversify risks in earnings. Franklin hopes to
flatten out fluctuations in revenues by expanding into non-
financial areas of operations. Franklin hopes that funds
generated from traditional banking operations can be used
more effectively, for the total organization, in non-banking
areas.

      There are potential problems in this course of actions,
however. The non-financial areas could become the tail
that wags the dog. These areas could drain scarce financial and, especially, management resources from the primary
areas of earning power in the banking functions. Also,
poor performance in these areas could reflect negatively
on the image of the banking and financial groups.

2.   The formation of strong staff groups is a relatively
new occurrence in banking circles. Traditionally, the loan
officer had been king of the hill. The more innovative
banks provide non-financial officers with the opportunity
for advancement, however.

      This has provided one of the reasons for a decrease in
morale at Franklin. The traditional bank officers find
they must be subservient to policies generated by non-
financially-oriented, staff managers.

      The operation staff groups provide the organization
with a more balanced approach to banking. Areas such as
EDP can provide rapid access to portfolio analysis. This
will assist the banking officers in spotting potential opportunity or problem areas. Other staff functions, such
as the proposed econometric and management services groups,
if operated effectively, could add to the overall coordination and control of the organization.

      These operations are going to require infusions of
management talent, however. Overhead will rise, since
most of these areas do not directly generate revenues.
They could be instrumental in increasing profit margins,
however. The question that has yet to be answered at
Franklin is whether these staff groups will be effective
in their role as coordinators and advisors.

Note to Franklin National Corporation

The (C) through (H) segments of the Franklin National
series constitute an extensive note to the (A) and (B)
cases. A wealth of background data is provided in these
segments. The following is a brief description of the
information presented in the different sections.

      Franklin National (C) --presents financial data and
                              results on the 22 largest banks
                              or bank holding companies in
                              the U.S.

      R4anklin National (D) --compares Franklin's resultts
                              with those of the other top
                              banks in the nation.

      Franklin National (E) --presents an extensive descrip-
                              tion of the economy of Long
                              Island. Some economic data for
                              the rest of New York State
                              are also presented.

      Franklin National (F) --presents legislation and reg-
                              ulations pertaining to bank
                              holding companies. Permisable
                              diversification of these organ-
                              izations is also described.

      Franklin National (G) --presents banking statistics
                              for New York State for the per-
                              iod 1964-1968. These are ag-
                              gregated as well as broken
                              down by the 12 banking districts.

      Franklin National (H) --presents results of the commer-
                              cial banking system for the
                              period 1950-1070. Projections
                              for the period 1970-1980 are
                              presented.

COMPREHENSIVE CASES

This section of cases is designed to present situations cutting across the full range of corporate, profit oriented, strategic problems. As much as possible, all the traditional functional and conceptual planning areas are included.

The purpose is to present students with the types of situations facing top managers. In some of the cases, the top managers are at the division level. In these instances, however, planning has been decentralized to this level.

The cases are designed to demonstrate the complex, integrative nature of strategic planning. These cases, moreover, require an understanding of the problems involved with implementing strategic change. Typically, this type of case is presented at the late stages of the course. A thorough analysis of problems and solutions requires a broad based background in the concepts and application of strategic planning.

EMS Oil Company

Purpose

EMS Oil Company is primarily designed to explore the planning process at the lower levels of a large, broadly based organization. The managers at the divisional level at EMS have only recently been required to participate in long range planning. They are still trying to develop policies and guidelines to follow in setting up their plans.

The case does present objectives that have already been set by both corporate and divisional managers. A secondary purpose of the case is to have the students evaluate the objectives in light of the environmental conditions.

Past policies have to be considered when analyzing how EMS has arrived at its present position. This means that a thorough analysis of the effect of external factors on internal strategies is necessary.

Although the case is disguised, there is a large amount of published data on the industry. The EMS case, therefore, can also be used to provide a vehicle for testing the ability of the students to gather and evaluate information from other sources.

Finally, the organization structure at EMS is in a state of flux. The strategies and policies at the company are changing. Following Chandler's dictum that structure follows strategy, the case could be used to determine what kind of structural changes are required to be consistent with the evolving strategy.

Position in Course

The EMS Oil Company case should be presented early in the course. The problems are reasonably well-focused. The industry and its mechanism is well known to most students and sufficient data are available for others to understand external constraints.

The case can be used in those segments of the course dealing with the planning function at lower levels of an organization. It is particularly appropriate for use in those segments of the course dealing with evaluation of objectives or formation of action plans.

The objectives facing Mr. Rickets and his planning committee are well formulated. There is a clear cut, primary, financial objective. There are several constraining, secondary objectives as well. Students could be asked to test the consistency, feasibility, and acceptability of these objectives.

The planning committee also has to develop an action plan consistent with these objectives. Since their options are fairly constrained, this presents a good opportunity for testing action plan formulation relatively early in the course.

Finally, the case can be used in that segment of the course dealing with organization structure. The connection between strategic change and organizational structure can be traced through the past history and future projections in the EMS Oil Company case.

Key Issues

1. Development of actions consistent with set objectives.

2. The relationship of strategic change and organizational structure.

3. Relationship between short and long range planning.

Analysis

Marketing Planning in the Petroleum Industry:
The case presents an invitation to a management consultant firm from a close personal friend George Rickets, a division sales manager of EMS to sit in on a planning committee meeting. The purpose of the meeting is to evaluate the proceedings and suggest policies and procedures for the future.

Headquarters demands that ROI at the divisional level be improved 125% by the close of 1974. This is the primary objective.

The company was founded as a regional firm in the 1920's. Rapidly expanded into other domestic regions and all over the world, it had over $2 billion in sales by 1973.

EMS operates on the profit center idea within the major products (petroleum, coal, chemicals, plastics). Each is subdivided by main activity (producing, pipeline, marketing), as well as geographically.

George's group is the South-Western marketing division, headquarters of petroleum operations. This division controls roughly 200 wholesale branches or agents and over 700 service stations throughout three states. These include independents, private ownerships, agencies and company operated ones (see exhibit 1 in the case for a breakdown).

169

Intensive competition with extensive government constraints are projected to continue in the future. In the
early 1940's EMS was the price leader with Conoco its
chief competitor. By the 1960's, Philips was sharing or
supplanting both leaders (Conoco and Philips both had had
the same growth pattern as EMS). Competition grew fiercer,
both nationally and regionally, among the large integrated
companies, the regional integrated firms, small independent
marketers, and discounters, with frequent extended price
wars.

Basically the price competition is the result of oversupply of crude petroleum. Jobbers are seeking legislation
to halt self-service gasoline distribution; service station
operators seek to regulate size and nature of price signs,
and some producers and distributors have been investigated
for conspiracy-in-restraint-of-trade. Consequently current
prices are about two cents below that of three years ago.

EMS has tried many marketing innovations. "A new company president and a new vice-president about eighteen
months ago have helped more EMS Company towards a 'new look'
throughout its management structure. Management seminars,
executive development programs, a change of the corporate
symbol, increasing emphasis upon communication at all levels
and new criteria for division management" evaluation have
been implemented. The major emphasis is now on "return
on assets used".

Due to general unprofitability of gasoline and oil in
the industry; an overseas 4-year payback requirement and
10 years at home, EMS is looking to other growth areas for
diversification to augment profits.

The planning committee comprised Rickets, three others,
and Turner from corporate headquarters as a consultant.
Corporate headquarters requires a 5 year plan within 60 days
designed to achieve 10% ROI.

Previously headquarters did all long range planning.
The present divisional involvement is the result of the
new vice president's directive.

A question and answer period brought the following
points to light:
i)   The 10% ROI requirement is AFTER taxes.
ii)   The regional annual budget already at headquarters
      is considered as the first year of the 5 year
      plan.
iii) To meet the headquarters requirements, retail
      outlets must average 12.6% return.
iv)   Planners have free reign in evolving a feasible
      plan.
v)   Present market value forms the basis for objec-
      tive ratio computation.
vi)   Unprofitable assets must be disposed of.

170

Specifically, the plan should incorporate the following assumptions: continued business and growth (exhibit 5 provides pertinent details helpful in this regard); 100% capacity must be assumed ie any additional gallonage (even ads) is an investment; every asset must be identified with its possible future use or add all assets by market and analyze; inflation must be assumed at 5% a year as well as a 50% tax rate -- no investment credit. The final plan must show total assets and its ROI. Action plans must be fairly explicit, including possible alternatives.

One suggestion involved selling and leasing back company owned properties. This would greatly improve the return on aassets. Questions were raised concerning the overall effect of such a move.

The meeting adjourned with a committee of four to prepare the draft proposal. A special projects representative was assigned to collate, write up and assist in preparing material for the plan.

Questions

1. Evaluate the EMS circumstances and planning activities to date.

2. What recommendations would you make to the planning committee to help them carry out the task of developing a five year plan?

3. Comment on the question of price leadership in the South-Western division.

Responses

1. EMS is structured along product lines at the top levels of the organization. Within product lines, the organization is split between the geographic marketing regions and the producing and transport divisions. This has been the traditional structure for the petroleum industry.

Prior to the time of the case, planning had been done at corporate headquarters. The plans were then passed down to the divisions to implement. The only planning function carried on at the division level involved standard budgeting procedures. Objectives had previously centered on gross sales and market share.

A new management team was bringing changes to all these areas, however. The primary objectives had shifted to return on assets (ROA). To implement this shift in objectives, top management is decentralizing part of the planning process. This decentralization appears to be incomplete in a significant area, however.

As noted previously, the objectives are still determined at top levels only. They are then passed down to
lower levels to develop action plans consistent with them.
It appears that the overall objectives are similar for all
regions and divisions. It could be that differing environmental conditions require different objectives.

Without the ability to achieve significant input to
the objective setting phase of strategy formation, decentralization of responsibility will be incomplete. A significant
problem will always be convincing the regional managers of
the feasibility and acceptability of the objectives before
they get down to developing an action plan.

Another, immediate, problem involves the timing of
the changes. Divisional management has not been given much
lead time in developing planning formats. They were initially told to develop their one year budgets. After
they were already implementing this budget plan, they were
then told to incorporate it into a five year plan. They
now have to submit these plans within sixty days. This
doesn't leave much time for managers who are unused to
doing their own planning to develop long range plans.

Overall, the changes being made by top management
seems to be consistent with a complex, competitive environment. The methods used to implement these changes leave
much to be desired.

2.   EMS division management must perform the following
analysis:
   i)   Do an economic analysis to understand the environ-
        ment and relate to the industry.
   ii) The market must be:
        a) qualitatively defined;
        b) quantitatively defined to show market poten-
           tial, market share of existing products, and
           market penetration with possibly new products;
   iii) Do a competitive analysis to know competitors,
        what they are doing and whether EMS is meeting
        competition;
   iv) Do a trend analysis to show what has happened at
        least five years back; what causes peaks, etc.,
        and covariance analysis to see what factors
        accounted for what variations;
   v)   Enumerate problems and opportunities and how to
        capitalize on them in both the short run and the
        long run;
   vi) Establish goals and objectives -- quantifiably
        dollars and cents targets by product line and
        market for each quarter and year;
   vii) Develop an action plan that includes detailed
        timing and personnel tactics;
   viii)Develop an evaluation or profitability analysis
        of the plan. A simulation is possible here.

172

3. The increased competitiveness had lead to a shift in price leadership. EMS formerly held the role of price leader. In this role, it was able to create a considerable degree of stability in the marketplace.

This kind of stability would be extremely suspicious now, however. The Justice Department frowns on that kind of pattern of price leadership. Given the increasing degree of regulation in the industry, these patterns tend to show up quite fast.

Basically, EMS, along with its competitors, has had to trade off price stability for a decreased threat of antitrust action. Also, the increased price competition has lead to an increase in gasoline usage. It is possible that the firms are able to better utilize their capacity. This at least should be checked. It is possible that maintenance of higher prices has been costing money. Events after the case show this not to be true, unfortunately.

Associated Chemicals

Purpose

The Associated Chemicals case presents large scale strategic planning in a microcosm. The case focuses on the problem of a division manager of a large, diversified petrochemical firm. Mr. Robbins, the manager, has been given the responsibility for developing a complete strategy for a new product.

The case should be used to demonstrate the interaction of all areas in the strategy formation process. Minimum guidelines have been set for the division. The product is well-defined, as are most of the problems. The case is a complex one, however, in the sense that it involves strategic questions over the full range of functional areas.

Organizational problems relating to responsibility versus authority can also be presented via this case. Attempts at implementing a matrix form of organizational structure to meet strategic objectives have been made at Associated Chemicals. Analysis of these attempts can bring fresh insights into the problems of evolving a structure consistent with strategic change.

Position in the Course

The case presents a complex set of strategic problems. The problems are fairly well defined, however. This combination of factors suggests that Associated Chemicals is well suited as a lead off case for that segment of the course dealing with complex, implementation-oriented cases. Alternatively, the case could be used as the last of the cases in analysis/formulation stage of the course.

In either event , the students will need more than introductory knowledge of the strategy formation process to provide a well rounded analysis of problems and solutions. The Associated Chemicals case, therefore, should probably be placed someplace at the middle of the course. From that point of view, it would make a good test case. Much of the material is presented in the case. It provides a good transition from strategy formation to implementation.

Key Issues

1. Responsibility versus authority in a complex organizational structure.

2. Development of new product strategies in a dynamic, high technology industry.

3.   Problems of evaluating long term, strategic projects with short term measures.

Analysis

In September 1966, a new capital request for iso-chlorathane, a new chemical product, was made. Jim Robbins, a division manager with the chemical group, was worried about the effect of this and other problems facing his division.

The market for iso-chlorathane was exploding. 1965 forecasts through 1969 had revealed no capacity problem. The 1966 forecast showed sales capacity constrained by the middle of 1967, however. The process technology was changing, moreover, and raw materials shortage existed for the present process.

Robbins was also extremely concerned over a current 60% - 80% plant cost overrun for plexon, originally estimated at $10 million. This was another product produced by the division.

Associated Petroleum was an international firm engaged in all aspects of the oil industry.

Structure: The firm operates in six areas: i)exploration and production, ii)transportation, iii)refining, iv)marketing, v)chemicals, and vi) research.

Chemicals mainly functioned domestically with three divisions: i)petrochemicals, ii)industrial chemicals, and iii)synthetic fibers and resins. In 1965 chemicals contributed 13% of total corporate sales revenue.

Corporate operations are decentralized. Central management evaluates managers through a ROI performance appraisal.

Industrial Chemicals: This division was basically organized along functional lines. An operations group was formed to coordinate the division's activities.

Operations was essential since Industrial's many products served other company divisions as well as outsiders as end products, intermediate products, and raw materials, hence the necessity of formal planning and coordination.

To expedite this function, the department was divided into product groups, e.g. "first stage" chemicals and intermediate stage chemicals. Each group played a vital role in the capital planning process.

The product groups had to forecast the need for additional capacity and present a detailed proposal (volume, kind of process, capital required and timing) to the divisional management. The divisional management, on approval, sought final decision from the corporate finance committee.

The relationship between the product groups and the functional departments was that of joint responsibility for product development. The group manager was the only person who could "hire and fire" the men directly under him, however.

Rewards and Punishments: According to Bill Stalzer, performance data, past and present, are available on employees but appraisals on data are not automatic. The important thing is how individuals face problems and future performance is what counts.

While a manager's evaluation includes the development and training of subordinates, quantitative measurements are not available on these grounds. Though emphasis is on subjective criteria, actual performance against standards is also counted.

Functional Chemicals: This group operated from the headquarters building in Houston, Texas. In 1965, this group had 10 products valued at over $50 million. Jim Robbins, 42, formerly assistant manager of Industrial Chemicals, is the manager.

Iso-chlorathane: in April, 1966, Jim Robbins explained that iso-chlorathane was "taking off". 12 firms produced this product in the U.S. 6 of them had 75% of the market. Concerned about over-expansion, Associated had consistently increased its capacity in bits and pieces. At this date, it was selling at its capacity level output (265 million pounds).

The major point is that the base of the present technology was changing from prime gas to feed gas with capital investment per pound practically unchanged. Even though the feed gas technology is new and untried and provides a limited choice of precesses, a look at the manufacturing costs is enlightening. Feed gas costs 2¢ to 4¢ per lb. versus 6¢ to 8¢ per lb. for prime gas. The future obviously belongs to ffed gas-based iso-chlorathane, at this point in time.

After failing to build a feed gas pilot plant in 1966, the functional chemicals group met with R&D on the situation. R&D outlined the major one of their problems as the need for a new sensing device and coupling device using a bonded metal and a special steel with super-tensile strength which happens to be on allocation (govt. controlled). This would take about 14 weeks to secure. Many of their problems with materials were found to be solvable in the Division's other departments.

Associated's major competitor had already bought the new technology from Japan, and Jim Robbins started to negotiate for licenses for the new process, all to no avail.

In April 1966, the functional group sales were 30% below plan. In May, the Engineering Coordinator requested engineering help desperately, to assist in various projects including iso-chlorathane.

In June, the marketing forecast indicated even greater demand for iso-chlorathane. In the market place, price competition had intensified, however. Given current prices and processes, a new plant (prime gas) will reduce ROI from 14% to a0% in 1971. With a feed gas plant at Baton Rouge, ROI is projected to be about 21% in 1971.

Robbins feels corporate strategy places emphasis on being ahead of competitors' labs and being first with low-cost plants. His R&D was still behind expectations, however.

As of June, sales were 81% of plan.

In July R&D made a breakthrough that they felt would allow putting the feed-gas plant on line in late 1969.

Prime gas shortage affected the iso-chlorathane situation. Purchasing Department said the world market was short of it, but the real point is that, with the feed gas process just around the corner, no one would expand their present, prime-gas capacity.

The July 11th meeting to consider alternatives came out with the following: i)send detailed problems to engineering and R&D, ii)mutually agreed trade-offs between iso-chlorathane and nylostyrene, iii)buy iso-chlorathane domestically and overseas if possible, iv) high pressure operations are using 10,000 more pounds of prime gas per day for the same output, v)equipment designed for prime gas process cannot be used for feed gas process.

In August, iso-chlorathane was out of the limelight because i)Robbins was occupied with evaluating a major Associated acquisition, ii)industrial chemical division was busy with assimilating a small manufacturing company recently acquired, iii)it was apparent that the plexon cost over-run would be much more than anticipated.

On the bright side, functional sales to date were 83% of plan and industrials 87%. An engineer had been specifically assigned to work on iso-chlorathane. In September, the new engineer proposed an "interim" expansion to provide the needed capacity through 1968.

Robbins saw three alternatives to the dilemma.
i) Pressure the firm to settle the iso-chlorathane issue.
ii) Shift his group's focal activity from iso-chlorathane.

iii) Get assigned to manage the new acquisition as "a graceful exit from a messy situation".

Questions

1. Evaluate the effects of Associated Chemical's organizational structure on the planning process.

2. Evaluate the three alternatives presented by Jim Robbins at the end of the case.

Responses

1. The organizational structure at Associated Chemical has serious flaws from the point of view of the planner. Basic management principles have been violated in the organization.

There are many instances of violations of unity of command. In setting up a matrix xtructure, top management has allowed both the functional and project managers to retain authority over members of the project group. This leads to split loyalty on the part of group members.

The types of suthority exercised by the managers adds to the problems, moreover. The functional managers have the sole authority for hiring and firing. They also initiate salary and promotion procedures.

The project managers, on the other hand, are required to fill in evaluation forms on the subordinates. Essentially this means that the project manager, through his report, will provide a significant input into the advancement process for these subordinates.

The project managers were also competing with the functional managers. Both shared responsibility for results. It is pointed out in the case that project managers and marketing heads both were responsible for sales. This was true for other areas as well.

This diffusion of responsibility lead to a decrease in control and coordination. Managers at various levels didn't really know who was in charge. They also had the ability to lay the blame for failure at someone else's feet.

2. The alternatives presented range from extremely pragmatic and self-serving to a reasonable start to a long range solution. The first solution makes good, long term sense. It requires close coordination between functional and product groups. It would also lead to better coordination and planning between the different product groups. In addition to this alternative there would have to be assistance from the internal users of iso-chlorathane who

can draw from the stocks of the product at will. This increases the problems in planning production needs. Return on investment is supposed to be the primary objective of the firm. Robbins will have to base his report on this basis.

The second alternative presents, at best, a compromise and retreat from his problems. The lack of attainment of group objectives is partly due to lack of overall planning on the part of Robbins. He has failed to set, and communicate, priorities. He jumps back and forth between projects. His subordinates apparently don't know which is most important at any given time.

The second part of this alternative also lacks foresight. The feeling that lack of capacity causes no harm does not consider the possibility that a competitor might find the breakthrough that Robbins' organization has failed to find. This would lead to a disastrous loss of market share.

Alternative three, unfortunately, is one that is frequently taken by managers in this position. Since evaluation is based on short term results, this type of action would probably work once. As a long term solution, it is clearly not in the best interests of Associated Chemicals. Also, the new manager of his project group would quickly realize the mess he had inherited. The new manager would probably try to shift the blame back to Robbins as fast as he could. This alternative clearly has the biggest risk of backfiring.

Clemens Super Market, Inc.

Purpose

Clemens is a complex, integrative case. It is designed to present the full range of functional and conceptual issues found in strategic situations. The problems present in this case include financial, marketing, organization, operations, competition, social issues and the economy.

The setting of the case, a relatively small company, permits ready identification of the problems, as well. The structure of the organization and of the external market is much easier to analyze in this well defined situation than in a much larger organization such as the Gulf and Western case. The problems, although complex in nature, are much more focused in the Clemens case.

This case cal also be used to demonstrate both the flexibility and constraints of the relatively small business. It presents a discussion of a broad spectrum of strategic, policy considerations faced by a small, but growing, super-market chain.

Position in Course

The case is well suited to demonstrate the full panoply of strategic problems. To perform a thorough analysis of the Clemens case, students will need a fair degree of exper-tise in both strategy formulation and implementation.

The case should be used in the latter portion of the course. Because of the size of the organization, the Clemens case is well suited to be the lead in case for the implementation section of the course. Changes can be made in the firm without too many complications. Clemens is in fairly good shape. There are extensive strengths and oppor-tunities. That provides a solid base to overcome the or-ganizational weakness and market threats. The problems are not insurmountable. For these reasons it is a good case for the students to test their strategic formation and implementation skills.

Key Issues

1. Transition from family control to professional management.

2. Competitive threats facing a relatively small company in an industry dominated by giants.

3. Development of plans for growth in a slow growth industry.

Analysis

Clemens is a chain of five supermarkets located in a suburban area of southeastern Pennsylvania to the north and west of Philadelphia. The firm is privately held. Most of the stock is held by two cousins, Jim and Abe Clemens. A small portion of stock is held by other top management personnel.

Current Problems:

The immdeiate question facing Clemens management is what to do with the Broad Street Store located in Lansdale. It has strong sentimental attachment to the owners since it was the first of their present chain. The management is also afraid of what reaction might be, both inside and outside the organization.

The store is the only supermarket in an area inhabited by many older residents of the area. It may be difficult for some of these residents to get to an alternative supermarket. There is also a fear of reaction to the closing of a store of what had been a rapidly expanding company in recent years. Finally, Clemens has built a reputation as a family-oriented organization with its employees, as well as its customers. The contraction in size, if only temporary due to the expected openingof a new store, would mean a lot of shuffling of present employees. It should be noted that there are no unions representing any Clemens employees, although there have been organizational attempts with extremely poor results.

Long Range Problems:

The current situation is symptomatic of more basic problems at Clemens. It is undergoing changes in management style. The two Clemens cousins are slowly relinquishing control to new, younger managers. This transition has been relatively unplanned, however.

Dave Stauffer, the executive vice-president, noted that no formal planning structure exists in the organization. It is apparent, however, that the firm is willing to take advantage of opportunities that present themselves, such as opening stores at new shopping centers.

Management claims that they plan their sites to be in the path of expanding population patterns. Increasing competition from the large chains, as well as independents, is making it harder to stumble across potential sites as has been done in the past. Also, the cost of land and construction precludes the company or the Clemens family from building their own shopping centers. More management time will have to be spent on locating and evaluating potential sites in the future.

Management strangth is still thin, however. The vice president of store operations is brand new. The other two top managers have been with the organization much longer, but their positions are poorly defined and contain a great deal of overlap.

Dave Stauffer says that one of his tasks is to keep abreast of technological and marketing advances in the industry. He feels he has the flexibility, due to size, to jump on board new trends developed by the major competitors. So far, he has been fast and lucky enough to do this. He notes, however, that he has no control over major competitors entering Clemens' primary market and "overstoring" the area. The big chains can afford this kind of cut-throat competition for an extended period of time, as with A&P's WEO campaign and resulting heavy price competition by all competitors in Clemens' immediate market area.

Finance:
Despite this competitive situation, Clemens' return on sales of 1% is four times greater than the industry average for the northeastern United States. The question remains whether Clemens can climb back to its traditionally higher return on sales shown by the following synopsis of past results.

	Sales (000)	Profits (000)	Return on Sales (%)
1973	$18,200	$183	1.00
1972	16.800	161	.96
1971	16,100	291	1.81
1970	15,100	250	1.65
1969	12,100	185	1.55
1968	10,500	173	1.65

The following presents a summary of Clemens' current financial position:

Current Ratio	1.49	low, tight
Acid Test	.756	low, tight
Debt/Equity	1.15	high
Inventory Turnover	12 days	fast, high
R.O.E.	9.5%	good

The firm has been able to maintain a good return on equity by using a large amount of both short, and long term debt relative to equity. This eliminates their ability to borrow for future expansion, however. Their mortgages have approximately 16 years to go based on current payout. This further limits them to using a lease method of financing. Leasing could get more expensive, however, and limits their choice of sites.

Also, most of the equity account is found in retained earnings. This says that while little new stock has been

182

sold, the owners have been willing to plow earnings back into the firm. The question remains as to how long they will be willing to tie up their estates in the company, considering their advancing age. (This is inferred from the history section, which notes they helped the original founder in the late '20's and 30's. They are both about 60 years of age).

This all leads one to question the firm's ability to continue to expand in the short run. Their considerable cash flow ($500,000) is largely accounted for by note payments and needs for increased working capital.

Organizational Objectives:
There also appears to be disagreement as to the desireability of major expansion. Dave Stauffer and Carl Rhoads have different views on the ability and advisibility of major new expansion.

This is all the more important since they are now the two executives most responsible for the expansion process. This is a further symptom of the lack of planning and organizational structure within the firm.

Basically, Clemens suffers from the problems of most small, growing organizations:
1. Management talent.
2. Capital inflow is restricted due to desire for control.
3. Planning is short-term -- at best.
4. They are at the mercy of large, strong, well-balanced competitors.

The company has built up employee and customer loyalty as evidenced by its growth and profitability. Only if they can make the transition to a professionally managed organization, will that growth and profitability continue.

Questions

1. What should management do with the Broad Street Store?

2. What organizational problems face Clemens in the short run? In the long run?

3. What are the competitive threats? How can growth be maintained?

Responses

1. The Broad Street store has clearly seen its best days. Although it can be argued that, since the store is still very profitably, it is clearly a draw on the resources of the organization. The key question that should be considered is where can the resources of the firm best be used.

Clemens does not have unlimited resources. The organization is committed to the new Center Square store. The equipment currently in the Broad Street store, with minor changes, can be used at the new store. This means, however, that the Broad Street store must be closed fairly soon.

There are significant problems to be encountered in closing the store. The employees and customers have to be convinced that there will still be a Clemens to work and shop at. The Main Street store is only a mile away. It is much larger and provides plenty of free parking. The Souderton store is also only about five miles from the Broad Street store, as well. In any event, to close must be consistent with the family image of Clemens which they have been so successful in imparting to the general public.

It might be of interest to note that the store was closed. All employees were transferred to the store of their choice, even though this did allow some temporary increases in overhead. There was some immediate, negative, reaction by customers. This passed by, very quickly, however. Of particular interest is the fact that only six months after the closing, the Main Street store was registering higher volume than the two stores combined had registered before the closing. Management felt they had been able to transfer all the Broad Street customers to the Main Street store. This required an increase in the size of the Main Street store within the following year.

2. In the short run, Clemens is faced with a problem of a fuzzy distinction between roles. There is considerable overlap between the three, second level managers. This overlap can also be seen at the next level where two of the buyers are also department managers in the store. These problems are typical of relatively small organizations, however. It just does not have the luxery of specialists to cover all functions.

The long run problems are more complex, however. There is little depth of management. Also, the two Clemens cousins have not planned for their own replacement. They appear to be grooming Dave Stauffer to take over full operations, but not very well. The positions of the various store managers have to be clarified, as well. There is too much shared responsibility at the store level between buyers and store managers.

3. Competitive threats are not severe in the short run. This was proved in the recent price competition move by A&P. Clemens was able to maintain their sales and income growth. They still had a much higher return on sales than their large competitors.

Their competitive advantage has been their local, family image. They also have been able to predict the direction of population trends. This has enabled them to get in and establish themselves before competition. They are running out of fresh territory, however. They have reached out for about eight to ten miles in all directions from the Lansdale starting point.

Also, competition from the large chains is starting to catch up with them. More stores are either planned or being opened in their current territory.

There is still a "hole" open for expansion just north and west of Lansdale. This would give them a full circle of stores around the central headquarters.

Clemens can still generate additional sales, and income growth, through enlarging their current stores. This is somewhat limited, however, since most are near the industry standards for a modern, efficient store. All stores, however, are in plazas where there is room for expansion.

The one other area for growth is in diversification. Other chains have added drug and discount stores to increase sales. Clemens could conceivably add a drug and cosmetic store to the current stores. This might create problems with the leases in the plazas they don't own, however. It should be pointed out that alcoholic beverages are sold only through state-owned liquor stores so that this avenue of growth is not open to Clemens.

The problem with any extra growth plans is clearly with resource availability. Clemens, as noted before, is short of management. It also does not possess a large amount of financial resources. Any bad decisions could be disastrous to the organization. Their larger competitors can afford to absorb the losses of a bad decision on location. Clemens cannot!

Assignment: Evaluate Clemens present strategy. What recommendations for change would you seek?

CLEMENS SUPERMARKETS, INC.

AN ANALYSIS

INTRODUCTION

The close of 1973 saw many changes in the supermarket industry. Traditional policies, procedures, and assumptions were challenged... expansion plans and programs were reconsidered ... the unlimited abundance symbolized by supermarkets was threatened ... consumers changed their buying patterns ... and the industry will never again be quite the same.

The food industry has rarely operated in an atmosphere of greater uncertainty and uneasiness. However, there are a number of favorable signs: (1) consumers are better informed, (2) experiences show that realistic margins can be re-established, (3) overall supplies will be adequate, and (4) growing realization that improved coordination and cooperation in the industry will have universal benefits.

The retail food industry is the largest in the U.S., with sales of $115 billion in 1973. Over 21% of the disposable income dollar goes for food. Operating margins in 1972 were disastrously low, reflecting the attempt to adjust to A & P's new discount policy.

In the area of growth it is projected that expansion will continue, competition will intensify, and some areas will be overstored, (Clemen's is concerned about overstoring). In the future, more independents and small chains are expected to become affiliated with wholesalers. Some industry analysts are expected to become affiliated with wholesalers. Some industry analysts are also predicting more independents either merging or going public and wholesalers moving into operating their own retail stores. Either way, supermarkets will have to diversify more and more to other fields to secure a larger share of the market.

New construction will level off with a 5% increase to store size from 28,500 to 32,000 ft.² and newer larger stores will achieve a better product mix.

Management responsible for supermarket operations will accelerate their search for cost cutting techniques and operational economies at all levels. This is due primarily to continuously rising expenses and stepped up price competition putting severe pressure on margins and profits. Even so, only limited increases in profit-ability can be expected.

It is anticipated that non-food items will be the fastest growing merchandise line because of its high margin and profitability. Convenience and specially prepared food items are also expected to grow rapidly.

In summary, the external environment facing Clemens' portends that there will be larger and fewer new stores, a definite, but slightly abating, margin squeeze, increased competition and competitive pressures, a leveling off of real dollar sales, increased use of new technology, and a large move to diversify with non-food items.

OBJECTIVES

A thorough analysis of Clemens' Supermarkets, Inc, has revealed that they should subscribe to a certain set of objectives. These objectives and recommended strategies are outlined in exhibit 1.

CLEMENS' CORPORATE ORGANIZATION typifies the small corporation having an informal structure, a loosely defined chain of command, and in some instances, loosely defined responsibilities. The problem here is that Clemens has long since outgrown this type of organization, and with 100 employees and $18 million annual sales spread over five stores, they are in need of a more efficient, well defined, and explicit organizational structure to function more effectively.

Exhibit 2 shows the proposed new Clemens Corporate Structure. The analysis made showed that the older Clemens cousins should be phased out of the day-to-day operations before age does it for them, and that a titular position of executive vice president with full day to day, intermediate, and long range decision responsibility and authority should be created.

The analysis further showed that the informal structure that now exists should be replaced with a more straight line, formal organization with the ultimate responsibility being in the hands of the EVP.

One of the first areas of planning that must be formalized is that of store location analysis and shopping center location decisions. Through analysis, we have carefully concluded that it would be best, for financial reasons, for Clemens to limit expansion, and contain themselves to the Mongomery and Bucks county areas. Factors to be considered before a location decision is made included the economy of the area, trading area size, population trends and characteristics, income levels, street and highway systems, area competition, and shopping center analysis. The latter included investigating present tenants and mix, possible location within the center, attractiveness of facilities, and management. A saturation analysis for actual store location feasibility, to determine if there is room for profitable expansion in an area, is then started. Because of limited finances, and because there is a definite tendency for supermarkets to be more profitable when located within a shopping center, we suggest Clemens lease in these centers, preferably with stores such as Clover, who also have a reputation to maintain.

Another area of planning involves remodeling and internal expansion. In order to successfully undertake these operations, it is necessary to look at both consumer trends and product mix potential for saleability and margin. The problem is to decide what is profitable, what consumers will buy, and how to arrange it in the best possible store layout.

The consumer statistics and analysis show that meats, produce, and dairy items are best for expansion, along with the new areas of bakery, deli, and general merchandise. Store layout should capitalize on these areas. The new store layout (Loewy designers) which we suggest (exhibits 7 and 8), takes into consideration consumers, gross margins, and trends. In such a case where remodeling is not feasible in this manner, we suggest basic ideas be carried through as much as possible.

With a full time marketing manager, we suggest a budget of 1% of sales for Clemens versus 0.8% for the industry. Two important considerations for Clemens will be store image and advertising content and timing. Because 83% of consumers do their grocery shopping at more than one store, and because store loyalty has been eroding in the industry, it will be necessary for Clemens to retain customers, and capitalize on their distinct personality of family. Loyalty has eroded because of the difficulty for stores to achieve a distinct personality, the area Clemens has plenty of, in quality, service, and image. For this same reason, and because it has not nationally increased sales, Sunday openings should be discouraged.

Ad content should heavily promote family image, while appearing on those days with most supermarket exposure, Wednesday.

COOPERATION WITH WHOLESALERS

As wholesale prices outpace retail prices for food, retailers must find ways to cut cost. We recommend that Clemens form a closer working relationship with Thriftway Foods, Inc., a subsidiary of the Fleming Co., and Hatfield Packing Co. This should help Clemens to take advantage of economies of scale, increase productivity, and be more responsive to consumer demand. The increased number of items carried by wholesaler makes it necessary for wholesalers and retailers to coordinate advertising, merchandising, and product strategies. The cost saving that this cooperation will **bring** can be translated into increased profits for both the retailer and wholesaler as economies of scale, rising transportation cost, construction cost, and wage cost make it necessary to find more ways to reduce expenses. Clemens can also use the computer facilities of Thriftway Foods to produce various reports for them. Clemens can also use Thriftway's expertise to develop a POS (point of sale) check out system for the future.

NEW TECHNOLOGY:

New equipment such as: four tier frozen food cases, electronic scales, and automatic slicers will help to increase the low productivity of the retail food workers. New techniques such as central breaking and pre-packing meat should also help to cut labor costs, which have been rising at a faster rate than productivity.

The biggest breakthrough, however, has been the introduction of the Universal Product Code (UPC) and Point of Sales (POS) systems. This combination has been hailed as the managers' dream and the greatest innovation to hit retail food stores since the cash register. This system is more expensive than a mechanical system but it offers cost savings and management information which should offset its cost in faster through-put and more efficient operations.

EXHIBIT I

SHORT RANGE OBJECTIVES

* Close the Broad Street store

  * mount effective PR campaign to overcome any adverse reaction

  * refurbish equipment for use in new store

LONG RANGE OBJECTIVES

The <u>primary objective</u> of Clemens is many-faceted. Si Ply stated, it is to:
* Make a profit as measured by a 1% return on sales, while at the same time

  * remaining competitive

  * maintaining a family image

  * providing excellent customer service.

In order for Clemens to achieve these objectives, it is recommended that they undertake the following:

1. Re-organize their corporate structure into a more functional, well defined, efficient organization with more efficient and explicit analytical planning, including such things as store location analysis, layout, new product lines, etc.

2. Make use (or better use) of voluntary co-op organization to increase customer service and reduce costs.

3. Further reduce costs by utilizing new technology such as:

   * point of sale terminals

   * pre-packaged meats

   * new distribution methods

4. Expand internally by expanding product line to include:

   * non-food items

*   deli

*   bakery

*   specialty and prepared food items

EXHIBIT 2

NEW CLEMENS ORGANIZATIONAL CHART

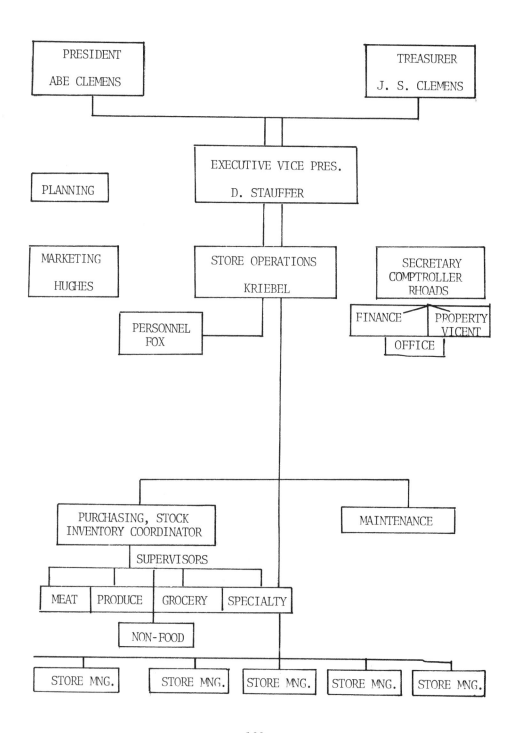

Gulf and Western Industries, Inc.

Purpose

The Gulf and Western Industires case presents the full range of strategic problems. It is designed to bring out the problems of maintaining a pattern of growth in sales and earnings.

Gulf and Western is a conglomerate business organization. The case, therefore, demonstrates the problems facing a highly decentralized, diversified organization. These problems focus on the ability of top management to coordinate the operations of the various subsidiaries owned by Gulf and Western.

This case also demonstrates the problems associated with trying to convince an external group that their strategy is feasible and effective. The objective of the organization is supposedly maximization of shareholders' wealth. To do this, they must maintain a high stock price. This requires investor and especially investment analyst confidence. The external constraints presented in this case are at least as considerable as the internal constraints.

Position in Course

The Gulf and Western case is designed to be presented at the end of the course. The complex and integrative nature of the problems requires a thorough understanding of the strategy formation and implementation process.

Those segments of the course most appropriate include that period when the students are expected to tie together all the concepts of the course. In this respect, the Gulf and Western case provides an ideal vehicle for demonstrating the effectiveness of the matrix approach proposed by the Boston Consulting Group as discussed in the text.

Another area where this case clearly would fit would be concerned with mergers and acquisitions. A major part of the growth strategy followed by Gulf and Western involves growth through external means.

All of these areas, however, are typically presented in the late stages of the course. The complexity of the case, moreover, lends itself to a group effort. Given the size of the organization, a great deal of expertise and time is required to thoroughly analyze and solve the problems faced by Gulf and Western Industries.

Key Issues

1. Problems of maintaining growth in a dynamic orgaa-
    ization.

2. Control and coordination in a conglomerate organ-
    izational form.

3. Necessity of acceptance of organizational strategy
    by external groups.

4. Criteria for mergers and aquisitions for success-
    ful growth.

Analysis

Gulf and Western Industires, Inc., by 1973, is a model
of the conglomerate organizational form. The firm is involved in eight different industry groupings.

This was not always the situation, however. The firm
started offering products in the automobile after parts
market. The present name was adopted in 1967. The modern
form of the organization is the direct result of the thoughts
and values of two men. The dominant role has been played
by Charles Bluhdorn. Assisting him has been John Duncan who
is currently President of G&W.

History: The original base for expansion was the formation of the American Parts System (APS). This group
competed in the spare parts market, primarily with the
National Auto Parts Association, its only real national
competition. Management at G&W proceeded to put together
an organization that manufactured and sold a full range of
automobile spare parts. The primary method used to build
the organization was aquisition or merger.

After 1961, G&W decided to diversify from the auto
parts market. The major switch in emphasis came in 1965.
G&W purchased New Jersey Zinc Company. This increased
sales by almost 50%. More important, it placed the company
in a basic industry. Diversification continued with purchase of firms first in plastics, then into leisure. The
next major aquisition was Paramount Pictures, in 1966.

The two major aquisitions, New Jersey Zinc and Paramount, were looked on with amazement by most analysts. Both
were high risk moves. Both turned out, at least in the
short run, as successes. Sales, and more important, income
rose steadily.

G&W added to basic industries and leisure time products over the next several years. It also diversified into
food, paper and building products and general consumer
products. 1968 marked the entrance into financial services.

The list of subsidiary companies, either wholly or partly owned, is rather lengthy and is outlined in the case. Similarly, a list of officers and directors of the parent is presented in the case.

Merger and Aquisition Criteria:
Two of the more interesting aquisition attempts pursued by G&W are also descriged in the case. They provide examples of the policies followed by top management in seeking mergers or aquisitions.

Madison Square Garden, similar to the earlier G&W aquisitions, seemed like a poor aquisition. It had been losing money. Bluhdorn and Duncan felt it had potential, however. They aquired slightly less than 20% of the stock of the parent. In 1972, G&W decided to boost its holdings to over 20%. Top management felt that the real estate holdings of Madison Square Garden provided tong term potential earnings. The added shares boosted G&W's ownership in Madison Square Garden to 28%. This allowed G&W to include a share of Madison Square Garden's earnings on its income statement. The ownership was described purely as a long term investment, however.

In 1973, G&W management decided to go after the A&P company. A tender was made to increase its share of A&P from 4% to approximately 19%. A&P top management fought the tender through court actions. After consideration, G&W management decided to give up its bid for A&P. It retained the shares it had purchased, on the open market, at a paper profit.

These two situations exemplified the aquisition policies in force at G&W. The primary objectives were to increase sales and earnings. If necessary, however, long term results might necessitate divestiture. A guiding constraint of its aquisition policy included the feeling that active, and vocal, opposition of any move would mean that G&W would back off from any plans.

Mr. Bluhdorn stated that he felt that timing was a key ingredient in aquisitions, however. He felt that management "must move fast when the opportunity presents itself."

G&W was organized into eight operating units. They are:
1. Auto Replacement Parts
2. Consumer Products Group
3. Financial Services Group
4. Food Products Group
5. Leisure Time Group
6. Manufacturing Group
7. Natural Resources Group
8. Paper and Building Products Group

195

Finances:
Although each of the groups drew up its own statements
and budgets, these statements are consolidated at corporate
headquarters. The groups were evaluated on their earnings
and sales growth. The parent share price had improved considerably from the low point of 1972 when stock sold for $10
per share. It still only commanded a price/earnings multiple of 9 on future earnings, however (stock price in
January, 1973, was $55).

The following provides a summary of operating statements:

	1972	1971	1970	1969	1968
Sales (000,000)	$1,670	$1,566	$1,630	$1,564	$1,331
Profits (000,000)	$ 69	$ 56	$ 45	$ 72	$ 70
E.P.S.	3.30	2.63	2.00	3.15	3.13

Current Ratio	2.45	2.41
Acid Test	1.16	.88
D/E	.84	.78
R.O.E.	10.2%	9.0%

Preliminary data for 1973 indicated a sizeable income in
operating results.

Organization:
G&W subsidiaries were organized on a decentralized
basis. Top management at the parent exercised control of
overall objectives. They evaluated subordinates on the
basis of sales and earnings results.

The top managers were characterized as individualists.
They were extremely entrepreneurial by nature. They were
primarily interested in long term, policy oriented decisions. They left operating decisions up to subordinate managers.

Future Operations:
Mr. Bluhdorn felt the future held only opportunities
for G&W. He stated that the firm was free from cyclical
problems. G&W had diversified to the extent that stagnation in one area would be offset by superior gains in
another. He pointed to the economy in 1973 as exemplify-
ing this situation. High interest rates might hurt the
financial group. This inflation would aid natural resources
however. He also felt that the high deby incurred by
the total entity wasn't too much of a burden.

Questions

1.   Evaluate the criteria for mergers and aquisitions
     followed by Gulf and Western Industries.

2. How has Gulf and Western adapted its organization to
    the objectives of a conglomerate?

3. Why has the stock market failed to react to the earn-
    ings preformance of G&W?

Responses

1. G&W proudly bills itself as a conglomerate. The défin-
ition of a pure conglomerate has typically been a firm that
has as its sole objective, increase in earnings per share.
It is not limited by geographic, consumer, product, or
service market.

     In this respect, G&W has held true to the conglomerate
with its aquisition criteria. Unfortunately, this is not
the sole criterion for aquisitions. Mr. Bluhdorn states
that size, in terms of assets and sales, have also been key
criteria.

     Its earnings criteria are interesting from a strategic
point of view. It purchases part or all of companies on
the basis of anticipated results. This is consistent with
good planning practices.

     G&W has the annoying habit of dropping potential aquis-
itions if they are actively, and vocally, opposed by relatively important groups such as regulators or management
of the firm to be aquired. As we state in the text, strategy formation involves selling others on the need for
strategic change. This often leads to a test of wills. The
point is that if the firm feels that a situation is worthy
of investment, it should be willing to fight for that investment decision.

     A secondary criterion for aquisition involves manage-
ment strengths. G&W desires management of aquired companies to be able to operate in a semi-autonomous atmosphere.
Analysis of management strengths, however, takes a back
seat to the potential for future profits for the industry.

2. As G&W has diversified its holdings, it has found it
more difficult to control and coordinate its organization.
Mr. Bluhdorn found early in his strategy that he couldn't
possibly be expert in all investment areas. The decision
by top management was to highly decentralize decision
making.

     Overall financial decisions are made at the corporate
headquarters. Operating decisions are made by group or
subsidiary management, however. G&W has had to rely on managers of aquired firms to continue to operate these organizations.

     G&W has aquired such a large number of firms that it
has had to place them in broadly defined industry groups.

While this allows for a degree of synergism, it also adds a layer of management between corporate headquarters and the subsidiaries. This, along with decentralized decision making, has led to a continuing need for strong, independent managers.

3.   The key problem facing the analysts concerns the believability of G&W financial statements. Earnings in a conglomerate such as G&W are not the same as cash flow. An example would be the investment in Madison Square Garden. While MSG was losing money, G&W held its investment below 20% of MSG stock. This allowed it to only note dividends as earnings on a consolidated income statement. When profits were projected at MSG, Bluhdorn decided to raise the stake in the company to over 20%. This allowed G&W to flow its "share" of earnings straight through to its consolidated statement. This occurred despite the fact that dividends would not be paid for some time.

Earnings per share, a key factor in investment analysis, often did not track well with total earnings. G&W often paid for aquisitions with stock. This leads to problems of comparability of earnings, particularly where convertible issues are used.

Finally, the high leverage position of G&W worries many analysts. Particularly, in this period of high interest rates, this high debt position is very costly. It might be extremely difficult to roll this debt over, if necessary.

The basic complaint has been distrust of the extreme diversification of G&W. This is partly the result of the poor performance of several of the original conglomerates such as LTV and Litton. In this respect, G&W is being hurt by the performance of others. Its own performance has not always been above suspicion, however. The difficulty in evaluating the statements and objectives of a different type of organization, such as G&W, has also led to downplaying the future value of the firm by outside analysts.

SAMPLE STUDENT REPORT

Assignment: Evaluate the current strategy
             facing G&W. Prepare modifications
             for the future.

GULF & WESTERN INDUSTRIES, INC.

Gulf & Western, Inc., ("G&W") is today a large conglomerate (ranked 79th in 1973 Fortune) which is comprised of eight semi-autonomous sub-operating groups. From 1966-1969 G&W grew primarily through acquisition. Since 1970 growth has basically been internal with the acquisition option used when management felt it was justified.

A review of the present G&W environment is important because it sets the parameters of our proposed five-year plan. Internally, we follow a pattern of diversification without concentration. We still have a young and knowledgeable management group, much of which is comprised of personnel from companies we have acquired. These men have the specific knowledge of their industries that we must keep if we are to continue to grow. Management controls 20% of the common shares and another 12 1/2% is owned by five investment companies friendly to management. Thus, we are in a strong position to maintain control of G&W. By providing centralized services such as inventory control, legal expertise, and financial advise to our sub-operating groups, we have been able to eliminate much overlap within these units. Since our current ratio for 1973 is 2.15:1 and our quick ratio is 1.03:1 we feel we are not facing any immediate short-term financing problems. Furthermore, our land holdings, in excess of 1,500,000 acres, give us great flexibility as far as future growth is concerned. Certainly, we face internal problems, one of which is to develop reliance on a strong corporate staff rather than rely primarily on Charles Bludhorn, John Duncan and David Judelson. However, our long-term debt/equity ratio is 1.64:1 which means we are not in a strong position to borrow.

Externally we have several opportunities open to us. With demand for our natural resources such as zinc, wood products, and sugar (sold out through 1975) so strong, we are in a good position to continue growing internally. Also, current EPA regulations indicate a possible source of expansion within our Auto Replacement Parts group. High interest rates pose a real threat to us today, particularly within our Financial Services group. Furthermore, the present image of conglomerates to both the financial district and the federal government is a problem that has hindered us in raising money and in acquiring new companies. Through 1973 we are faced with federal price controls that hinder us in attaining price increases where needed. With the above in mind, we are now able to move onto our statement of objectives.

OBJECTIVES

1. Achieve an annual minimum 15% growth rate in earnings per share.

2. Maintain a 5% increase in sales for the next three years and an 8% increase for the following two years.

3. Increase return on investment at an annual rate of 1/2 of 1%.

4. Develop new top management talent. Achieve a minimum of two capable replacements by 1978 for each executive committee

member.

5. Grow primarily through internal expansion of current holdings with acquisition of new companies not being ruled out. Major emphasis will be placed on the Consumer, Manufacturing, Natural Resources, Paper and Building, Food and Auto Replacement Parts Sectors. We want to reduce our heavy reliance on the Financial Services and Leisure Time Sectors.

6. Increase our precentage of ownership above 20% in selected companies that will increase our consolidated earnings per share figures. Resources for this undertaking will be from the divesture of stocks held in those companies not meeting our standards for consolidation.

In order to achieve our objectives, we intend to implement the following strategies:

1. Automotive Replacement Parts Sector: With the government requiring new environmental control equipment, a whole new field has been opened. For example, the catalytic converter, which will be on 80% of the 1975 automobiles, loses its efficiency with the burning of leaded gasoline. We anticipate a large replacement market and intend to develop a converter and have it available by mid-1975. Further, the expansion of the foreign automotive parts business will be investigated. We have learned that automobile batteries are a scare commodity in Europe. Our manufacturing facility in Italy could be expanded to meet this demand by the end of 1974. Accordingly, we anticipate sales increase of 10% annually over the next five years. This will be aided by the increased demand for automotive parts and greater efficiencies in our distribution and warehousing systems.

2. Natural Resources Sector: G&W will continue to actively explore for new mineral deposits both in the United States and abroad to supplement present reserves. We will also by early 1975 increase plant capacity by 15% if the Cost of Living Council allows us to raise the price of zinc from $.21 1/4 to $.30 per pound. We anticipate a 15% growth rate in operating income for each of the next two years and 5% for each of the following three years.

3. Paper and Building Materials Sector: A 10% increase in annual operating income over the next five years is expected. This will be accomplished through an increased demand for our products due to the existing paper shortage, continued plant renovation, and an increased marketing effort on the more profitable grades of paper.

4. Manufacturing Sector: G&W projects an increase in earnings of 10% to 12% annually over the next two years and thereafter a leveling off at 5%. Increased emphasis on the development and production of components vital to the generation and transmission

of energy will be one of the contributing factors to the attainment of our projection. Continued cost reduction through improved methods in manufacturing procedures will also aid. We look for the passage of the Alaskan Pipeline Bill because we are in an outstanding position to supply pipe and related pumping equipment and would anticipate $50 to $100 million in sales volume directly related to this venture.

5. Leisure Time Sector: By syndicating the Mission Impossible series, we project that Paramount will receive $100,000 in revenue for each of the 150 episodes. We plan to seek the syndication of other successful series for television such as The Brady Bunch, Mannix, Love American Style, and The Odd Couple. We also plan to expand film distribution programs that do not involve the capital risk involved in the production of films and to develop more commercial enterprises for pay television and theater operations. In an effort to reduce downside risk, we plan to seek out more co-investors and co-producers for Paramount. These plans will be implemented in 1974 and can be handled with existing resources. We expect flat to slightly lower earnings for the next two years. Further-out projections are difficult to make due to the uncertainty of the direction of the economy.

6. Financial Services Sector: We plan to complete the development of our on-line computer system which should greatly reduce costs and increase operating income. The cost will be $20,000,000 which has been budgeted and has already been 50% expensed. We plan to develop broadened financial and related services in Europe similar to our arrangements in England by late 1975. Due to high interest rates forecasted for the next two years, we do not anticipate an increase in operating income.

7. Consumer Products Sector: We anticipate increasing our market share in little cigars from 9% to 15% through increased marketing efforts. Increased sales will cover the expense. We also plan to enter the more expensive cigar market through acquisition of interests in South America in 1974. In 1975 we are looking to the development of complementary products to be distributed through present channels. We expect a 2% increase in operating income over the next two years and a 2% to 3% increase thereafter.

8. Food Products Sector: Our plan is to expand our cattle and vegetable operations in the Dominican Republic by 10% which should contribute to their domestic beef supply as well as to a potential export market. Due to heavy demand, we plan to increase our capacity in the production of sugar and its by-products in the Dominican Republic by the cultivation of presently unused acreage, due to be implemented by September 1974. In 1975 we plan to investigate diversification into real estate development such as resorts and condominiums. We presently have substantial real estate holdings but will have to go outside to get expertise in the land-development and land-leasing areas. Our other alternative is to sell the land and let others develop it. We expect an increase

in operating earnings of 8% to 9% per annum over the next five years. Success in diversification efforts could raise this projection to 10% to 12%.

9. Development of a Formal Training Program (Operational by late 1975): We will attempt to insure promotability to the next management level by a formal training program. The program will be hierarchical in nature. Each manager will be evaluated by his superior as to his potential for advancement based on performance and competency. Those showing the greatest potential will be offered the opportunity of formal management training at company expense.

Thus, in spite of the fact that the two most profitable sectors will not be contributing as heavily in the next two years, we believe our efforts in the other sectors should be instrumental in achieving our objectives.

Management In The Future-ORACLE

Purpose and Position in course.

A traditional problem encountered with the case
method has been that all information is dated. The
students find it difficult not to use perfect hind-
sight of what actually happened. Often, they feel
constrained in their analysis and choice of solutions
by this knowledge.

The section under Management in the Future is
designed to overcome these problems. The introductory material presented in the short story "A Sun
Invisible" sets the stage forth assignment. It gives
general background material on the key individuals
in the ORACLE case. The story also describes the
general environment within which organizations must
operate in the year 2519.

The ORACLE case is designed primarily to demonstrate the problems faced by an entrepreneur who is
rapidly losing control of his organization. Operation
s are growing exponentially. The top manager has to
develop an organization strucure to allow for this
growth instead of hinder it.

A side issue in the ORACLE case involves the
development of action guides which subordinates may
follow in dealing with alien environments. Questions
of selection and training of subordinates also arise.

The case should be presented at the latter stages
of the course. It has been used successfully as a
wrap-up case to demonstrate what strategic requirements will be necessary in the future. It also provides a lighthearted finale to, what often is, a
difficult, and heavy course to conceptualize. References should be made to similar situations in the
other cases presented. The top manager at Solar Spice
and Liquors, Mr. Van Rijn, can be likened to Mr. Roth
at Franklin National Bank. The company itself can be
likened to Gulf and Western Industries with its far
flung enterprises.

Analysis.

Mr. Van Rijn, owner of S.S.&L., has just come off
of a successful operation with alien beings who threatened his trading empire. Mr. Van Rijn has operated his
inter-galactic trading company in a highly entrepreneurial node since its inception. He deals exclusively

204

in products that are associated with spices and liquors.
He holds the monopoly rights for trading in these
products, from the Polesotechnic League. It was a
rather tenious monopoly arrangement, however. If he
shows signs of not being able to control and coordinate
his efforts, there will be someone else available to
take over the task-and the monopoly.

The case takes place in the year 2519. O.R.A.C.L.E.
is a consulting group that has been asked to help Mr.
Van Rijn develop policies for future expansion. Since
Mr. Van Rijn only operates on the fringes of explored
space, coordination is extremely difficult. He operates in this highly uncertain area because he feels that
the potentially high rewards justify the high risks
involved. It should also be noted that Mr. Van Rijn
enjoys taking high, but calculated, risks.

One can picture the geographic area in which S.S.
&L. operates by thinking of an apple. At the core of
the apple is the earth. Much of the fruit represents
explored space. If the apple were to have a relatively
thick skin, this would represent the part of space
where S.S.&L. operates. Now think of the apple growing
inexorably, day by day. That volume occupied by the
thick skin would be growing exponentially. This, then,
is at the heart of Mr. Van Rijn's problem. How does
he control and coordinate the activities in his area
of operations.

Several interesting solutions have been posed for
this problem. Typically, students will propose the hiring of more, new factors such as David Falkayn (described in A Sun Invisible). Discussions centering on these
recommendations sent in on several related problems.

1. How to find this type individual?
2. How to select him?
3. How to train him?

Typically, the finding problem centers on raiding
other employers. This is at best a short term solution. An innovative suggestion has been to look at the
ranks of cashiered military officers and non-coms. They
might fit the right requirements.

Once found, a decision must be made as to the
specific individuals to select. Usually, students will
suggest a personality profile of existing factors on
Mr. Van Rijn himself. The problem is that profile
matching looks for norms. The kind of individual
sought is supposed to be one who is extraordinary. He
probably would not fit any norm, even if one could be
put together.

Other suggestions might center on giving the applicants a case study to solve. Those applicants that arrive at the highest number, as well as the most innovative, methods of solving the problem would be selected.

The final problem of training presents the most difficult questions to answer. We are just now starting to attempt to train entrepreneurs in schools of business. We really don't know how successful these efforts will be. Possibly student inputs would be valuable for our own efforts here.

To bring the students back to the present, similarities between Mr. Van Rijn's situation and modern organizations might be noted. It should be pointed out that, in this era of multinational organizations, and rapidly changing environments, the problems faced by Mr. Van Rijn are not all that far-fetched. The students should be aware of these problems, since they may soon be facing them.

ELTON COLLEGE*

Internal Expansion in an Institution of Higher Learning

<u>Analysis</u>

TOPICS FOR DISCUSSION:

Forces promoting internal academic expansion leading to new
courses, new programs, new departments or other divisions; problems
created by rapid expansion in programs, curriculum planning, and faculty and administrator staffing; interpersonal relations among subject
matter specialists; the interaction among "growth minded" faculty ad-
visers, heads or chairmen of departments or other divisions; the
"wisdom" of academic administrators; the role of the Board of Trustees,
and its prerogatives with respect to internal academic development,
plans and policies.

COMMENTARY:

1. As a warm-up exercise, it might be interesting to have some discussion of the possible thinking and action that led to the design of the
business administration program. This might include such topical areas
as the following:

    a) Educational philosophy of a business administration
        education, in general, and in the geographical area
        of influence of the college,

    b) general and specific objectives of the business
        administration program, and

    c) general and specific objectives of each subject area
        indicated.

In terms of action, were catalogs of other colleges and universities examined? Were the officers of the American Association of Collegiate Schools of Business Contacted? Were the needs of businessmen
in the area determined? What weight should be assigned to them? Just
how is a curriculum constructed, and what is the role of the faculty in
the process?

Was the decision to offer the business administration courses at
the Junior and Senior levels, rather than have them integrated with the
arts and sciences courses for four years, the proper one? Why?

---

*Prepared by Associate Professor Roy Ashmen, College of Business
and Public Administration, University of Maryland.

(It is not a purpose of the case to offer a completed curriculum, with specific course titles, with the idea of having students appraise or critize it).

2. In the matter of staffing, such questions as the following may be raised:

   a) Are there cycles in the demand and supply of instructors of business administration, in general? of particular subject areas? Are there long-term trends?

   b) What is the "market place theory" of salary level determination for entry positions? What is the relationship to the salary level of incumbents?

   c) What are the more important correlates of the differences in salary levels at the various institutions of higher learning?

   d) What is the procedure for making openings known to potential candidates for collegiate teaching positions?

   e) What is included in the process of evaluating a candidate and hiring a college teacher?

3. Regarding the uncompleted curriculum for the last half of the Senior year --

   a) What action would you have taken at the faculty meeting in the spring semester: If you had been the Dean? The Division Head? The Chairman of the Faculty Council?

   b) In view of the action taken at the faculty meeting, assume that you have been appointed Chairman of the Special Committee, what would you have your committee members do in the matter of thinking, collecting, material, making contacts, and in writing the report?

   c) What options might Dr. Dyke, Head of the Department, be thinking about prior to receiving the report, and what might some of his thoughts be regarding the possible consequences of selecting one option or another?

   d) Would it be wise for Dr. Dyke to attempt to allay the immediate potential interpersonal relations problem among his faculty members by deciding to offer a course in business policy (including managerial economics) to be taught by himself?

4. Was the operation of the program in business administration started too quickly by the Board of Trustees? (Recall that the first classes need not be started until March 15, 1966). Speculate on the motivation for placing the whole program into operation so quickly. What problems

might this have created for the College? For the new Department?

5. What is the role and function of the Board of Trustees of a College? (As an outside assignment, attempt to answer this question for your particular institution).

Counter Attack on Health Maintenance Organizations

Pupose and Position

This incident is designed to present problems associated with gaining the acceptance of the need for strategic change. It demonstrates the concept that stategy formation is a social/political process as well as an intellectual process. Problems associated with compromising a strategy to get it accepted are also aptly demonstrated with this case.

The case should be used at the early stages of the course. It is designed to be used in a one hour time period. If it is to be used in a longer period, it can be expanded through the use of a role playing session. Different members of the class could be assigned the roles outlined in the incident.

Analysis

A consulting firm, Iconoclast consulting unlimited (I.C.U.) has been asked to submit a proposal for a County Health Reorganization Plan. I.C.U. had computer models it thought would be applicable. It also had a consulting group which had just come off one assignment that could be used immediately on this project. They could give a discount to the Planning Consortium if the contract were signed soon.

The Planning Consortium presented a list of four questions at an initial meeting with I.C.U. members. The members of I.C.U. also sized up the members of the Consortium present at the meeting as to who would be helpful and who would be a hinderance.

After the meeting, I.C.U. drew up a tentative action sequence for the Consortium. They also prepared a proposal using computer models to evaluate the environment for the Consortium.

They found at the next meeting a great deal of resistance to the proposal, the committee members were pleased with the proposal, but the Consortium President was opposed for some reason. I.C.U. stated that any delay would require an increase in the price. The reason for the low price was because of a few week slack period between consulting projects by the I.C.U. health team.

I.C.U., upon evaluating its problems discovered that there was considerable political motivation behind the delay. Questions of resource allocation, minority rights as well as pure political power plays were apparently involved in the decision. I.C.U. was faced with reevaluating the entire project. They had to consider whether they ever felt it worthwhile to continue to pursue the project.

Questions

1. What errors did I.C.U. make in pursuing this project?
2. What alternatives are open to I.C.U. at the end of the case?

Responses

1. The major error that I.C.U. managers committed in pursuing this project was in not doing their homework before the project. They discussed the project with a committee of the Consortium. They failed to consider any other elements than those presented by the committee. They also failed to interview the president of the Consortium who was not a member of the Committee.

Moreover, they failed to even consider the implication of the project on the various constitueacy groups involved. This occurred, despite the fact that much of the funds for any project would come from public sources.

I.C.U. should have at least considered some of these problems when it was first approached. They were, after all, asked to test the validity of a report that had already been submitted by another agency. When this occurs, most consultants would immediately consider the political implications as to why a review was being sought. This was not done until it was too late.

Basically, I.C.U. is looking at planning as an intellectual exercise. The political problems involved are being overlooked. They have to be considered if any recommendations are to have any chance of being implemented. This, of course, assumes they pursue this project and are selected.

2. The alternatives now open to I.C.U. managers are to either pursue or drop the project. If they drop the project, they should fully explain to their backers with in the Consortium why they are following this course of action.

If they pursue the project, the first order of business is to determine all parameters involved. They must realize that all the parameters are not necessarily quantifiable. They don't all fit into neat, computerized models.

The managers at I.C.U. went into the project because they saw an easy way to fill up some slack time. They offered their services cheaply and were then treated the same.

If they pursue the project, they will have to take a more professional attitude. The project should be approached as any other project would be. It should be priced the same as nay other. It should be given the same thorough analysis of the environment that they hopefully give to all projects.

Metal Specialties, Inc.

Purpose and Position

The Metal Specialties, Inc. (MSI) case describes a situation involving poor planning of an expansion move. It should be used to present the integrative nature of the strategy formation process.

It demonstrates how actions in one area of an organization end up affecting the total organization. It also shows the effect of lack of coordination and control in the implementation of strategic change.

The incident described at MSI should be used early in the course. Idealy, it should be used in conjunction with material in the text as the basis for discussion of the above mentioned problems. Those instructors who use a lecture format at the early stages of the course could use this incident as an example for their comments.

Analysis

MSI was a small firm ($1 million sales in 1968) producing a line of proprietary and competitive products. It decided to expand using existing personnel or wider basis. The extra effort was to be rewarded with stock in the new company. The owners, John and Bill Jason believed this was a viable strategy.

The various managers found they could not devote full efforts to both continuing efforts and expansion plans. The new operation, Metal Fabricators, Inc., caused such a drain, that it threatened the financial strength of M.S.I. The creditors required its termination and a turnaround at MSI. Otherwise, they threatened to foreclose.

George Kelly, an "Ivy Leaguer", was brought aboard to strengthen the sales department at MSI. After making some progress at increasing sales, he demanded control of the company and a larger salary.

Subsequent actions by George Kelly brought his motives at the organization into a new light though he knew the firm needed business even at a break even price, he had knowingly bid too high on a large project. It was also learned that George was not utilizing management talents in the sales area.

It was determined that George Kelly's salary would be increased, but that his responsiblities would be shared by a sales committee. George Kelly felt that this was an affront. He soon resigned. His only salesman soon resigned, as well.

One member of the executive committee, intuitively felt something was wrong. He finally figured that George Kelly was trying to steal the company by seeing that losses continued, even at a small rate, until the creditors foreclosed and he could then buy it for its debts.

After George left, the top managers and owners all pitched in to develop sales. Within two months the firm was once again profitable.

The discussion should center on the fortune of the owners to plan their expansion moves. The Jason brothers failed to control and coordinate the efforts of the total organization. They delegated authority without really noting what responsiblities or objectives were expected of subordinates. Communication within the organization only occurs apparently when a crisis develops.

The question of the motives of George Kelly is open to debate. It could be that he really was trying to steal the company. It's also possible that he was simply upset at not being rewarded as well as he believed he should. In any event, the discussion should focus on the planning problems as opposed to Kelly's motives.

THE MEEDIAM BROADCASTING COMPANY ---- Image Change in a Highly Competitive Market*

Analysis

TOPICS FOR DISCUSSION:

Competitive dynamism in a local radio broadcast market; optimum number of radio stations in a market; market segmentation and product differentiation; concept of image, and image measurement techniques (questionnaire, focused group interview, semantic differential and other kinds of rating scales; innovation in radio broadcast programming; broadcasting research, especially radio audience analysis; FM vs. AM radio program formats, and comparative profile analysis of listeners; role of push and pull strategies in station promotion; the buyer-seller dyad in a local market; "canned" sales talk vs. creative selling; recent FCC radio station rulings; radio broadcast station trends (industry statistics).

COMMENTARY:

At the next meeting, the discussion at times became intense as differing points of view were espoused. The following is representative.

It was argued that some change was needed to combat the higher quality of OFTD and its more varied resources. And, that they should emulate some of OFTD's sports and review offerings (despite the fact that this is not original). Also, they might re-institute interspersed "talk" shows. A change in the FM format to music might be tried so that a listener to AM could switch to TEED's FM music offerings when he had heard the news. But how effective would the talk show be and what type of music would best complement the news format. How to integrate into programming?

What to really change to? The news was being swamped by the new competitor. Competition in music stations was even more intense, the field being saturated in this metro market. If the programming was changed, the station might likely lose a good part or even all of its identity.

Changing an image would not be easy, and would take time and money. An attempt to take on OFTD's image may be disastrous. And they were faced with a large, competitive music market. However, TEED may not wish to ignore completely the music market in its problem review as one alternative or partial solution.

_____

*Prepared by Associate Professor Roy Ashmen, College of Business and Public Administration, University of Maryland.

It was pointed out that TEED still had little or no competition in news on the FM band, and in view of the expanding FM market, the FM programming should be kept strong as this market had long-term potential. It was observed that some loss of TEED market position may realistically be in real danger as long as OFTD had significant overlap. Audience prospects for both stations could now be considered substantially similar.

It was suggested that it might be to TEED's advantage to re-allocate the amount of time it devoted to each of the various news segments in an effort to distinguish itself in one field, e.g., national, or local, or international.

When the discussion turned to the sales force, there seemed to be more agreement among the officers. It was believed easier to revamp sales force than to create a new image for the station. No radical change in organization seemed to be needed. The salesmen must be provided with answers and facts to combat OFTD's competitive surge. They should be equipped with up-to-date and relevant selling points to present to prospective customers. Better selling aids than flip charts should be available. How do salesmen answer prospective clients who ask "How much money will your station advertising make for me?"

Regardless of the change in format, if any, salesmen's activities needed to be upgraded. Salesmen must be more attuned to the needs of individual customers, and must design their "pitches" to answer customers' questions (this requires some market research to provide a data base). Canned sales pitches must be eliminated. The sales staff should try to merchandise the station's advertising.

TEED needs to develop perceptual differences between itself and its new "all-news" competitor. One suggestion here was to have salesmen stress the local, more established theme to potential advertisers. Local news and local events could be stressed since TEED is more of a local station than OFTD. The promotional strategy could attempt to increase audience loyalty to TEED. Perhaps the use of a known disc jockey would be useful for local interest. (It is to be immediately noted that this is a reversion to a former practice).

The station could find itself in a position where its best bet would be to disband all AM broadcasting and concentrate in the FM audience market. Some points in favor are: TEED has 20,000 watts as opposed to OFTD's zero; the number of rivals with all-news on FM is reduced; the select (?) type of audience will allow advertisers more concentration of appeals; it would be less difficult to define the type of audience reached. Also, funds from the liquidation could be used for research and program improvement.

Rather than disband AM broadcasting, a less radical move would be to shift emphasis to FM. By putting all its expertise (marketing and management) into the FM band, it might be able to build a unique quality market. If a person has a choice of AM and FM, will he be drawn to the better quality sound, assuming similar programs? Do persons with FM equipment tend to be more affluent? Better informed? (If checked by research, this could be presented to advertisers as a plus factor).

On the other hand, the salesmen could represent the station to re-tailers and other advertisers as broadcasting on both AM and FM, and that this is a distinct advantage. Advertisers could broadcast on two radio stations -- TEED-AM and TEED-FM at no extra charge, thereby reaching two market segments. This assumed simulcasting.

In order to follow an acceptable course of action in its policy formulation and strategic planning, the answers to a number of questions were preferably on the basis of facts obtained by good research and analysis. How should the station allocate or re-allocate its resources? Should more salesmen be added? How should present salesmen be retained? Should the sales force effort be concentrated on large accounts? Why do time buyers in the market assume that the amount of money the station can make for them is calculable? Are methods available to trace sales response to specific radio commercials? What are the characteristics and differences between AM and FM listeners? What is the nature of the advertiser station-switching in the market? Other than programming format, what is the chief competitor doing differently?

In general, what should be the short-run policy and strategic plan of radio station TEED? What are some of the important factors it should take into consideration in its long-run planning?

FINAL COMMENTARY:

The President and other officers of the Meediam Broadcasting Company held a third meeting at which certain steps were taken. After heated discussion and argument had subsided somewhat on the question of changing the image of the station through a change in program format, calmer decision-making prevailed.

The image of an all-news station had been built up over some years and the station still had a large loyal listening audience. It was decided to expand its sources of national and international news by use of an additional wire service and by affiliation with the news service of a radio station group.

Another step was to add a number of part-time local correspondents situated at strategic spots where newsworthy events and ideas arose or could arise.

Station TEED operated on both the AM and FM bands, although its AM operation was about one-fiftieth the power of that of OFTD. The wattage on its FM operation was about 40 percent of OFTD's AM power. The Meediam Broadcasting Company executives decided to apply to the Federal Communication Commission for an increase in FM station power to equal the AM power of OFTD. Although it took some time for this to be approved, it finally came through. TEED's AM station operated only in daytime; sign-on was at sunrise, and sign-off at sunset. However, this allowed it to reach the commuting group driving to and from work. Furthermore, its use of a simulcast system enabled the newscasts on its AM station to be carried as far as that of OFTD's via its FM broadcast system. Its FM broadcasting was on a 24 hour basis. The station covered both local and national news at least twice during each hour, averaging about 15 minutes each at a time, with local starting about quarter after the hour and national and international at half on the hour. In addition, it added features and commentators and included some name newscasters weekday mornings. The all-news program of the AM station is simulcast in the daytime and continues through the night with the FM.

(It may be of interest to note that in 1973 the FCC, in a move to encourage more voices and diverse programming, ruled that an AM station could duplicate only 50 percent of its programming on FM, the same ruling it had set aside in 1972 to permit classical music stations to survive).

FAIRFIELD FOODS, INC.

Role of Top Executives in Advertising Agency Selection

ANALYSIS

TOPICS FOR DISCUSSION:

The concept of an advertising agency; evaluation of agency services; selection of a new agency; executive involvement in the advertising process and client-agency relations; advertising campaign management and implications for the "marketing concept."

BACKGROUND COMMENTARY:

1. An advertising agency has been defined as " an independent business organization composed of creative and business people who develop, prepare and place advertising in advertising media for sellers seeking to find customers for their goods and services.

The way the advertising normally receives its compensation is distinct from other consulting organizations. The commission system is still the traditional and most widely used method of compensating advertising agencies. Agencies pay for space and time used on behalf of advertisers at the "card rate" less a certain discount, usually 15% and bill them at the card rate. Thus it appears that agencies receive their basic compensation from advertising media rather than from advertisers. But it is the advertiser who pays the agency the total amount the agency receives. Hence it may be a mistake to say media pay agencies. The money agencies deduct from advertisers' payments in the form of media commissions is never in the hands of any medium. The medium simply allows the agency to make the deduction.

2. The modern, and especially larger, advertising agencies perform not only the strictly advertising services such as copy writing, art work, production, time and space procurement, advertisement placement, and so on, but other promotion and marketing services. These include sales promotion, publicity and public relations, aid in stimulating reseller effort, package design or redesign, creation of merchandise displays, and marketing research, among others. The larger agency is enabled to be objective in its counsel and free of captive opinion. It can develop marketing knowledge and skills in any and all areas of business and apply them to develop the opportunities facing advertisers. It can truly be a partner with the client in sharing and implementing the "marketing concept."

Prepared by Associate Professor Roy Ashmen, College of Business and Management, University of Maryland.

3. With regard to the evaluation and selection of advertising agencies, a survey of 400 executives in companies using agencies revealed the following:

Evaluation of a New agency includes
the participation of the:

        Advertising directors in . . . . .   89%   of the companies
        Presidents in. 70%
        Sales managers in. 54%
        Executive V-P in 48%
        Marketing directors in 43%
        Sales promotion managers in. . . .   29%
        Public relations directors in. . .   18%
        Product managers in. 14%

The responsibility for selection of
a new agency rests with the:

        President in . . . .   35%   of companies
        Advertising directors in 30%
        Sales directors in 11%
        Management committees in 8%
        Executive V-P in 6%
        Marketing directors in 5%
        Board chairman in. 3%
        Public relations directors in. . .   2%

According to the results of this study, several executives in most companies participated in the actual evaluation. But the final agency selection usually was made by an individual -- most often the president, and next most often the highest advertising executive. This then turns out to be a top level decision. Furthermore, more than a third of the respondents indicated that they re-evaluated their present agency's services constantly, continually, or every day, and 44% said that their companies conducted annual formal reviews of the agency's contribution to the total marketing effort. ("How Agencies Find New Business," Printers' Ink, June 10, 1960, pp. 35-38).

4. The use of a checklist in selecting an advertising agency is not uncommon. Some companies use a rating scale with rating points adding to 100. Criteria are grouped under several headings as, for instance, agency history, marketing services, and handling of the remainder of the points is divided approximately between the other two categories. Items under marketing services might be creative, media, sales promotion, merchandising, production, research, product publicity, and campaign planning. Other items might be manpower, experience, contact, growth, and marketing concept. Some companies study the product and account history.

5. The possible loss of a good client is always of concern to an agency. Thus an agency should be sensitive (most are) to signs of an

advertiser's dissatisfaction with its performance. The agency must constantly subject itself to certain acid test questions: Does it have all the skills needed or wanted? Is it giving the service expected? Does it have enough offices for client's purposes? What is the track record on creative ideas that worked? What is behind client's rejection of agency recommendations, if so? Why is it getting harder to come to agreement on work, if so? If client is not spending enough money for advertising, why not? Does client think agency is making too much money for services given? Is client getting too many services for the money? When client's sales decline, what can agency do to prevent becoming a scapegoat? And many more. Advertising is a highly personal business and the personal relationships are at the center of client-agency relations. People work closely together and often under great pressure, striving for results within a limited time period. If the creative type person is more volatile than others, friction can develop with the resulting loss of harmony and the subsequent search for a new advertising agency. Of course, a change in management of a company can also result in the desire to have a new agency for one reason or another.

CASE COMMENTARY:

1. Fairfield Foods, Inc., a large processor and canner of fruits and vegetables, has developed and tested a new fruit juice blend "NEKTA Punch" to be marketed. As the performance of the company's advertising agency has been questioned, the president has directed that new agencies be considered to handle the company's advertising. Several agencies have made presentations and a report has been prepared.

2. The student can readily note and select the advantages and disadvantages of the several candidate advertising agencies (See Exhibit I). A solution which offers a straight listing of the pro's and con's and a decision regarding which agency to select is necessary but not sufficient. The longer term matters and larger issues pertain to the company organization and policy formulation as well as the role of executives.

3. The case lends itself to a written assignment outside of class. If so used, the following format may be specified. Analyses and solutions will vary. (See Exhibit II).

EXHIBIT I

ADVANTAGES AND DISADVANTAGES OF EACH AGENCY

Advantages:

A. Agency A

1. High rating for originality
2. Possess considerable creative potential
3. High on efficiency
4. Direct association with a radio and television organization

B. Agency B

1. A creative agency
2. Rapport the highest of the five
3. Excellent performance on clients' accounts

C. Agency C

1. Best man of agency would serve as Fairfield's account executive
2. A reliable group with which to be associated
3. Impressive account management area
4. Had excellent rapport with Fairfield's executives
5. Virtual non-turnover of personnel
   a. Implies qualified personnel
   b. Also implies personnel are pleased with their positions
6. Had exceptional knowledge and ability in the media field
7. Special assignments could be handled to complete satisfaction

D. Agency D

1. President impressive
   a. The creative head
   b. A leader in thought as well as authority
   c. Well prepared to discuss almost any facet of advertising
2. Personnel well qualified
   a. Executive vice president knows his job in account management
   b. Proposed account supervisor showed keen interest in precise, analytic expression with a lack of pretense
   c. The creative director combines creative writing with art ability
      1) He is given credit for most successful advertising campaign for a new line of women's cosmetics
3. Agency is capable of determining the communication problem and developing something worthwhile and saying it in a way that will interest the market you are trying to reach
4. Other corporations had high praise for agency

5. High in top management efficiency as well as rapport
6. Personnel turnover is stable
7. Seems adequately staffed to cater to Fairfield's versatilities
8. Has a fine caliber of performance on their present accounts

E. Agency E

1. Fairfield's present agency
2. Been with Fairfield Foods, Inc. for twelve years

Disadvantages:

A. Agency A

1. Creative head is uncertain about the amount of time to allot
    to Fairfield Foods, Inc
2. Quality of leadership might well be on the whimsical side
3. Creative potential would seem to have limitations for Fairfield
4. Media planning potential seems questionable

B. Agency B

1. Approach to things does not have the probity and penetration
    of other agencies
2. Were a bit haphazard about the points they made and conclusions
    they drew
3. Advertising ideas really did not take any direction
4. Originality of thinking not as strong as other agencies
5. Potential for leadership not impressive
6. Top management efficiency not as high
7. Media capacity and flexibility of services only adequate

C. Agency C

1. Possibly too young to meet all of Fairfield's needs
2. Client account handling not considered to be outstanding

D. Agency D

1. No apparent bad points are presented

E. Agency E

1. Proposal had little to do with effective advertising
    a. Failed to relate to development of a broad dynamic
        advertising campaign
2. Large personnel turnover
3. New creative director seems devastatingly unsuited for his
    new broader responsibilities
    a. Presentation was nothing new but was derived from a
        two year old speech
    b. Seemed to dodge the challenge of speaking for Fairfield
        though advertising in a way that would distinguish it
        to the consumers

4. Marketing statement appeared to drown the advertising proposal
5. New copywriter assigned to Fairfield was not present at the agency's presentation
6. Lack of coordination between agency and company
7. Agency's contribution to company during last two years was less than satisfactory
8. Copy staff deteriorating

EXHIBIT II

AN EXAMPLE OF A WRITTEN CASE SOLUTION

FAIRFIELD FOODS, INC.

1. Statement of the Problem: Should the Fairfield Foods Company choose one of the advertising agencies presented, given the data presented by the advertising director and the present status of their marketing organization and, if so, which one should they chose.

2. Decision: Fairfield Foods, Inc. should concentrate their efforts on establishing an effective overall marketing organization, listing their marketing objectives and strategies, and, while this is being accomplished, retain the services of Agency "D".

3. Analysis:

Advantages:

A. Some of the basic questions which can not now be answered, but for which answers are necessary for the effective operation of both the marketing and advertising programs include:

(1) What are the basic marketing objectives of the firm (sales volume) and how do they relate to both the corporate objectives at one end of the spectrum and the advertising objectives at the other?
(2) What will be the specific objectives of the advertising program, its strategies, and what specific skills are necessary to accomplish both these goals and those of the overall marketing program?

(a) In this respect the criteria established by Adams is a good attempt at defining the qualities an agency must possess to perform satisfactorily for Fairfield Food. The criteria do not appear to contain any objective measures for evaluating proposed advertising plans.
(b) Since $50K is to be spent on the commercialization of "NEKTA PUNCH" its place in the overall advertising scheme would be necessarily explained in the written objectives and strategies.
(c) Since the firm has no marketing research organization, it might be best to evaluate each agency in that department.

B. Given the lack of stated objectives and strategies it could be assumed that they were there and had been considered in establishing the criteria. Regardless, it appears necessary to choose a new agency given the dissatisfaction with (1) the previous method of choosing and

224

(2) past performance. Competition will not allow the firm to wait on deficiencies in the internal organization.

C. Evidence that the incumbent agency is not giving adequate attention to the firm's requirements include:

(1) Change-over in account executives
(2) Apparent inability of new account executive to work with groups of people having divergient views.
(3) Inability of agency's management to keep its word.

D. Advantages of Agency "D" over others include:

(1) Apparently Mr. Bowers is an excellent account executive and, since he is a fourth partner, should remain fairly stable.
(2) Excellent rapport between agency and firm
(3) Good media ability allows satisfactory handling of special assignments
(4) Agency "A" does not appear to be as solid in overall planning.
(5) Agency "B" lacked so many of the criteria as to preclude it:

(a) leadership is not adequate
(b) lack of direction, something the firm needs
(c) inability to establish turnover rates

(6) Agency "C" clearly is the only competitor to the chosen one. They have the best account man and were equal to agency "D" in all except creative ability.

DISADVANTAGES:

A. It does not appear that Mr. Adams has any method of evaluating the effects each agency will have on sales volume other than an overall, hopefully beneficial, trend. The subjective nature of the criteria precludes the really effective analyzing of different proposals.

(1) There is a possibility that the speed of the decision would result in choosing the wrong agency thus necessitating change again in the near future with the resultant loss of continuity. (Therefore, keep present agency and continue to look?)
(2) A poor advertising effort might reduce the effectiveness of the new product.

B. Agency "C" does have the best account man and is almost equal in other aspects to agency "D". Finally, it was Mr. Adams who allowed the situation to deteriorate to its present level. It might be better to get a marketing director and incorporate all marketing efforts into one division. It is fairly obvious that this needs to be accomplished and that a good competent man might be able to turn around the firms sales trend by introducing new techniques.

4. Conclusion: It is apparent that the time is not there to allow a

complete reorganization prior to choosing an advertising agency. The immediate problem is to choose an agency and attempt to get a cohesive program launched. During this time however, it will still be necessary to organize the marketing functions under one division and hopefully get some more objective standards for evaluating performance. At this point in time, given the criteria and data presented by Adams, agency "D" is superior in most respects to the others.

5. Recommendation: Fairfield Food Inc. should immediately notify Agency "E" that its services are no longer required and retain the services of Agency "D". At the same time the President should start a search for a marketing executive to head the marketing division of Fairfield Foods, Inc. This individual should be given responsibility for establishment of objectives and strategies for these subelements.

SAVOR STORES, INC.

Information Search Prior to Purchase and
Capital Investment

Analysis

TOPICS FOR DISCUSSION:

Classification of industrial goods; models of industrial purchasing; defining the specific industrial purchasing task; the information search process; making the purchasing decision; new task, unique procurement, capital investment, and the role of major executives.

BACKGROUND COMMENTARY:

Classification of Industrial Goods

Each year a vast array of industrial goods are used either directly or indirectly in the production and distribution of other goods and services by many industries. One way to summarize the aggregation of industrial goods is to classify them as follows:

A. Capital Goods
    1. Installations
    (a) buildings and land rights
    (b) major equipment
        (i) custom-made
        (ii) standard
    2. Accessory equipment
        (tools and equipment that facilitate
        production or office activities)

B. Expense Items
    1. Components and materials
        (a) raw materials
        (b) component parts and materials
    2. Supplies - maintenance, repair and
        operating supplies
        (MRO items)
    3. Services

In general, the nature of the demand for industrial goods is different in many respects from the demand for consumer goods. Some of the major differences between the general industrial market and the general consumer market could be enumerated by students. In this way,

_____

This teaching note was prepared by Associate Professor Roy Ashmen of the University of Maryland.

some of the interesting and significant contrasts could be brought out.

General Models of the Industrial Purchasing Process

At this point in time there are only a few models of the industrial buying process available in the literature. Two recently published models are discussed in this section beginning with one devised by Webster.

Webster's Model

In connection with his concern about the lack of an industrial buyer behavior "theory," Webster has developed a model of the industrial buying process which he feels is only the start toward rationalization of the industrial buying process.[1] According to Webster (as noted above) plenty of descriptive detail is available concerning the industrial buying process, however, a model is presently needed to structure this information so that important variables and causal relationships can be identified.[2] In Webster's model the buying process is separated into four segments which are described in summary below:

(1) Problem Recognition – A buying situation is created by the recognition of a problem which can be solved when there is a perceived difference between goals and actual performance, and can be caused by a change in either goals or performance. Goal-setting and problem recognition are influenced by personnel and impersonal factors, both internal and external to the buying organization. . . .

(2) Buying Responsibility – Buying decisions are made by individuals working as part of an organization. The assignment of buying responsibility is influenced by industry, company, market, product, and individual factors. . . .

(3) The Search Process – Individuals have more or less routine methods for gathering information for the purposes of identifying alternative problem solutions and establishing criteria for evaluating buying alternatives. Search can result in a change in goals, and goals serve as selection criteria. As search becomes more complex and considers new information sources, it also becomes more costly. Cost and time factors constrain the amount of research.

(4) The Choice Process – The final stage in

industrial buying decision is the selection
of one or more suppliers. The choice process
is closely related to the search process--
the order in which alternatives are
identified influences the final decision.
. . . (This last segment consists of three
stages: vendor qualification, comparing
offerings with specifications, and comparing
offerings with each other).[3]

Regarding work involved in constructing a general model, Webster,
has stated that

. . . (his) attempt to construct a generalized
model of industrial buying behavior was
frustrated by the basic complexity of the process
and led to a conclusion that each of the several
stages of the buying process--problem recognition,
research, evaluation of alternatives, and choice--
could best be attacked individually.[4]

Attention will now be turned to a second general model of the
organizational buying process.

Marketing Science Institute Model

A more recent analytical framework of the industrial buying process has been formulated by Robinson, Faris, and Wind in connection
with a research study of three manufacturing firms sponsored by the
Marketing Science Institute.[5] They have entitled their model the
Buygrid Framework. This model has been widely used in the literature
subsequent to its publication. The basic framework is shown in Figure
1 below.

FIGURE 1

The Buygrid Analytic Framework for
Industrial Buying Situations

	Buy Classes		
Buy Phases	New Task	Modified Rebuy	Straight Rebuy
1. Anticipation or recognition of a problem (need) and a general solution.			
2. Determination of characteristics and quantity of needed item.			
3. Description of characteristics and quantity of needed item.			
4. Search for and qualification of potential sources.			
5. Acquisition and analysis of proposals.			
6. Evaluation of proposals and selection of supplier(s).			
7. Selection of an order routine.			
8. Performance feedback and evaluation.			

Source: Patrick J. Robinson, Charles W. Faris, and Yoram Wind, Industrial Buying and Creative Marketing (Boston: Allyn & Bacon, Inc., 1967), p. 14.

In the Buygrid Framework, buying situations (buy classes), are separated into three categories: new task, modified rebuy, and straight rebuy. The characteristics which distinguish these categories are (1) newness of the problem to the buying influences and decision-makers, (2) information requirements of the buying influences and decision-makers, and (3) new alternatives given serious consideration by the buying decision makers.

The new task situation is the most complex and challenging buying situation involving the greatest number of buying influences and decision-makers, the greatest need for information and the widest consideration of alternatives. On the other hand, the straight-rebuy situation involves no consideration of new alternatives, the problem is not new and very little information is required. The modified-rebuy situation lies between the other two in terms of problem newness, information requirements, and consideration of alternatives.

Also, in the Buygrid Framework, the fundamental activities of the procurement process are divided into eight buy phases as shown in Figure 1 above. Some of the phases may occur simultaneously but, they tend to follow in sequence. It may be difficult in practice to determine precisely where one phase ends and another begins. Sometimes a redefinition of the problem will occur which will cause a recycling of the buy phases process.

In a straight rebuy situation the **buy** phases are passed through rapidly and routinely while in the modified rebuy situation **the** phases are passed through less rapidly, and in the new task case the phases are least rapidly covered.

In general, during the early phases of the buying process, key roles are played by corporate staff personnel. Supervisory personnel in the using department play key roles when the decision process moves to where the requirements become more explicit. The purchasing department normally plays the major role when negotiations with vendors are initiated.

CASE COMMENTARY:

It would seem that Savor's information search was extremely thorough. Six months after the storage system was in use, all persons concerned were extremely pleased with the racks and the new storage facility in general. They were proud of the decision process that led to the purchase from Stak-Rite. (Whether the passage of time will inject qualifications into the situation or even dissatisfaction remains to be seen).

The study team engaged in an information search not only to make a purchase decision and a capital investment but to solve a problem. The uniqueness of the purchase for Savor removed the decision from the scope of purchasing or procurement per se.

In order to solve the storage problem, Mr. George had to become somewhat knowledgable in the area of warehousing. His search for information, though rather unstructured, was highly instrumental. He was unfamiliar with the area. Would it have been possible for him to have provided more structure to the information search? Trade journals are a valuable source of information in such a situation. Yet Mr. George consulted only one Journal, Material Handling Engineering. However, he did make good use of personal contacts, the Materials Handling Institute Trade Show, and visits to storage installations to inspect various techniques and equipment in use. As a result, Mr. George did learn a great deal about warehousing, which is what he had set out to do.

Once the decision was made to stick with conventional materials handling equipment and some sort of rack storage system, the pre-purchase activity became highly structured. Requests for initial bids were sent to 18 of the 22 Rack Manufacturer's Institute members. The exclusion of only four manufacturers from consideration may be considered indicative of the overall thorough search for information. Eleven vendors submitted initial bids. One, with an exhorbitant bid, and one who had not given enough information, were then eliminated. In making the cut from nine to five, the company depended almost exclusively on the knowledge and experience of Mr. Borgman. The quality of the decision-making process at this stage rested entirely on Mr.

231

Borgman's evaluation of the various vendor's products. This is easily the point at which Savor had least control over the decision.

The study team then visited five installations; and, after seeing Stak-Rite's product, stopped considering any other vendor. The opinion may be ventured that this is the weakest point in all the pre-purchasing decisions in this case.

By asking for a final bid from Stak-Rite, Savor was able to obtain: (1) a $30,000 reduction in cost from the initial bid and, more importantly, (2) new ideas for the design of the storage system with the objective of more efficiency and flexibility in operations.

Again, it seems important to stress that Savor had set out not to make a purchase but actually to solve a problem -- a storage problem. Problem solving of this type requires ideas. The final negotiating period between vendor and purchaser is often an excellent source of new and original design ideas. Yet Savor severely limited its source of these ideas by only taking one vendor into this final negotiating stage.

All told, the information search process, from start to placement of the order, took a little over one year and a half.

FOOTNOTES

[1] Frederick E. Webster, "Modeling the Industrial Buying Process," Journal of Marketing Research, Vol. II (November 1965), pp. 370-76.

[2] Ibid., p. 375.

[3] Ibid., p. 375. (Webster has indicated specific research needs and opportunities in connection with each segment in his model.)

[4] Frederick E. Webster, Jr., "Industrial Buying Behavior: A State of-the-Art Appraisal," in Jack L. Taylor, Jr. and James F. Robb (Eds.) Fundamentals of Marketing: Additional Dimensions, Selections from the Literature (New York: McGraw-Hill Book Company, 1971), p. 207.

[5] Patrick J. Robinson, Charles W. Faris, and Yoram Wind, Industrial Buying and Creative Marketing (Boston: Allyn & Bacon, Inc., 1967). Research data from a fourth firm was included from Wind's dissertation which emphasized source loyalty.

APPENDIX 1 TO CHAPTER 7

SOLUTION TO PROBLEM I

The following are the calculations needed for arriving at Net Present Value (NPV) decisions:

Year	NPV of $1 Received in Year ...	Net Present Value of Returns Strategic Move A	Strategic Move B	Strategic Move C
1	.9346	$ 14,019	$ 46,730	$28,038
2	.8734	39,303	34,936	21,835
3	.8163	48,978	20,407.5	16,326
4	.7629	41,959.5	15,258	11,443.5
		$144,259.5	$117,331.5	$77,642.5
Initial outlay		−100,000	−125,000	−75,000
Net present value		$ 44,259.5	−$ 7,668.5	$ 2,642.5

If only one strategic move can be chosen, A should be the one. If resources are not that limited, A and C should both be followed, since they both offer positive net present values, i.e., they both offer returns greater than the cost of capital to the firm.

APPENDIX 2 TO CHAPTER 7

SOLUTION TO PROBLEM II

P = Probability
Worst = Worst outcome
Best = Best outcome
Res = Research
A = product A
B = product B
EV = Expected Value

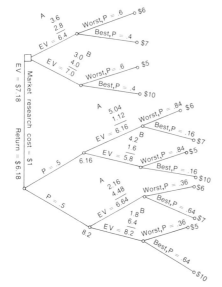

Product B with no
market research provides
the best solution.

$P[\text{Worst}] = .6 \qquad P[\text{Best}] = .4$
$P[\text{Res A/Worst}] = .7$
$\therefore P[\text{Res B/Worst}] = .3$
$P[\text{Res B/Best}] = .8$
$\therefore P[\text{Res A/Best}] = .2$

$$P[\text{Worst/Res A}] = \frac{.7 \times .6}{(.7 \times .6) + (.2 \times .4)}$$

$$= .84$$

$\therefore P[\text{Best/Res A}] = 1 - .84 = .16$

$$P[\text{Worst/Res B}] = \frac{.3 \times .6}{(.3 \times .6) + (.8 \times .4)}$$

$$= .36$$

$\therefore P[\text{Best/Res B}] = 1 - .36 = .64$

Alt. 1 $\begin{cases} .6 \times 6 = 3.6 \\ \qquad\quad + \; = 6.4 = EV \\ .4 \times 7 = 2.8 \end{cases}$

Alt. 2 $\begin{cases} .6 \times 5 \; = 3.0 \\ \qquad\quad + \; = 7.0 = EV \\ .4 \times 10 = 4.0 \end{cases}$

Alt. 3a $\begin{cases} .84 \times 6 = 5.04 \\ \qquad\qquad + \; = 6.16 \times .5 = 3.08 \\ .16 \times 7 = 1.12 \end{cases}$

Alt. 3b $\begin{cases} .84 \times 5 \; = 4.20 \\ \qquad\qquad + \; = 5.80 \\ .16 \times 10 = 1.60 \end{cases}$

Alt. 3c $\begin{cases} .36 \times 6 = 2.16 \\ \qquad\qquad + \; = 6.64 \\ .64 \times 7 = 4.48 \end{cases}$

Alt. 3d $\begin{cases} .36 \times 5 \; = 1.80 \\ \qquad\qquad + \; = 8.20 \times .5 = 4.10 \\ .64 \times 10 = 6.40 \end{cases}$

Alt. 3a + Alt. 3d = 7.18
Alt. 3 − cost of information =
7.18 − 1 = 6.18

STRATANAL

The STRATANAL program discussed in the text is presented below. The program listing is one that has been used on a Control Data Corporation 6400. It requires a on line, interactive, time share mode to operate.

The only user requirement is knowledge of the case being analyzed. The program will ask a series of questions, depending on user responses, the program will either follow a predetermined series of questions or present a series of optional questions.

All responses must be made on one line. If a series of responses is requested for a question, this will be noted by a number preceeding the line of the response.

The only word not allowed in a general response is the work "NONE". This is because the word "NONE" is reserved for a special purpose. If the user feels he has answered a particular question to the best of his ability, he may type in the word "NONE" and the program will proceed to the next question.

The program can be used with any corporate strategy oriented case.

The program will have to be used in conjunction with the job cards in use at the computer center utilized. A programming consultant at the computer facility should be able to provide these easily.

```
      PROGRAM PROG1(INPUT=101B,OUTPUT=101B,TAPE98=101lB,              000100
     1TAPE5=INPUT,TAPE6=OUTPUT)                                       000110
      DIMENSION TTS(10)                                               000120
      LOGICAL INDEX,SWITCH                                            000130
      INTEGER R(13,21),F(10,7)                                        000140
      LOGICAL INDEX,SWITCH                                            000130
      INTEGER R(13,21),F(10,7)                                        000140
      INTEGER W(18,2),TTS                                             000150
      INTEGER PI                                                      000160
      INTEGER B(101)                                                  000170
      INTEGER T,IA,IS,TI,G,H,Q                                        000180
      DIMENSION G(3)                                                  000190
      INTEGER NONE(5),SEED,X(10),STRT                                 000200
C     STRT IS FILE STRATEGY                                           000210
      INTEGER QSTN                                                    000220
C     QSTN IS THE QUESTION FILE                                       000230
      INTEGER TYPE                                                    000240
C     TYPE IS THE TYPEWRITER UNIT                                     000250
      INTEGER KEYB                                                    000260
C     KEYB IS THE KEYBOARD UNIT                                       000270
      INTEGER RESP                                                    000280
C     RESP IS THE LINE NUMBER IN THE RESPONSE FILE                   000290
C     THE INTEGER IDENTIFERS *QSTN* AND *RESP* ARE THE               000300
C     MAJOR INDEXES TO THE PORTIONS OF THE WORKING DATA SET          000310
C     FOR THE QUESTION FILE AND THE RESPONSE FILES RESPECTIVELY      000320
C     THEY SHOULD NOT BE CHANGED.                                    000330
      INTEGER PMT                                                     000340
C     THE CHARACTER THAT PRINTS AS AN *O* IS A BACKSPACE             000350
      LOGICAL LINE(133)                                              000360
      INTEGER AA(5)                                                   000370
      INTEGER AA1,AA2,AA3,AA4,AA5                                     000380
      EQUIVALENCE (AA(1),AA1),(AA(2),AA2),(AA(3),AA3),(AA(4),AA4)     000390
      EQUIVALENCE (AA(5),AA5)                                         000400
      DIMENSION H(5)                                                  000410
      DIMENSION Q(13)                                                 000420
```

236

```
      C     RESP IS THE RESPONSE FILE                            000430
            COMMON TT,TTS,W,T,B,AA,KEY,F,H,R,G                    000440
            COMMON Q                                              000450

 40         DATA NONE/4,1HN,1HO,1HN,1HE/                          000460
            DATA SEED/43921/                                      000470
            DATA STRI/98/                                         000480

            DATA QSTN/0/                                          000490
            DATA TYPE/6/                                          000500
            DATA KEYB/5/                                          000510

 45         DATA TYPE/6/                                          000500
            DATA KEYB/5/                                          000510
            DATA RESP/1001/                                       000520

            DATA PMT/2H   /                                       000530
                                                                  000540
      C                                                           000550
      C     FORMATS
 902        FORMAT (1XI2,*:      *)                               000560
 903        FORMAT (* LIST THE MAJOR ASPECTS OF ANOTHER ALTERNATIVE*/) 000570
 904        FORMAT (1X)                                           000580

      C                                                           000590
      C     INITIALIZE                                            000600
            CALL INITIAL                                          000610

            G(1)=0                                                000620

            G(2)=0                                                000630
            G(3)=0                                                000640

            H(1)=0                                                000650
            H(2)=0                                                000660
            H(3)=0                                                000670

            H(4)=0                                                000680
            H(5)=0                                                000690
 65         DO 1 K=1,13                                           000700

  1         Q(K)=0                                                000710
            T=1                                                   000720
            II=1                                                  000730

            TA=1                                                  000740
            TS=1                                                  000750
 70         WRITE (TYPE,1710)                                     000752
```

237

```
1710 FORMAT(*0WELCOME TO TEMPLE STRATANAL.*/* PLEASE PICK A NUMBER*,    000754
    1* FROM 1-99999 AND ENTER IT (HERE).*/2H *)                        000756
         READ (KEYB,1720) SEED                                          000758
   C                                                                    000759
1720 FORMAT(I5)                                                         000760
         CALL UNIF(SEED)                                                000770
   C                                                                    000780
   2     CONTINUE                                                       000790
         DO 20 KEY=2,44,2                                               000800
         WRITE (TYPE,904)                                               000810
         CALL IXGSTR(B,QSTN,KEY)                                        000820
         CALL RDWDS(KEY+1,AA,LENGTH)                                    000830
1001 FORMAT (*KEY=*,I3)                                                 000840
   C     AA(5) IS PRE ANALYSIS                                          000850
         GO TO (101,102,103,104,105,106,107,108,109),AA5               000860
   C     OUTPUT QUESTION                                                000870
   C                                                                    000880
 101     Y(1)                                                           000890
         CALL PUTSTR(B,TYPE)                                            000900
         GO TO (101,102,103,104,105,106,107,108,109),AA1               000910
   C                                                                    000920
 102     Y(2)                                                           000930
         CALL IXGSTR(B,QSTN,KEY+50)                                     000940
         CALL PUTSTR(B,TYPE)                                            000950
         AA(1)=5                                                        000960
         AA(2)=16                                                       000970
         AA(3)=16                                                       000980
         AA(4)=16                                                       000990
         IF (AA(5).EQ.7)AA(5)=8                                         001000
         IF (AA(5).EQ.8)AA(5)=7                                         001010
         GO TO (101,102,103,104,105,106,107,108,109),AA5               001020
   C     INPUT ANSWER                                                   001030
   C                                                                    001040
 103     Y(3)                                                           001050
         CALL GETSTR(B,KEYB)                                            001060
         CALL PUTSTF(B,RESP)                                            001070
         I=I+1
         CALL ANALYS(AA(2),B)
         CALL ANALYS(AA(3),B)
         GO TO 20
```

```
C        Y(4)                                          001080
104      W(TA,1)=T                                     001090
         DO 1041 J=1,10                                001100
         WRITE (TYPE,902) J                            001110
         CALL GETSTR(B,KEYB)                           001140
         WRITE (TYPE,904)                              001150
         IF(.NOT.INDEX(B,NONE))GO TO 1043              001160
         IF(J.LT.3.AND.AA(2).EQ.10)GO TO 40            001170
         W(TA,2)=T                                     001180
         TA=TA+1                                       001190
         GO TO 20                                      001200
1043     CALL ANALYS(15,B)                             001210
         CALL PUTSTF(B,RESP)                           001220
         T=T+1                                         001230
         CALL ANALYS(AA(2),B)                          001240
         CALL ANALYS(AA(3),B)                          001250
         GO TO 1041                                    001260
C        FOUR                                          001270
40       CALL IXGSTR(B,QSTN,KEY+50)                    001280
         CALL PUTSTR(B,TYPE)                           001290
C        SEVEN                                         001300
1041     CONTINUE                                      001310
         W(TA,2)=T                                     001320
         IA=IA+1                                       001330
         GO TO 20                                      001340
C        Y(5)                                          001350
105      DO 1051 I=1,10                                001360
         IF (I.GT.1)WRITE (TYPE,903)                   001370
         X(I)=TS                                       001380
         DO 1052 J=1,10                                001390
         WRITE (TYPE,902) J                            001400
         CALL GETSTR(B,KEYB)                           001430
         WRITE (TYPE,904)                              001440
         IF (.NOT.INDEX(B,NONE))GO TO 1053             001450
         IF(J.EQ.1)GO TO 20                            001460
         GO TO 30                                      001470
```

239

```
145   1053  CALL ANALYS(15,B)                                              001480
            CALL PUTSTR(B,STRT)                                            001490
            TS=TS+1                                                        001500
      1052  CONTINUE                                                       001510
      30    WRITE (TYPE,904)                                               001520
      1051  CONTINUE                                                       001530
150         GO TO 20                                                       001540
      C     Y(6)                                                           001550
      106   DO 1061 J=1,10                                                 001560
            IF (X(J).EQ.0)GO TO 80                                         001570
      1061  CONTINUE                                                       001580
155   80    X(J)=TS                                                        001590
            DO 1062 J=1,10                                                 001600
            WRITE (TYPE,902) J                                             001610
            CALL GETSTR(B,KEYB)                                            001640
160         WRITE (TYPE,904)                                               001650
            IF (INDEX(B,NONE))GO TO 20                                     001660
            CALL PUTSTR(B,STRT)                                            001670
            TS=TS+1                                                        001680
      1062  CONTINUE                                                       001690
            GO TO 20                                                       001700
165   C     Y(7)                                                           001710
      107   CALL NEWFILE(2,7,PI)                                           001720
            GO TO 1091                                                     001730
      C     Y(8)                                                           001740
      108   CALL NEWFILE(4,8,PI)                                           001750
            GO TO 1091                                                     001760
170   C     Y(9)                                                           001770
      109   CALL NEWFILE(5,10,PI)                                          001780
      1091  IF (PI.EQ.1)GO TO(101,102,103,104,105,106,107,108,109),AA1     001790
175   20    CONTINUE                                                       001800
            END                                                            001810
```

```
      LOGICAL FUNCTION INDEX(STR2,STR1)              001820
      INTEGER STR1(1),STR2(1)                        001830
      L1=STR1(1)                                     001840
      L2=STR2(1)-L1                                  001850
      IF (L2.LT.0) GO TO 202                         001860
C     SEE IF WE CAN FIND A MATCH                     001870
      KB = L2+1                                      001880
      DO 20 K=1,KB                                   001890
      DO 10 J=1,L1                                   001900
      IF (STR1(J+1).NE.STR2(K+J)) GO TO 20           001910
10    CONTINUE                                       001920
      INDEX=.TRUE.                                   001930
      RETURN                                         001940
20    CONTINUE                                       001950
202   INDEX=.FALSE.                                  001960
      RETURN                                         001970
      END                                            001980


      SUBROUTINE PUTSTR(STRG,UNIT)                   001990
      INTEGER STRG(1),UNIT                           002000
10    FORMAT(1X,100A1)                               002010
20    FORMAT(1X)                                     002015
      LEN=STRG(1)+1                                  002020
      WRITE (UNIT,10) (STRG(K),K=2,LEN)              002030
      WRITE (UNIT,20)                                002035
      RETURN                                         002040
      END                                            002050
```

```
        SUBROUTINE GETSTR(STRG,UNIT,INDX)                            002060
        INTEGER UNIT,STRG(1),INPUT(100),BLK,NONE(6)                  002070
        LOGICAL LINE(133),BK                                         002080
        DATA BLK/1H /                                                002090
        DATA NONE/4,1HN,1HO,1HN,1HE,1H /                             002100
        DATA BK/1H /                                                 002110
10      FORMAT (100A1)                                               002120
        READ (UNIT,10) INPUT                                         002130
        IF (EOF(UNIT)) 60, 15, 60                                    002140
        DO 20 K=1,100                                                002150
        L=101-K                                                      002160
15      IF (INPUT(L).NE.BLK)GO TO 30                                 002170
20      CONTINUE                                                     002180
        STRG(1)=0                                                    002190
        RETURN                                                       002200
30      CONTINUE                                                     002210
        STRG(1)=L                                                    002220
        DO 40 K=1,L                                                  002230
40      STRG(1+K)=INPUT(K)                                           002240
        RETURN                                                       002250
        ENTRY IXGSTR                                                 002260
        DO 50 K=1,133                                                002270
50      LINE(K)=BK                                                   002280
C       CALL RDWDS(INDX+UNIT,LINE,LENGTH)                            002290
C       NOW THE UNIT NUMBER IS THE MAJOR OFFSET IN THE WORKING DATA SET 002300
        DECODE (100,10,LINE) INPUT                                   002310
        GO TO 15                                                     002350
60      DO 70 K=1,6                                                  002360
70      STRG(K)=NONE(K)                                              002370
C       IF THE ATTN KEY WAS HIT IN RESPONSE TO A QUESTOION, NONE     002380
C       IS THE ANSWER                                                002390
        RETURN                                                       002400
        END                                                          002410
```

242

```
      SUBROUTINE PUTSTF(STRG,UNIT)                        002420
C     THIS SUBROUTINE WRITES ON THE WORKING DATA SET      002430
C     IT CHANGES THE VALUE OF THE *UNIT* PARAMETER SO THAT 002440
C     WHEN IT IS CALLED AGAIN IT WILL WRITE ON THE        002450
C     NEXT LINE OF THAT SEGMENT OF THE                    002460
C     WORKING DATA SET.                                   002470
      INTEGER S                                           002480
      INTEGER BLK                                         002490
      INTEGER UNIT,STRG(1)                                002500
      LOGICAL LINE(133)                                   002510
      DATA BLK/1H /                                       002520
      S=STRG(1)                                           002530
      DO 20 K=S,99                                        002540
 20   STRG(K+2)=BLK                                       002550
      ENCODE (140,30,LINE)  (STRG(M),M=2,101)             002560
 30   FORMAT (100A1)                                      002570
      CALL WRITWDS(UNIT,LINE,133)                         002590
      UNIT=UNIT+1                                         002600
C     INCREMENT THE UNIT NUMBER, IT IS NOW THE INDEX      002610
      RETURN                                              002620
      END                                                 002630
```

```
        SUBROUTINE NEWFILE(AA,BB,CC)                      002640
        INTEGER Q(13)                                     002650
        INTEGER F(10,7),H(5),G(3),R(13,21)                002660
        INTEGER TTS(10)                                   002670
5       INTEGER Z(100),AA,BB,CC                           002680
        INTEGER RA,CC,TTM1,TT,W(18,2),TTS,TYPE,RESP,TTM   002690
        INTEGER B(101)                                    002700
        INTEGER AX(6)                                     002710
10      INTEGER T                                         002720
        COMMON TT,TTS,W,T,B,AX,KEY,F,H,R,G                002730
        COMMON Q                                          002740
    C   DATA TYPE/6/,RESP/1000/                           002750
    C   ABOVE DEFINED I/O UNITS                           002760
        RA=1                                              002770
15      CC=0                                              002780
   10   IF (RA.EQ.3)GO TO 90                              002790
        P=W(AA,2)-W(AA,1)                                 002800
        IP=IFIX(P*UNIF(0))                                002810
        TTM1=TT-1                                         002820
20      DO 20 M=1,TTM1                                    002830
        IF (TTS(M).NE.IP)GO TO 20                         002840
        RA=RA+1                                           002850
        GO TO 10                                          002860
25 20   CONTINUE                                          002870
        TTS(TT)=IP                                        002880
        II=II+1                                           002890
        TTM=W(AA,1)+IP                                    002900
        CALL IXGSTR(Z,RESP,TTM)                           002910
30      CALL PUTSTR(B,TYPE)                               002920
        CALL PUTSTR(Z,TYPE)                               002930
        CC=1                                              002940
90      RETURN                                            002950
        END                                               002960
```

244

```
      SUBROUTINE ANALYS(DB,EB)                              002970
      INTEGER B(101)                                        002980
      INTEGER TTS(10)                                       002990
      INTEGER W(18,2)                                       003000
      INTEGER AA(6)                                         003010
    5 INTEGER S(21)                                         003020
      INTEGER F(10,7),H(5)                                  003030
      INTEGER R(13,2)                                       003040
      LOGICAL INDEX                                         003050
      INTEGER Q(13)                                         003060
   10 INTEGER EB(101),Z(101)                                003070
      INTEGER NONE(5)                                       003080
      INTEGER G(3)                                          003090
      INTEGER QUES,TYPE,KEYB                                003100
      INTEGER P                                             003110
   15 INTEGER DB                                            003120
      COMMON II,TIS,W,I,B,AA,KEY,F,H,R,G                    003130
      COMMON Q                                              003140
      DATA NONE/4,1HN,1HO,1HN,1HE/                          003150
      DATA QUES/0/                                          003160
   20 DATA TYPE/6/                                          003170
      DATA KEYB/5/                                          003180
  904 FORMAT (1X)                                           003190
      DATA S/1,1,1,3,3,13,13,13,12,11,11,10,10,9,8,5,6,7,7/ 003200
      N=0                                                   003210
   25 IDB9=DB-9                                             003220
C                                                           003230
      GO TO (110,111,112,113,114,115,116),IDB9
    C Y(10)                                                 003240
  110 IF (J.GT.2.OR.(J.EQ.2.AND.PR.EQ.1))GO TO 116          003250
      CALL FOLLOW(AA(4),EB,P)                               003260
   30 IF (J.EQ.2.AND.P.NE.1)GO TO 1101                      003270
 1102 PR=P                                                  003280
      GO TO 116                                             003290
 1101 CALL IXGSTR(B,QUES,KEY+50)                            003300
```

245

```
35          CALL PUTSTR(B,KEYB)                                        003310
            GO TO 1102                                                 003320
      C     Y(11)                                                      003330
      111   DO 1111 M=1,7                                              003340
            IF (INDEX(EB,F(1,M)))GO TO 1112                            003350
40    1111  CONTINUE                                                   003360
            GO TO 116                                                  003370
1112        IF (G(1).NE.0)GO TO 1113                                   003380
            WRITE (TYPE,905)                                           003390
            G(1)=1                                                     003400
45          CALL GETSTR(Z,KEYB)                                        003410
            GO TO 116                                                  003420
1113        IF (G(2).NE.0)GO TO 1114                                   003430
            WRITE (TYPE,906)                                           003440
            G(2)=1                                                     003450
50          CALL GETSTR(Z,KEYB)                                        003460
            GO TO 116                                                  003470
1114        IF (G(3).NE.0)GO TO 116                                    003480
            WRITE (TYPE,907)                                           003490
            G(3)=1                                                     003500
            CALL GETSTR(Z,KEYB)                                        003510
            GO TO 116                                                  003520
55    C     Y(12)                                                      003530
112         P=IFIX(5.*UNIF(0))+1                                       003540
            IF (N.EQ.4)GO TO 116                                       003550
            N=N+1                                                      003560
60          IF (H(P).NE.0)GO TO 112                                    003570
            H(P)=1                                                     003580
            WRITE (TYPE,904)                                           003590
            DO 1121 M=1,4                                              003600
            CALL IXGSTR(Z,QUES,4*P+96+M)                               003610
65          CALL PUTSTR(Z,TYPE)                                        003620
            CALL GETSTR(Z,KEYB)                                        003630
            IF (INDEX(Z,NONE))RETURN                                   003640
1121  CONTINUE                                                         003650
```

```
70        GO TO 116                                             003660
   113    CONTINUE                                              003670
   114    CONTINUE                                              003680
   115    DO 1151 M=1,21                                        003690
          IF (.NOT.INDEX(EB.R(1,M)))GO TO 1151                 003700
75        P=S(M)                                                003710
          IF (M.LT.7.AND.DB.EQ.14)P=P+1                        003720
          IF (Q(P).EQ.1)GO TO 1151                             003730
          CALL IXGSTR(Z,QUES,120+P)                            003740
          CALL PUTSTR(Z,TYPE)                                  003750
          CALL GETSTR(Z,KEYB)                                  003760
80        Q(P)=1                                                003770
          RETURN                                                003780
   1151   CONTINUE                                              003790
   116    RETURN                                                003800
   905    FORMAT (* WOULD YOU BE MORE SPECIFIC */)             003810
   906    FORMAT (* PLEASE BE MORE SPECIFIC*/)                 003820
   907    FORMAT (* HOW WOULD YOU KNOW THAT HAD OCCURED */)    003830
          END                                                   003840
```

247

```
      SUBROUTINE FOLLOW(YD,ZY,IP)                      003850
      LOGICAL INDEX                                    003860
      INTEGER PY,PZ                                    003870
      INTEGER YD,IP                                    003880
      INTEGER AZ(1),ZY(10),BZ(10),CZ(10)               003890
      INTEGER INPUT(21)                                003900
      INTEGER KEYW                                     003910
C     ABOVE DEFINED KEYWORD + DATA FILE                003920
      EQUIVALENCE (INPUT(1),AZ(1)),(INPUT(12),CZ(1))   003930
      DATA KEYW/2000/                                  003940
  907 FORMAT (I2,10A1,10I3)                            003950
      DO 1 K=1,10                                      003960
    1 BZ(K)=0                                          003970
      DO 20 K=1,107                                    003980
   15 CALL RDWDS(KEYW+K,INPUT,LENGTH)                  003990
      IF (.NOT.INDEX(ZY,AZ))GO TO 20                   004000
      DO 30 M=1,10                                     004010
   30 BZ(M)=BZ(M)+CZ(M)                                004020
   20 CONTINUE                                         004030
      PZ=1                                             004040
      PY=YD                                            004050
      DO 40 M=2,10                                     004060
      IF (BZ(M).LE.BZ(PY))GO TO 34                     004070
   25 PY=M                                             004080
      GO TO 40                                         004090
   34 IF (BZ(M).GT.BZ(PZ))PZ=M                         004100
   40 CONTINUE                                         004110
      IP=0                                             004120
      IF (YD.EQ.PZ.OR.YZ.EQ.PY)IP=1                    004130
   30 RETURN                                           004140
      END                                              004150
```

```
          SUBROUTINE INITIAL                                              004160
          INTEGER AA,B,F,G,H,Q,R,I,II,IIS,W                               004170
          COMMON TT,TTS(10),W(18,2),T,B(101),AA(6),KEY,F(10,7),H(5),R(13,21)004180
         $ ,G(3),Q(13)                                                    004190
          INTEGER INPUT(2),IN2(10),IN3(5)                                 004200
     C    DEFINE FILES                                                    004210
          INTEGER QSTN,KEYW,CARD                                          004220
          DATA QSIN/1/                                                    004230
          DATA KEYW/2000/                                                 004240
          DATA CARD/98/                                                   004250
     C    FORMATS                                                         004260
     907  FORMAT (I2,10A1,10I3)                                           004270
     908  FORMAT (I2,12A1)                                                004280
     909  FORMAT (I2,9A1)                                                 004290
     910  FORMAT (I3,10A10)                                               004300
     911  FORMAT (I4,5I3)                                                 004310
     C    INITIALIZE SIS FILE                                             004312
     C    CALL SISSET                                                     004314
     C    READ THE F AND R ARRAY                                          004320
          READ (CARD,909)F                                                004330
          READ (CARD,908)R                                                004340
     C    READ KEYWORD AND DATA FILE                                      004350
          LINE=1                                                          004360
     10   READ (CARD,907)INPUT                                            004370
          IF (INPUT(1).EQ.99)GO TO 19                                     004380
          CALL WRTWDS(KEYW+LINE,INPUT,210)                                004390
          LINE=LINE+1                                                     004400
          GO TO 10                                                        004410
     C    READ THE QUESTION FILE (PART 1)                                 004420
     19   READ (CARD,910)INDX,IN2                                         004430
          IF (INDX.EQ.999)GO TO 29                                        004440
          CALL WRTWDS(INDX,IN2,100)                                       004450
          GO TO 19                                                        004460
```

249

```
C     READ THE SECOND PART                        004470
29    READ ((CARD,911)INDX,IN3                    004480
      IF (INDX.EQ.999)RETURN                       004490
C     RETURN, ALL DONE                             004500
      CALL WRIWDS(INDX,IN3,50)                      004510
      GO TO 29                                      004520
      END                                           004530


      FUNCTION UNIF(I)                              004540
      X = I                                         004550
      IF (X .NE.0.) CALL RANSET(X)                  004560
      UNIF = RANF(DUM)                              004570
      RETURN                                        004580
      END                                           004590


      SUBROUTINE SISSET                             004600
      COMMON/SISBLK/FET(22),IERR,BUFF(2000),IKEY,IREC(21)   004610
      CALL STFETF(FET,4HDATA,IREC,210,50,BUFF,2000)  004620
      CALL STKEYF(FET,IKEY,0,1HI,30)                004630
      CALL OPNEWF(FET,IERR)                         004640
      DO 110 I=1,14                                 004650
110   IREC(I) = 10H                                 004660
      IKEY = 0                                      004670
      CALL INSRTF(FET,50)                           004680
      ICR=10HR                                      004682
```

```
      ICN=10HN                                               004684
      CALL OPNOLF (FET,ICR,ICN,IERR)                         004690
      RETURN                                                 004700
      END                                                    004710


      SUBROUTINE WRTWDS(IK,IR,NC)                             004720
      COMMON/SISBLK/FET(22),IERR,BUFF(2000),IKEY,IREC(21)    004730
      DIMENSION IR(1)                                        004740
      IERR = 0                                               004750
      IKEY = IK                                              004760
      NW = FLOAT(NC)/10. + .99                               004770
      DO 110 I=1,NW                                          004780
  110 IREC(I) = IR(I)                                        004790
      CALL INSRTF(FET,NC)                                    004800
      IF (IERR .EQ. 0) RETURN                                004810
      IF (IERR .NE. 14) GO TO 200                            004820
      IERR = 0                                               004830
      CALL RPLACF(FET,NC)                                    004840
      IF (IERR .EQ. 0) RETURN                                004850
      PRINT 1000, IERR                                       004860
 1000 FORMAT(*OREPLACE SIS ERROR NO.:*,I4)                   004870
      STOP                                                   004880
  200 PRINT 1010, IERR                                       004890
 1010 FORMAT(*OINSERT SIS ERROR NO.:*,I4)                    004900
      STOP                                                   004910
      END                                                    004920
```

251

```
      SUBROUTINE RDWDS(IK,IR,NC)                                004930
      COMMON/SISBLK/FET(22),IERR,BUFF(2000),IKEY,IREC(21)       004940
      DIMENSION IR(1)                                           004950
      IERR = 0                                                  004960
      IKEY = IK                                                 004970
      CALL ACSSKF(FET,NC)                                       004980
      IF (IERR .NE. 0) GO TO 200                                004990
      NW = FLOAT(NC)/10. + .99                                  005000
      DO 110 I=1,NW                                             005010
  110 IR(I) = IREC(I)                                           005020
      RETURN                                                    005030
  200 PRINT 1000, IERR, IKEY                                    005040
 1000 FORMAT(*0ACCESS SIS ERROR NO.:*,I4,*,  KEY=*,I6)          005050
      STOP                                                      005060
      END                                                       005070
```

252